Also by Thomas P. McElroy, Jr.

The New Handbook of Attracting Birds

This is a Borzoi Book published in New York
by Alfred A. Knopf

THE HABITAT GUIDE TO BIRDING

Illustrated by Matthew Kalmenoff

Alfred A. Knopf New York 1974

THE HABITAT GUIDE TO BIRDING

Thomas P. McElroy, Jr.

This is a Borzoi Book published by Alfred A. Knopf, Inc.

Copyright © 1974 by Thomas P. McElroy, Jr.

All rights reserved under International and Pan-American Copyright Conventions. Published in the United States by Alfred A. Knopf, Inc., New York, and simultaneously in Canada by Random House of Canada Limited, Toronto. Distributed by Random House, Inc., New York.

Library of Congress Cataloging in Publication Data
McElroy, Thomas P.   (date)   The habitat guide to birding.
1. Bird watching—United States. I. Title.
QL682.M33   1974   598.2'073'0973   73–9945
ISBN 0–394–47492–9

Manufactured in the United States of America
First Edition

1787829

To Tommy and Wendy

*and grandchildren everywhere, with
the hope that they, too, may
thrill to the flight of the eagle,
know the beauty of the cardinal,
and revere the cathedral tones
of the wood thrush.*

Contents

A Guide
to the Habitat Lists

A Guide
to the Illustrations

Preface

The sudden realization that man is inherently dependent upon the related functions of the natural community has, in part, initiated a great resurgence of interest in all outdoor activities. People are searching for fundamental truths—the basic laws of survival and their meanings in terms of human welfare and happiness. Some seek answers in the remoteness of the backcountry; others must challenge the beckoning peaks of high mountains; and others find a degree of solitude in plying wilderness waterways. But for many, the most meaningful rewards are found in following the lives of birds, for birds have represented the enduring qualities of life since eons past.

Although I have been interested in birds since childhood, I must admit that I find it somewhat difficult to pinpoint those qualities which sustained my interest over so long a period. Perhaps I was content, in those formative years, to add a "new" bird to my list, to know where the oriole or kingbird nested, to thrill at the swift flight of a hunting hawk, and to find solace in the bell-like tones of the thrushes as I returned from my woodland wanderings. The birds were there, and I was content to have them as my daily companions.

Even in this most casual form of acceptance, bird watching was a deeply satisfying experience. In more recent years, however, I have become increasingly aware of more significant attributes to be found in observing wild birds in their natural habitats. Also, the dimension of concern has been added; birds are recognized as the earliest and truest indicators of environmental change. I am not alone in these discoveries, for there is a growing human force, informed and inquisitive, whose intellect cannot be satisfied by the mere facts of existence alone. This is especially true relative to the comparatively new science of ecology. Where the relationships of life and environment are involved, this new force demands positive answers. In the case of bird watching, it is no longer sufficient to say the wood thrush is a brown speckled bird of the forest. Why is it there? How does it survive? What does it contribute to the total forest community? The answers to such indicative questions carry the bird watcher beyond the staid practice of merely listing recognized species.

Recognizing these facts, this book, then, is manifold in purpose. Primarily, its intent is to improve one's skill and to increase one's pleasure as a birder. The pursuit of these objectives is through an innovative approach to the whole field of bird watching: that birders can be helped in locating, identifying, and understanding birds through a knowledge of their physical adaptations and behavioral patterns as associated with the habitats in which they live. Also, this book is based on the premise that birds are an important functional unit in the total natural community, and that through the understanding of these functions and the community, the birder can pursue his interests with a keener knowledge and find greater personal rewards.

This book also recognizes the hypothesis that one or more species of birds can be found in every conceivable type of habitat, no matter how specific we may be in designating the habitat's scientific nomenclature, or how careful we are in delineating its boundaries. Birds are everywhere, and this fact alone injects the element of evolutionary mystery and provides innumerable ecological equations to challenge the most curious of intellects.

From this myriad of adaptations, relationships, and similar habitat characteristics, I have fashioned the basis for this book.

Birds are not distributed uniformly throughout any geographical area. Each species survives best in a certain type of habitat because of adaptations and specialization by generations of its ancestors. Habitats differ greatly in their biological and physical characteristics. Some support large numbers of a few species; others sustain lesser numbers of a greater variety. Recognizing these differences in representative habitats of the eastern half of our continent, from the tundra to the semitropics, it soon becomes evident that the techniques of locating, observing, and identifying birds will vary somewhat from one habitat to another. Also, the kinds of preferred clothing and equipment for watchers will differ as they progress from forests to marshlands to seashores. In chapters pertaining to specific habitats, I have included certain field techniques (including the use of equipment) that will make birding in each area an enjoyable and rewarding experience. In addition, I have devoted an entire chapter to field techniques in general, and another to the important matter of selecting and using binoculars and scopes. The beginning bird watcher may wish to read these two chapters (16 and 17) before going on to the rest of the book.

And in the preparation of this book I have not neglected the aesthetic appeal of bird watching, for it is this emotional quality that lures most of us afield.

Mostly, this book has grown from my many years of watching birds, and from my keen interest in the ecology of our land. But I hasten to acknowledge those whose work has made bird watching such an easy pursuit to follow. Generations of scientists have given us a system of organization —a scientific classification and nomenclature for birds of the world. Men such as Edward H. Forbush, Frank M. Chapman, Arthur Cleveland Bent, and Alexander Sprunt, Jr. have given us detailed life histories; Andrew J. Berger, Josselyn Van Tyne, and Olin S. Pettingill, Jr. have developed comprehensive courses of study for the serious student; and Roger Tory Peterson, Richard H. Pough, and others have simplified the task of bird identification. And in a book of this kind, one cannot ignore the efforts of Eugene P. Odum, R. F. Daubenmire, Henry J. Oosting, Paul B. Sears, and other pioneering ecologists.

This book is largely a personal effort, but I am especially grateful to Olin S. Pettingill, Jr., Director of the Laboratory of Ornithology, Cornell University, for his interest and sug-

gestions for certain portions of the text; to Paul Knoop,
director of the Aullwood Audubon Center at Dayton, Ohio,
for his time afield with me; and to Hannah H. McElroy for
many months of patience and understanding. But mostly, I
am indebted to Blanche E. Getchen for many hours of assis-
tance in preparation of the final text, and to my editor, Angus
Cameron, for his continued guidance, inspiration, and enduring patience.

T . P . M .

Suggestions
for Using This Book

Birders are individualists, and their personal interests are quite diversified. Consequently, there is no singular technique or method of procedure for using this book. Its organization and content are such that it will be a source of help to the amateur and the experienced birder alike. The following notes and suggestions will explain the book's features and make it easier to use in the pursuit of personal objectives.

• The habitats included here were chosen because of their dominance in the eastern half of our continent and for their attractiveness to birds. They are grouped in a manner convenient to the bird watcher—what you may view from one place, or on one field trip.

• The names used in the text are from the *American Ornithologists' Union's Check-List of North American Birds*, 5th edition, 1957. For clarity and ease of use, in any extensive lists, birds are listed alphabetically, first by families (common names) and then by species. In most cases, the family headings include only those genera which are represented by one or more species in the list. For example, the family of "Crows, Magpies, and Jays" may be listed as "Jays" and followed by the species "Blue."

• Scientific names have been purposely avoided in most cases, and are used only where necessary for clarity.

• Birds described for identification (field marks, etc.) are males in spring plumage unless indicated otherwise.

• For information on a specific species, use the index. Often, the same species is referred to in several habitats. Details of characteristics and habits will be found in the most appropriate section of the text.

• The numerous illustrations in the margins are intended to be both atmospheric and informative. Mostly, they are applicable to the immediately adjacent text.

• You will soon become aware that this is not a complete treatise on bird identification. It is not intended to be, for this subject has been covered expertly by others. However, you will find information on methods of identification, and in some instances, field marks and characteristic habits will be pointed out as a means of applying these methods. This book will supplement your favorite field guide.

• Study the appropriate section when planning a field trip to a particular type of habitat. It will help you to know what birds to expect and what behavioral patterns to look for when studying various species. Also, this book will serve as a guide to the selection of habitats for locating specific species.

• Use this book as a follow-up to field trips and as a cross-check for notes taken in the field. Make this a personal book; additional border sketches and notes will enhance its personal value.

• Many of you may find this book an introduction to the ecology of bird communities. And so it was intended, for we cannot really know birds without understanding the environment in which they live.

THE HABITAT GUIDE TO BIRDING

Birds are an integral part of the American landscape, and their numbers and kinds vary as the landscape varies. Our lofty mountains with their adjacent rolling hills, our wide valleys with their meandering rivers, grasslands, and fields of grain, our sculptured coastlines and sandy beaches—it is to these panoramic wonders that birds add color, song, movement, and, above all else, life itself. The cry of sea birds along New England's coastline, the clatter of wintering geese on the back bays of Virginia's lowlands, the statuesque herons and egrets atop the cypress and the mangroves, the raucous call of crows above an Ohio cornfield—these things are as symbolically Americana as the physical terrain upon which they dwell.

America is especially blessed with birds, both in numbers and in varieties. Mostly, this population is not a static one, but one that changes with the seasons and with the environment.

As the cold days of winter settle upon the land, the song sparrows, catbirds, and towhees give way to the whitethroats and juncos. The field sparrows and bobolinks no longer feed upon the seed heads of foxtail and bluestem grasses; in their stead, we hear the tinkling of tree sparrows and redpolls. The daily preachings of the red-eyed vireo no longer resound from his woodland pulpit. The bluebirds (except the pair in the sumacs) have gone. The nest in the box elder is wind-blown and deserted; but the tree's winged seeds, hard-fast to the supple twigs, rustle

1 In Search of Birds

their defiance at the winter winds. Their fate is sustenance for evening grosbeaks and purple finches. Only now, in the quiet bleakness of winter, can we hope to see the snowy owl, or his miniature counterpart, the saw-whet.

Springtime brings a change in mood and tempo. Life is breathed into the earth once again, and it responds with a crescendo of song and the beat of birds on the wing.

All movement is northward. Flocks of tree swallows swirl in cyclonic fashion as they leave the sedges and shrubs where they roosted for the night. Gradually the flocks thin, and flight is resumed; they will feed as they travel. Waves of warblers progress from treetop to treetop as they rest and feed; their long flight will be resumed in the darkness of night. Everywhere, all across the land, birds are on the move, and the tide rolls ever northward.

In the fall, this great tide reverses itself; the flow of life is southward. The sandy spits along our sea beaches overflow with migrating shore birds. Thousands of ducks leave the sloughs and potholes of the Midwest and prairie provinces of Canada. And the warblers—their thin lisps in the stillness of the night reveal their myriad numbers—are on the wing again. But come the dawn and daylight hours, they can be seen flitting about the treetops in search of insects to replenish their energy for the coming night's long journey.

But it is during the warming months of summer, when birds are at home, that we can observe the excitement of their living. All activities seem to take on a hastening pace; there is so much to be done before chill winds once again force the departure of most species. For some, there is no need to hurry. The red-bellied woodpecker can spend days drilling his hole in the hard dry stub of a pine; he will not move with the cold. The goldfinches can remain in their social flocks; the milkweed pods will not release their down and seeds until early July. But for those who will leave in the fall, time is of the essence. There is territorial homesteading to be done, and a mate to be found. Hours will be spent in singing and warding off intruders. A hundred searching trips or more must be made to find appropriate nesting materials. Eggs must be laid and brooded, and thousands more forays made in search of food. The young must be taught to fend for themselves, and then, only then, may the pace of living be slowed. And slow it does, for there is a mysterious quiet about the sun-baked gardens and woodlands during the hot days of late summer. Old Red-eye now preaches to an unresponsive congregation.

Environmental changes also help keep much of our bird population in a state of fluctuation. Natural succession is slow, but nevertheless effective. A pond in the open, edged mainly with water lilies, may appeal to the pied-billed grebe and a few dabbling ducks. As grasses, sedges, cattails, and loosestrife begin to dominate the edges, these few species will be joined by others such as red-winged blackbirds, swamp sparrows, marsh wrens, and Virginia rails. The appearance of shrubs—willows, black alders, and buttonbush—will bring yellowthroats, song sparrows, catbirds, yellow warblers, and other shrub-loving species. If this natural succession were allowed to continue undisturbed, the forest would eventually be the permanent habitat of the pond's borders. Birds of the previous pond-edge communities would be gone; chickadees, titmice, vireos, nuthatches, ovenbirds, woodpeckers, and other woodland birds would be dominant.

When man enters the scene with his monstrous machines, environmental changes are apt to be radical. With a few swipes by a bulldozer or backhoe, a sand spit, a marsh, or a fencerow can disappear from the face of the earth. The sad part of such intrusions is this: there is little recuperative power in a habitat of concrete and steel.

But change is the essence of bird watching's appeal. From season to season, from mountain to valley, from field to forest, no matter when or where you go, there is a constant newness each time you are afield. Each type of habitat supports a different variety of birds. Birding knows no season, requires no license, and is of interest to all age groups. Birds belong to us all—free for the watching.

We think of a bird's habitat as being the place or particular type of area in which it has a habit of living. Actually, it is much more than that; it is a combination of interacting physical and biological (community) factors that produce an environment to which an individual species has become best adapted through innumerable generations. Each species remains in, or returns to, the type of habitat in which it was born. Although a certain habitat is often home to a variety of birds, we speak of each species as being best suited, and adapted to, a specific habitat. When all plants and animals within a given area are considered, we refer to the area as a community.

Most species of birds are so instinctively bound and so physiologically adapted to one type of habitat that they cannot tolerate environmental changes, nor can they survive by moving to a totally different habitat. Other species, however, are ecologically tolerant in varying degrees. In my home state of Florida, the Everglade kite faces possible extinction because of its complete dependence on a delicately balanced fresh-water habitat. It feeds exclusively on the fresh-water *Pomacea*. This snail breeds and thrives in the flooded shallows of the Glades. But man has entered the scene. Hundreds of miles of straight-line drainage ditches (ostensibly for flood control) and the indiscriminate use of pesticides have narrowed the habitat in which the snails and the kites can survive. By contrast, the robin is a most tolerant species; its food habits are not so specialized. I have seen it nest in the gardens and parks of the Carolinas, along the shrubby fencerows and woodland borders of New England, and in the openings of Quebec's northernmost forests. Still other species have a moderate tolerance for environmental changes. If we are to know where to find and watch birds, we should have a knowledge of these tolerances and of the dominating forces within the bird community. Why are the birds there? What attracts them? What are the relationships between species and selected home sites? An understanding of the functions within the bird community will make our trips afield more successful and more meaningful.

The bobolink returns to its home in a Wisconsin hayfield. It welcomes spring from the bobbing tip of a dried goldenrod stem, its song bubbling forth in a series of alternating high and low metallic notes. The wood thrush announces its homecoming from the deep shade of a Pennsylvania forest with a song of the flute—clear, mellow, and ending with a vibrato that fades into the shadowy depths. The American bittern claims its territory by "driving stakes" along the marshy borders of a remote lake in Maine. Everywhere across the land, birds return home in the spring to a particular biological niche in the outdoor community.

The bobolink may return to the very field in which it was hatched slightly less than a year ago. It does this not by choice, or by any calculated evaluation, but by instinct alone. The young bobolink is the culmination of all the inherited reflexes, responses, habits, and abilities of its parents and countless generations of its ancestors. Have they not made the great flight down the east coast of our continent and across the Bahamas to Jamaica? And then another five hundred miles across an islandless ocean to the shores of South America? Have they not spent a hundred thousand winters on the pampas of Argentina? Have they not returned to sing from a hundred thousand golden-rod stems? Have they not known fear at the screaming of a hawk, or the quiet passing of a fox?

Yes. All the experiences of living to be encountered by the young bobolink have been known countless times before. But unknowingly, and in an infinitesimal way, it will contribute to the inheritance that will assure the survival of future generations.

The wood thrush senses security in the cool shade of the forest. Its large eyes have developed a special keenness in the subdued light; it avoids the bright sunshine. It experiences little competition as it forages about the forest floor, flipping dead leaves aside with its bill, seeking crickets, grubs, spiders, ants, flies, and earthworms. Most of its woodland neighbors either are seed eaters or catch their insects at higher levels. The wood thrush is an understory specialist—it feeds low, perches low, and nests low. And always, its tawny back blends with the protective browns of the forest floor. Just as were its progenitors throughout the eons, it is a creature of the forest community. It takes, it gives, and it survives.

And the bittern, has it not always known the wetness of the marsh? Over the great span of time past, it has been so much a part of this wetland habitat that the striations of its plumage now mimic the reeds and grasses in which it lives. Unlike most herons, its way of life is solitary and secretive; it does not feed in flocks, nor does it colonize for nesting. It is a loner—a master of stealth and concealment.

And so it is with the ducks and the geese, with the hawks and the falcons, and with the warblers and the sparrows. And so it is with the plovers and the sandpipers, and with the terns and the gulls. Each species instinctively fulfills its destiny as an active member of the particular community to which it is irrevocably bound.

The Outdoor Community

To the human eye, the outdoor community in which birds live presents a deceptive façade of harmony and tranquillity. In reality, it is a composite of dynamic forces that function interdependently in the never-ending struggle for survival. It is not unlike the community in which man himself lives; it has its basement dwellers, street-level residents, and high-rise occupants; it has its own factories, shopping centers, police force, garbage collectors, robbers, and parasitic welfare cases. The community functions as a circuitous chain of events propelled by the energies of birth, competition, and death. The green leaves that have survived the competition for sunlight and are structured by the carbon they have taken from the air may satiate the appetite of a ravenous caterpillar; the life juices of the caterpillar may flow in the bloodstream of a newly hatched cuckoo; the cuckoo may strengthen the sharp-shinned hawk who, through his own demise, will eventually release the carbon for use by other green plants. Life within the community beats with a fundamental rhythm of natural laws. Birds are an essential part of this rhythmic beat.

There are numerous and varied physical and biological factors associated with each type of bird community that largely determine the numbers and varieties of species it can support. These factors, when divided into their innumerable components, associations, and relationships, form the basis for detailed ecological studies. Obviously, that is not the purpose of this book, but we should be concerned with the major and more recognizable factors of community structure. This will help us determine where we have the best chance of finding certain species and give us a working knowledge of what species we can expect to find in a particular habitat.

Plants—not birds or other animals—are the structural backbone of the community. Either directly or indirectly, they are the source of all energy necessary to maintain the lives of all organisms. In most communities, they provide food, home sites, and protective cover. From the minutest plankton to the most stalwart of trees, all plants are in some way involved in maintaining the rhythmic beat of life within the community. Plant growth, as we know, is subject to such climatic and ecological conditions as air temperature, precipitation, humidity, exposure, wind, light intensity, and soil composition. Plant groups that tolerate these conditions in various combinations determine the numbers and species of birds a particular community will attract and support. When a degree of uniformity is reached through a certain combination of these conditions, a corresponding degree of uniformity is reached in the plant life and in the animal life. These factors, along with topography and geographical location, constitute the basis for a specific type of habitat. These principles apply in both terrestrial and aquatic communities.

The importance and contributions of birds to a balanced environment are difficult to evaluate. Their associations with other animal and plant members of the community are so numerous and often so obscure, but nevertheless important, that ecologists may never unravel all the ramifications involved. However, we do know enough about these relationships to realize that birds are a significant part of the intricate web of all living things, including man. We know, for example, that such species as the bobolink, field sparrow, and junco consume tons of weed seeds every year. As far as community balance is concerned, the amount of seeds actually consumed has less significance than the thinning out and distribution of the various plant species from which they came.

In a forest, an elm tree succumbs to disease and the shade of a beech-maple canopy. Woodpeckers chip away

the bark in search of grubs and insects; they drill nesting cavities in the softer limbs and trunk areas. In doing so, they hasten the processes that will eventually return the tree to the soil. A limb breaks at a weakened spot and falls; rain water fills the cavities and helps the process of rotting; eventually, a wind storm tumbles the tree to the ground. Here it may serve as a drumming log for the ruffed grouse, or it may provide a temporary home for a chipmunk or a deer mouse. But now the bacteria and fungi take over, and gradually the elm is returned to the soil, releasing its carbon and other elements to be used once again.

Birds might be looked upon as the "middlemen" in the community's pyramid of numbers. Certain songbirds may rear a dozen or more young in a season, but the seeds, insects, and smaller animals upon which they feed are produced in tremendous numbers. Along with weather, disease, and other natural deterrents, birds act as a "lid" over these exploding populations. Vertebrates higher up on the pyramid aid in the same repressive controls over the songbird population through predation. Species such as vultures, crows, and gulls serve as community scavengers.

Aquatic communities tend to be less stable and not as easily defined as the terrestrial varieties. Nevertheless, the same ecological principles govern the survival of species, and birds are involved in many ways. A duck flying from one pond to another may carry a number of tiny floating duckweed plants on its body. In doing so it helps distribute and perpetuate its own food supply. A bittern feeding in the marsh may spear a minnow infested with tiny parasitic grubs, some of which will remain, live, and lay eggs within the bittern's mouth. As the bittern feeds, the eggs are washed into the water, where they hatch, feed, and eventually infest another minnow, thus continuing an intricate aquatic life cycle.

By now we know our bird population is widely distributed among a variety of habitats. We also know that feeding habits, nesting requirements, physiological adaptations, and other factors tend to limit many species to a certain type of habitat. This is especially true during the nesting season. During migration, when birds are concerned chiefly with travel routes, feeding, and resting, they can often be observed outside their normal nesting areas. Also, we should remember that the more pronounced natural communities seldom have definitive boundaries; more often than not, there is a transition zone (known as an *ecotone*) from one community to another. These ecotones often support more numbers and more species of birds than either adjacent community. For example, the transition zone between an uncultivated field and a hardwood forest may consist of the hardier field plants, a variety of shrubs and vines, and a number of young encroachment trees from the forest. This mixture of vegetation provides an abundance and variety of foods, nesting sites, and protective cover. In the eastern part of our country, this type of ecotone would attract such species as the field sparrow, song sparrow, cardinal, catbird, brown thrasher, yellow-breasted chat, rufous-sided towhee, indigo bunting, prairie warbler, and chestnut-sided warbler.

It now becomes quite obvious: the greater the variety of habitats we visit, the greater the variety of birds we can expect to find.

2 Habitats and Bird Identification

One or more species of birds are indigenous to every type of habitat on planet Earth, with the possible exception of some remote interior areas of Antarctica. And each biological niche within the larger habitats or communities supports a number of birds that have become adapted to its peculiar physical and biological characteristics. To understand why this is so, we must reach back into prehistoric times.

Scientists have proved beyond doubt that birds are descendants of the early reptiles. The skeletal forms of present-day birds and the fossilized remains traceable to intermittent periods are the basis of their proof. But why, how, and when these reptiles took to the air is speculated upon with a lesser degree of certainty. The most acceptable hypothesis is that certain reptiles first took to the trees because of competition for food and living space, and for their own safety. Then, over a period of millions of years, the physical adaptations that permitted jumping, gliding, and flight ensued in progressive order.

The oldest known bird fossil, *Archaeopteryx*, was found in a stratum of Upper Jurassic rock dating back some 140 million years. But the next fossil of record came from a stratum formed millions of years later. By the Eocene epoch, some 50 million years ago, the physical characteristics of birds approached their present form. Also, during this period, they probably made their most rapid advances in the processes of evolution.

One can only speculate on the number of birds in the past. All scientific evidence indicates there were greater numbers of species and individuals than presently exist. As the dinosaurs and other giant reptiles disappeared, the environment favored greater safety and proliferation of avian species. In addition, great physical changes on the surface of the earth produced new and varied habitats. Mountains were formed, islands rose from the sea, and great forests appeared but gave way to the grassland of the drier leeward side of the mountains. Birds radiated into the new habitats wrought by such cataclysmic changes. Not until the era of glaciers changed the relative uniformity of climate did birds suffer any drastic losses in the proliferation of species. The advance and retreat of glaciers is credited with starting the vast north and south movement of birds that is inherent in the migratory patterns of today.

Most species were limited to a specific range by such factors as the availability of food and cover, physical barriers, and climatic changes, and by their own adaptation to a specific type of environment. Woodlands, grasslands, and extensive marshes barred the natural distribution of species, even though comparable habitats may have existed beyond their distant boundaries. Some species were tolerant of greater temperature extremes than were others; some needed the longest of days in order to find sufficient food; and others needed consistent winds and thermals for prolonged flight.

As birds filled the various habitats, their tremendous numbers pressured the need for continued adaptation and specialization. In the forest, for example, different species occupy varying levels from the ground to the treetops. In the wetlands, we find waders, probers, skimmers, divers, dabblers, and other specialists. By selection (or perhaps by population pressures) each species has become adapted to the means of survival within a particular niche of each habitat. The physical features and characteristic habits, which developed over the eons and are needed to ensure this survival, are pronounced and visible; thus, they are a definite aid to bird identification.

The fact that birds do occupy every conceivable type

of biological niche, and that their kinds vary with each, makes bird watching an intriguing activity, and identification its most challenging objective. Recognition becomes the key to gratification.

Today, bird identification is comparatively easy, for the basic research has been done, and the results are available in compact field guides, thousands of photographs, and many excellent recordings. Every species indigenous to our continent is included in the recent field guides, and most of their songs are recorded for public use. In this chapter, and throughout this book, we are concerned mainly with identification as it relates to habits and habitat associations. Some emphasis is placed on the use of field marks, and on the recognition of songs and calls.* Following are some guides for recognizing birds by their location.

Birds on the Ground

Many birds spend a considerable amount of time on the ground, but here the mannerisms of various species are often quite different. The robin hops and runs across the lawn, stops suddenly, and cocks its head slightly to the side, watching for the slightest movement of a grub or earthworm. The grackle walks with a deliberate stride, but the mourning dove sort of "patters" along with short steps, bobbing its head back and forth as it goes. The ovenbird walks ever so quietly across the forest floor, its tail perked at a jaunty angle and flipping a bit with each step, but jays and sparrows travel on the ground by hopping. The sparrowlike water pipit walks, but it can be recognized by the constant bobbing of its white-edged tail and by its slender bill. Spotted sandpipers and waterthrushes also walk, but they "teeter" as though they were overweight in the front.

Woodland thrushes search for food by flipping leaves aside with their bills, but towhees and fox sparrows can be heard scratching amid the dry leaves of the forest floor. They do not scratch like a chicken, but hop back and forth, kicking the leaves aside with both feet.

* Additional information on bird identification will be found in succeeding chapters and in the Bibliography.

Some ground-feeding (or near-ground) species give clues to their identity by traveling in flocks. This is characteristic of tree sparrows, pipits, horned larks, snow buntings, and redpolls.

Perching birds offer the best opportunity to observe the distinctive characteristics and physical features of individual species. Flycatchers, for example, sit in a pronounced upright position—more vertical than similar species. By contrast, nighthawks and whip-poor-wills perch horizontally on a limb or wood fence; they have small weak feet, so they actually rest on their body feathers.

Birds in Shrubs and Trees

Notice the size and shape of the bill and tail (this is not at all difficult with a good binocular).

Seed-eating species, such as sparrows, finches, and buntings, have short, stubby bills.

The bills of cardinals and grosbeaks are thick and heavy, enabling them to hull and crack larger seeds.

The mandibles of the crossbills are actually crossed in scissorslike fashion. They are especially adapted to extracting seeds from the cones of our northern evergreens.

The woodpeckers have strong chisellike bills for "pecking" into wood.

Shrikes and sparrow hawks have hooked bills adapted to meat-tearing purposes.

Warblers and wrens have thin, sharply pointed bills for the purpose of catching small insects.

Not all birds "carry" or "hold" their tails in the same manner. Flycatchers have a tendency to droop or drop their tails below the angle of their bodies. Some, especially the phoebe, habitually flip their tails downward. Wrens cock their tails upward, often to a 45-degree angle or beyond.

Thrashers, mockingbirds, cuckoos, and grackles have long tails; the tail of the mourning dove is long and pointed.

Some birds—starlings, nuthatches, meadowlarks—have short, square tails. The tail of the mockingbird is rounded, the barn swallow's is forked, and the purple martin's is notched.

Certain species are expert tree climbers, notably woodpeckers, nuthatches, and creepers. The nuthatch is often seen coming down the trunk of a tree head first, giving it a unique advantage in spotting insects and grubs behind bits of bark that curl downward. The brown creeper invariably starts at the base of the trunk, clings close to the bark, uses its tail as a prop, and spirals its way upward. The woodpecker "hitches" its way up or down the tree; it also uses its stiff tail feathers as a supporting prop. The black and white warbler feeds in much the same manner as the brown creeper, but it hunts in either direction with equal facility.

Birds in the Air

The manner in which birds fly is one of the principal means of identification. The flight of some species is so distinctive that little else need be known in order to identify them.

Species such as robins, doves, cuckoos, and house sparrows fly in a straight line; woodpeckers, nuthatches, and goldfinches have a bounding or undulating flight.

Herons fly with a slow rhythmic beat; ducks must maintain a rapid wing beat for constant flight. Herons and bitterns fly with their long necks retracted, but ibises, storks, and cranes fly with their legs and necks fully extended.

Turkey vultures soar with their wings angled upward; the smaller black vultures and eagles soar with their wings much flatter—like a flying board.

Terns, kingfishers, ospreys, and sparrow hawks frequently hover in midair while hunting. Kingbirds, meadowlarks, and grasshopper sparrows have a fluttering style of flight.

The shapes of wings and tails are often distinctively outlined when birds are in flight, especially with the soaring varieties. It is one of the most helpful features in identifying the high-flying hawks.

Flight mannerisms and shape characteristics are also helpful in distinguishing families of similar-sized species, such as sparrows from warblers, and swifts from swallows.

The beaches and flats along the thousands of miles of our eastern coastline probably attract more birds in the course of a year than any other type of habitat. There is a special fascination in watching shore birds because they embody unique physical adaptations for survival in a great variety of biological conditions.

Birds along the Shore

Herons, egrets, and bitterns are large, long-legged wading birds that stalk their prey. Their long, pointed bills are adapted to spearing fish, frogs, and aquatic insects.

The roseate spoonbill is the most colorful of the long-legged waders. Its large spatulate bill is designed for sifting small fish, crustacea, and aquatic insects from the water and soft mud.

Among the smaller shore birds, dowitchers and sanderlings probe with their comparatively long bills, while plovers and turnstones pick at food on the surface. The turnstone's bill is curved slightly upward to aid in turning small stones, shells, and seaweed.

Avocets have long legs and long, upturned bills for the purpose of sweeping or skimming in the shallow waters of lake borders, flooded fields, and tidal pools; the black skimmer skims while on the wing.

Birds in the Water

Someone once said, "All ducks swim, but not all swimming birds are ducks." Other swimmers among our larger birds include swans, geese, brant, pelicans, gulls, cormorants, loons, grebes, anhingas, coots, and gallinules.

Because of light reflection and similarity in coloration, ducks and other "water birds" are frequently difficult to distinguish by color alone. Often, they can be most easily identified by their distinctive silhouettes, flight patterns, and field marks.

Each species of birds has a distinctive color pattern or physical feature that makes it distinguishable from other species. These prominent markings or features, known as field marks, include color patches, eye rings, wing bars, and the size and shape of bills, wings, tails, legs, and feet.

Using Field Marks

Field marks provide an effective means of distinguishing individual species within a family. The observer can determine by size and shape whether the bird in question is a hawk, heron, sparrow, or warbler, but beyond that point, other distinguishing features must be relied upon. In most cases, more than one feature, or field mark, is necessary for positive identification. For example, we cannot label the spring warbler we are watching as a Kentucky warbler just because it has an unstreaked yellow breast. If we check our field guides, we find there are a dozen other species that fit into this category, but the Kentucky warbler is the only one with black sideburns *and* yellow spectacles. Thus, the process of elimination, through comparisons, becomes an important factor in the use of field marks.

The beginning student will soon become aware of the fact that the most applicable combinations of field marks will vary according to families. For example, when we watch flying ducks, we are concerned primarily with wing and breast markings; with herons and egrets, the color of feet and legs is important; with terns, bills and caps must be considered. Five species of eastern thrushes are predominantly brown. They can be identified by the process of elimination—whether they have certain field marks or not. Rufous coloring, breast spots, eye rings, and cheek patches are the differentiating features. Warblers and sparrows are small and confusing, and a greater number of more specific field marks must be used. Here, we are concerned with such features as colorations, streaked or unstreaked breasts, wing bars, facial patches, eye rings, caps, and tail markings.

R. T. Peterson's *Field Guide to the Birds* is based primarily on the use of field marks. This method of systematizing the different visible features according to families, and the grouping of similar species within the families, is a most practical basis for the study and use of field marks as a means of identification. If you follow the Peterson system, you will become more adept at field identification as you become increasingly aware of *knowing what to look for*. For example, a sparrow lands on a bush in front of you; quickly, you note the breast is unstreaked, but that it does have a pronounced central spot. Instantaneously, you label it as a tree sparrow. The obvious question now is: How do I learn the field marks for so many species?

As in any learning situation, book knowledge becomes more meaningful, and is more easily retained, if accompanied by a means of practical application. If you know that tomorrow's trip will include a lot of bay ducks, some preliminary study of the field marks of the ducks you expect to see will be helpful. If you are going to the shore, study the sandpipers, terns, and other species you are likely to see along the beach. If you are planning a spring warbler hike, study the Peterson plates and accompanying text before you go. Once you actually see a bird as the book says it is supposed to be, you are likely to remember it on succeeding occasions. If you follow this practice—study the field marks of probable species before each field trip—you will be amazed at how the accumulated mental pictures will aid you in field recognition. Actually, it is unlikely that you will ever learn specific field marks for every species, but eventually you will know what to look for in each situation, and that is the key to being a good field observer.

Learning Songs and Calls

Many beginning bird students learn to recognize birds by sight quite easily, but they often experience a mental block when it comes to identifying them by songs and calls. This should not be, for it is just as simple to recognize a bird by its song (unless you are totally tone deaf—and very few people are) as by its shape or color; sometimes it's much easier.

The songs of birds are beautiful and exciting; they add much to the enjoyment of being outdoors. For the birder, their recognition is a must, for on most field trips (especially in the spring and summer) more birds are heard than seen.

I have taught many students to recognize birds by their songs and calls using the three steps that follow. If you are a beginner, or are having trouble learning and remembering bird songs, I recommend you give them a try.

Watch Birds Sing

This is probably the most helpful point of all: once you have positively identified the bird, *watch* it sing, and *listen*. As you listen, note its singing perch. Is it an exposed tree branch, or a utility wire? Is it a dead weed stem, or a fence post? *Watch* its singing attitude. Does it throw its head back and just let the song bubble forth, as the song sparrow does, or does it precede the song with some preliminary flutterings and contortions, such as the grasshopper sparrow frequently employs? Watching the bird sing—noting its singing perch and posture—will give you a mental picture that is easily recalled each time you hear that particular song. The song? The bird? It's an indigo bunting singing from the dead branch of a fencerow shrub!

Associations and Notations

We recall the name of a popular song by remembering the lyrics associated with that particular melody. Similarly, it is possible to recall the names of many birds by associating words with their songs. Of course, the easiest ones to remember are those that actually sing or call their own names such as the whip-poor-will, chuck-will's widow, bob-white, phoebe, wood pewee, and chickadee. Others are remembered by associating "sounds like" words or phrases with the songs. The examples given on the next page are more or less standards, and have been used by birders for many years. Their origin would be difficult to determine.

The use of words alone does not give you any indication as to whether one note is higher or lower than another, whether the notes are comparatively long or short, or which note or syllable should be accented. For this reason, you should develop a simple, personalized system of recording songs in your field notebook. As you associate words or syllables with a bird's song, you automatically memorize the rhythm; this becomes the basis for your notations. I use a simplified version of the system Aretas A. Saunders uses in *A Guide to Bird Songs*. The length of the note is indicated by the length of the line; the high or low quality of the note determines the line's comparative position. A wavering note or trill is indicated by a wavy line. Anyone interested in developing this system further should study Saunders's book.

For those of you who are musically talented (which I

RECOGNIZING BIRDS BY THEIR SONGS

Flycatcher, Least:	*"Che-beck."*
Ovenbird:	*"Teacher, teacher, teacher."*
Owl, Barred:	*"Who cooks for you?"* or *"Who cooks for you all?"*
Sparrow, Chipping:	*"Chip, chip, ip, ip, ipipippp."*
Sparrow, White-throated:	*"Ah, sweet Canada, Canada, Canada."*
Towhee, Rufous-sided:	*"Drink your tea,"* or *"See towhee."*
Warbler, Black-throated Green:	*"Trees, trees, murmuring trees."*
Warbler, Chestnut-sided:	*"I want to see Miss Beecher."*
Yellowthroat:	*"Witchity, witchity witchity witch."*

definitely am not), Schuyler Mathews's *Field Book of Wild Birds and Their Music* may be of some help in developing a personalized system. I think it would be a decided advantage to be able to jot down a few musical notes along with your various symbols and words.

The important thing is to develop your own system—one that you understand. You will be surprised at how many "strange" calls you can record in the field with enough accuracy for future identification. Some calls, like those of the bobolink and winter wren, are virtually impossible to record with a pencil, but once identified they are not easily forgotten.

The actual voices of most North American songbirds have been recorded on a number of records and tapes. (See the Bibliography for a list and details.) The use of these recordings is one of the most effective ways of learning bird songs. They are especially helpful when selected calls (of birds most likely to be seen and heard) can be listened to prior to a field trip.

Recordings

There are two points I would make regarding the use of recordings:

First, the listener should have a visual picture of the bird doing the singing. It does little good to hear the song of a bobolink if you haven't any concept of its size, shape, or color. For this reason, recordings are most effective when used in conjunction with slides, pictures, or field guides.

Second, keep the volume down. I recall walking into an identification session and hearing a song sparrow screech and groan like a subway train pulling into a station. For the song to be recognizable in the field, present it as naturally as possible. If you have a large group, they will just have to listen—a good introduction to field-trip etiquette.

Of all the natural habitats in the eastern United States, the hardwood forest is by far the most extensive. Extending from the borders of Canada, where it is in a constant struggle for survival with its coniferous neighbors, it spreads a verdant summer carpet southward across mountain and valley until it fades into the subtropic vegetation of the Gulf states. It reaches westward until inadequate rainfall and excessive transpiration cause it to surrender to the dominant prairie grasslands. From its primeval vastness of nearly half a million square miles, we have carved our great metropolises, our towns, our highways, and our farmlands. Yet despite these intrusions by man, and lacking most of its pristine state, the deciduous forest dominates our eastern landscape.

This great, green carpet does not enshroud the land in its entirety with any singular hue or texture. Stained and blotched by the trampling of three hundred years of "progress," it struggles constantly to regain its pristine beauty and structure. In all degrees of growth, there is evidence that the forest seizes every opportunity to reclaim the land for its own.

In the southern Appalachians, this struggle ends in a climax forest dominated by the cucumber tree, beech, tulip poplar, sugar maple, white oak, buckeye, and hemlock. This is the geographical heart of this vast forest realm. It is the oldest exposed land mass of the region, and scientists believe a similar forest has existed here since

3 Birds of the Hardwoods

Tertiary times. It is also believed to be the center of origin for many of the widespread hardwood species. Here there is a great variety of trees, and the biological associations are quite complex. There are perhaps twenty or more species (in addition to those just mentioned above) that could be part of a climax condition.

In the northern portions of this mixed mesophytic forest, the beech and the sugar maple strive for supremacy. As the broken forest reaches westward into Wisconsin and Minnesota, the beech gradually gives way to the basswood. A large portion of our eastern coastal forests were dominated by an oak-chestnut association until the Asian chestnut blight made its appearance in New York City in 1904. Forests along the mountains from New England to Georgia were affected by this deadly disease. A variety of oaks, tulip poplar, and some hickory are the prevailing species today. Even in the hardwood's most southern range, the oaks (in different varieties and association) preempt the enduring forest. Mixed with them are the gum, ash, dogwood, hackberry, and a variety of shrubs.

This great American forest, enriched with ecological diversity, provides homes, food, and shelter for numerous endemic species of birds and wildlife. Even man seeks its sanctuary, for it is in these same middle latitudes—where the hardwood forest flourishes in all its richness and beauty—that man has clustered in the greatest numbers.

Quiet and subdued in the cold grasp of winter, the leafless trees stand bleak and lonely in a steel-gray world. The pulse of life is slowed, and all but the hardiest of creatures lie snug in the torpor of hibernation. But there are those who must defy winter's cruelties and keep the pulse of life astir. The fox plies his stealth in the silence of the darkest night. His coat is thick and warm; he does not mind the cold as long as he can satiate his hunger. The tiny shrew, voracious and bloodthirsty, must hunt almost continuously in order to survive. Neither day nor season gives him rest from his foraging. The cottontail rabbit and the white-tailed deer browse upon the tender shoots of young trees and shrubs—the forest must not be choked by its own lush growth. The staccato hammering of woodpeckers resounds from hill to hill; there are no leaves to buffer its

SOME NESTING BIRDS OF THE EASTERN HARDWOODS

Chickadees and Titmice,
    Chickadee, Black-capped
    Chickadee, Carolina
    Titmouse, tufted
Creepers,
    Brown
Crows and Jays,
    Crow, Common
    Jay, Blue
Flycatchers,
    Acadian
    Great Crested
    Pewee, Eastern Wood
Gnatcatchers,
    Blue-gray
Goatsuckers,
    Whip-poor-will
Grosbeaks,
    Rose-breasted

Grouse,
    Ruffed
Hawks,
    Broad-winged
    Red-shouldered
Nuthatches,
    White-breasted
Owls,
    Barred
    Great Horned
Tanagers,
    Scarlet
    Summer
Thrushes,
    Veery
    Wood
Vireos,
    Red-eyed
    Yellow-throated

Warblers,
    Black and White
    Cerulean
    Hooded
    Kentucky
    Ovenbird
    Redstart, American
    Worm-eating
Woodcocks,
    American
Woodpeckers,
    Downy
    Hairy
    Pileated
    Red-bellied
    Sapsucker, Yellow-bellied

resonance. Chickadees and nuthatches join them in their search for grubs and insect larvae. Visiting grosbeaks, finches, and siskins reap a harvest of late-clinging seeds.

Life within the winter woodland continues—now dormant, now active. Not until the wandering Earth exposes its northern latitudes to the more vertical rays of the warming sun will life resume its hastening pace.

The coming of spring is inevitable. Slowly at first, and then with a resurgence of life that fills the forest with the colors, the sounds, and the aromas of a newborn season, spring emerges.

In the low wetlands, the skunk cabbage and the marsh marigolds have thrust through the mucklike forest floor; the maples are tinged with red, and the spicebush spreads a yellow haze through the valley. The "kon-kor-reee" of the male red-wing can be heard along the stream's marshy borders. Higher on the ridge, the aspens are draped with fuzzy gray catkins. The ruffed grouse relishes them and welcomes the change in diet. The black and white warbler is there, too, searching the trees for the first hatch of insects. The first butterfly of spring, the mourning cloak, emerges from its winter cocoon and flashes its golden-edged wings. And the sweet smell of arbutus is wafted on the warming winds along the sunny hillside.

Now the flow of spring surges in every forest vein. The bloodroot and the hepatica are in bloom; May apples, wild columbine, Solomon's seal, and bellwort must make their maximum growth before the closing forest canopy deprives them of sufficient light. The fringe-loving dogwood wraps the forest in a tattered ribbon of white. The songs of birds resound from every level—the ovenbird from the forest floor, the wood thrush from his low perch, and the scarlet tanager from the highest tree. There are warblers and vireos, grosbeaks and orioles, flycatchers and buntings. The rushing tide of spring has reached its crest.

Spring: the season of flowers, songs, mating, birth, and growth—the season of life renewed!

Spring: the season that beckons the inherent traits of man—the season when those of us who are interested in birds must answer the woodland's call!

As you leave your car and the sterile ribbons of concrete behind you and step into the cool shade of the forest, you are entering the most dynamic of all outdoor communities. You walk down the trail, rest on a decaying log, and survey the green world about you. Everything you see, hear, touch, or smell is in some way involved in a life-building pyramid of ecological events necessary for the forest's survival. The birds you came to watch fill a significant niche in this mounting struggle for life's energy.

The square foot of soil beneath your feet is a compact mass of energy that is being produced, stored, and used simultaneously. Its tiniest creature, the soil bacterium, makes its bid for dominance by the simple and rapid procreation process of dividing itself into two complete individuals every half-hour or so. Biologists tell us that if all the offspring of one such bacterium survived, their bulk would be larger than the earth in less than a week. As the soil lives, the energy cycle of control evolves. Protozoa and fungi are the most abundant, but they are preyed upon by mites, springtails, millipedes, and other animals. Earthworms, beetles, weevils, ants, larvae, and grubs build the pyramid higher. They, in turn, are subject to predation by shrews, moles, mice, and ground-feeding birds. Many of the larvae are transformed into insects and spend their adult lives amid the green foliage. Now the insect-eating birds help maintain the ladder of diminishing numbers. The pyramid is now above ground, and the energy-producing processes begin building toward the pinnacle.

The leaf-brown floor of the deep forest is home to the most mysterious and secretive of our woodland birds. The call of the ovenbird resounds loud and clear with unmistakable tones—a call of "teacher, teacher, teacher," that grows progressively louder. But this ecstatic song is deceptive as to distance, and the bird is not easily found. The woodcock is so secretive and blends so well with the forest floor that it can spend an entire nesting season near a well-traveled pathway without being discovered. The ruffed grouse sits tight and unnoticed until it explodes from near the intruder's feet with a startling whir of pounding wings.

Like the wood thrush, the ovenbird and the woodcock have comparatively large eyes adapted to the subdued light of the shaded forest. The ovenbird likes to sing from a log or fallen limb that gives it a slight elevation above the forest floor. This is where it is noticed most often. Once it is found, there is nothing reticent about its actions. If one watches quietly, it will continue to sing, or it can be observed walking across the matted leaves, flipping them aside in search of insects. The walk is deliberate and accompanied by a "jerking" or "wagging" of the tail. This action has resulted in such colloquial names as "wagtail warbler" and "woodland wagtail." The diet of the ovenbird consists mainly of the small creatures found in the upper strata of the forest floor—earthworms, slugs, snails, beetles, weevils, aphids, crickets, ants, and spiders. It also includes some flying insects.

The ovenbird gets its name from the type of nest it builds—an ovenlike structure, roofed over and with a single entrance. It is built on the ground, usually near an opening in the forest or along an old trail, making flight approach easier. The nest is built of a variety of materials including dead leaves, rootlets, bark, moss, and grass. It is lined with fine plant fibers or hair. The nest is so well camouflaged that it is usually discovered by flushing its occupant. Even then it is not found so easily, as the oven-bird will leave the nest and walk several feet away before taking flight.

Woodcocks are rather crepuscular in most of their habits. It is during the twilight hours that we see them settling into the alder and maple bottomlands. They come in singly—not in flocks. They must find soils well supplied with earthworms, for this is their main source of food. They are early spring migrants moving northward with the receding frost line; arrival in New England is as early as the latter part of February or the beginning of March.

The woodcock is a chunky quail-size bird with a long bill. The upper mandible is sensitive and somewhat flexible, enabling the woodcock to feel and capture earthworms by probing. Its large eyes, set well back on the head, are out of the way and allow it to see in all directions when in this rather precarious feeding position. Being mostly nocturnal, the woodcock is rarely seen in the actual process of feeding, but its tracks and borings are often visible in the low flat mudlands.

The dead-leaf coloring of the woodcock, its principal means of protection, gives it a deep trusting sense of security. It is a tight sitter and will not flush until nearly stepped upon; then it zigzags through limbs and treetops and settles down again 50 yards or so away. When it is nesting in a depression of brown leaves, one can look intently at the nesting site without seeing anything unusual. Not until the large eye is noticed is it possible to discern the shape of a bird. The woodcock has a spectacular courtship ritual. Since it takes place mostly in the darkness, it is described in Chapter 15, "Birds in the Night."

The woods of spring are filled with the exuberant sounds of life, but none is so profound as the drumming of the ruffed grouse. The male seeks a large log on which he can strut and display his prowess—and this he does in a grand manner. First he puffs out his chest, ruffs a ring of neck feathers to frame his profile, and expands his banded tail in fanlike fashion. He then struts back and forth on his stage like an egotistical performer surveying his audience. The wings are extended and held momentarily. All is quiet. The baton falls, and the performance begins. With a forward and slightly upward stroke of the wings, he compresses a pocket of air against his inflated chest. The resulting boom resounds through the forest. The drummer pauses for an instant; all seems well and the beat continues. Slowly, at first, it reverberates, and then with a rapidly increasing blur of wings, until the final flourish echoes like the muffled roll of distant tom-toms.

Wallace Byron Grange describes the ruffed grouse's drumming as: "Thrump! Thrump! Thrump!" "Thrump —— Thrump —— Thrump — Thrump — Thrump – Thrump – ThrumpThrumpThrump ThrumpThrumpThrumpThrump-Thrump-p-p-p-p-p-pppp ppppppppp!"

Arthur Cleveland Bent writes of it as: "the throbbing heart, as it were, of awakening spring."

The diet of the ruffed grouse is quite diversified, consisting of nuts, seeds, buds, catkins, foliage, wild fruits, and a variety of insects. During the summer months, when the birds are rearing a brood of young, they feed mostly on or near the ground. The young leave the nest as soon as they are dry. Their mother teaches them to forage among the leaves for worms, beetles, larvae, flies, ants, snails, and spiders. Strawberries, blueberries, dewberries, and low-growing blossoms and buds are also a part of their summer diet.

The female grouse is a very protective mother. I remember an occasion when I surprised a female leading her brood across an old lumber road. She immediately fluffed her feathers, spread her tail, and went into a charging rage. When this failed to deter me, she feigned a broken wing and went fluttering off across the forest floor. Her ruse worked. I was so busy watching her performance that I didn't notice the chicks disappear into the surrounding cover. I've no doubt that such a devoted mother could give an inquisitive snake or small mammal a rough reception.

Adult ruffed grouse are primarily browsers. The buds

and flowers of aspen, hazelnut, birch, and apple are favorits foods. They also relish the leaves of clover, sheep sorrel, wintergreen, greenbrier, and numerous woodland plants.

It is an interesting, and sometimes humorous, sight if one is lucky enough to see grouse in the process of "budding." They will fly onto the limb of a favorite tree and proceed to pick the buds one after another. They work their way out toward the tip of the limb (where the most buds are) until they have to employ all sorts of contortions to keep their balance on the flimsy branches. Finally they give up, fly to a new limb, and start the process over again.

When the day's light fades from the forest, and most of its diurnal creatures have quieted for the night, the bell-like tones of the wood thrush peal from the darkening depths. In the Northeast and along the middle ridges of the Appalachians, this hour of song is sometimes shared with the veery, whose treble flutelike song spirals downward with a distinctive "whree-ur, whree-ur, whree-ur, whree." Both species are primarily ground feeders, but there is a decided difference in their feeding habits. The wood thrush is a thorough hunter; it hops across the forest floor turning over leaf after leaf as it searches for insects. The veery seems more impatient; it will fly to a low limb, log, or stump, hop down to the ground, and feed momentarily. It will then fly to another low perch and repeat the process. The veery undoubtedly covers a wider feeding range than the wood thrush, but perhaps not so thoroughly.

The two thrushes also differ in the way they build their nests. Again, the veery likes to stay slightly above ground level. Lacking a low stump, tree crotch, or bit of brush, it will often build a mound of dead and rotting leaves, sometimes as much as a foot in height. The cuplike nest is lined in the center with dry leaves, rootlets, and plant fibers. The wood thrush prefers to nest 6 or more feet above the ground in understory trees and shrubs. The forked crotch of a dogwood limb is a favorite location. Its nest is somewhat like that of a robin. It uses mud to bind together decaying leaves, rootlets, grass, and weed stems. The wood thrush has the singular custom of placing one or more pieces of something white (rag, paper, or a bleached leaf or grass blades) in the exterior edge of the nest. The reason for this is still a matter of conjecture, but the most plausible explanation suggests this peculiarity is an attempt to break the recognizable contour of the nest. This theory is further substantiated by the fact that brooding females, or fledglings still in the nest, will point their heads upward and display their white throats when disturbed.

Ground-nesting species are subject to the controlling law of predation. Eggs and young are sought by snakes, raccoons, foxes, skunks, weasels, and other creatures that prowl the forest by day or night. Survival is largely a matter of protective coloration and the instinctive understanding of how to use it.

We think of the forest as being shadowy—even dark— but light is one of the most predominant forces within this woodland realm. Growth is controlled largely by surface areas exposed to light. As springtime advances and the rising sap pushes the swollen buds into leaf, plants compete for the direct rays of the sun. Gradually the canopy closes, and the forest is "roofed over" with a lacy pattern of overlapping leaves. This green roof now becomes a controlling factor in the climatic changes and living conditions within the forest. It not only influences the amount of light reaching the understory, but affects the temperature and humidity as well—physical factors that modify, or in some way become a part of, the intricate life cycles of all woodland creatures.

The yellow-bellied sapsucker welcomes this resurgent flow of the trees' sweet juices. They will be a stable part of its diet throughout the growing season. The green leaves, tender and abundant, become the basic link in countless food chains that transport the forest's energy on a circuitous route of interdependence. It is the time of insects— the time when their myriad numbers threaten to denude the forest of all living matter. But it is also the time of birds—the time when they, too, are at the peak of their abundance. Permanent and summer residents expend their energy in preparation for the ensuing nesting season. They are joined by a flood of transients wending their way

northward. Birds are present in such numbers and varieties that every niche of the forest is subject to their specialized hunting techniques.

The sapsucker sets its trap by drilling a hole in the bole of its favorite tree. It drinks the sap and eats the cambium, the tender layer between the bark and hard wood. The hole is drilled at a slightly downward angle, and acts as a miniature reservoir. When this reservoir overflows, and the sap runs down the tree, the sapsucker is very careful not to get this sticky substance on its body feathers. (If you watch a sapsucker feed, you will notice that only its feet and the spiked tips of its tail touch the tree.) The dripping sap attracts ants, moths, and a variety of other insects; ants are an important part of the sapsucker's diet. Numerous birds find an easy meal among the trapped insects; the ruby-throated hummingbird and the Baltimore oriole will sometimes drink from the tiny reservoirs.

During the nesting season, when the demand for food is greatest, the sapsucker's drillings are more numerous. It will drill a series of holes in its "orchard," and tend them as prudently as a New Englander would tend his sugarbush.

The trunks and limbs of forest trees are subject to the close scrutiny of a variety of birds especially adapted to this purpose. The tiny brown creeper starts at the base of a tree and spirals its way upward, hitching along in woodpecker fashion. With its long, curved bill, it probes into deep crevices and behind bits of scaling bark, where it finds small beetles, weevils, ants, spiders, and the larvae, pupae, or eggs of numerous insects. The white-breasted nuthatch searches the tree from a different angle; it starts high and works downward in a head-first position. The black and white warbler, unlike most other members of its family, hunts extensively on the trunks and larger limbs of trees. It is like both the creeper and the nuthatch in its actions; it would just as soon feed coming down the tree as going up. Also, it will leave the trunk of the tree, dart into the air, and catch a flying insect in typical warbler style. The woodpeckers inspect the trees from still another viewpoint; with their chisellike bills, they will drill through the bark in search of cambium-feeding and wood-boring grubs. Tanagers and wood pewees patrol the upper reaches of the larger trees.

The forest's multilayered canopy is subject to increasing hordes of rapacious insects. They are present in such numbers and varieties that every tree and shrub is a potential victim of their foraging. There are leaf-chewing and leaf-mining specialists; others are specifically adapted to eating wood or seeds. Populations are kept within reasonable balance mostly by climate and the abundance of their enemies, especially birds.

Vireos, flycatchers, and certain warblers are common birds of the deciduous woodlands, and they find this great variety of insects much to their liking. The vireos and warblers are quick of flight and are persistent hunters. The flycatchers are watchers; they sit on a favorite perch and dart into the air to catch passing insects. The red-eyed vireo and the redstart (warbler) are the two most abundant birds of our eastern hardwoods. It is reasonably safe to say that every deciduous woods, large or small, from northern Florida to the Canadian border will have at least one pair of nesting red-eyes. They are sometimes joined by other vireos—the white-eyed, the yellow-throated, the warbling, and, in the northern hardwoods, the Philadelphia. But none is so plentiful as the red-eyed. The redstart is at home in the second-growth woodlands from Georgia and Alabama to the Gulf of St. Lawrence and central Manitoba.

Other species of warblers particularly partial to this diversified habitat include the hooded, worm-eating, cerulean, Kentucky, and waterthrush (warbler). Invariably, the Kentucky warbler is found in the low, moist bottomlands, and the waterthrush along woodland streams. The cerulean is a bird of the treetops, and by contrast, the hooded and worm-eating prefer understory thickets.

The great crested flycatcher is the largest member of its family to nest in our eastern woods. It is nearly robin-sized in length, but not quite so plump, and is easily recognized by the long rufous tail and yellowish breast. This is the only flycatcher we will find nesting in cavities. Like the wood thrush, the great crested flycatcher has adjusted to the encroachment of civilization. It will often abandon its woodland habitat to nest in old orchards and open parklands. The same could be said of the least flycatcher; it, too, can be found in the open woods, orchards, and groves. The Acadian flycatcher and the wood pewee still prefer the shaded woodlands, but the phoebe often nests under bridges and the eaves of buildings. The smaller fly-catchers are distinguished best by their calls, as the birds are quite similar in shape and coloration. To me, the Acadian says "wits-see" with a rising inflection, while the least flycatcher has a definite and choppy "che-bek." The phoebe and wood pewee are quite similar in appearance, but each one calls its own name, making recognition quite easy. The phoebe has a phonetically correct "phoe-be." The wood pewee whistles a slow, drawn-out, "pee-a-wee."

The scarlet tanager, the summer tanager, and the rose-breasted grosbeak are among the most colorful of our woodland birds. Both species of tanagers are sometimes referred to as "the guardians of oaks," for it is among these dominant trees that they like to nest and feed. They consume large quantities of insect eggs, larvae, moths, beetles, weevils, caterpillars, and other infectious creatures to which the oaks are a helpless host. Both tanagers are nearly starling size. The males are red, but the male scarlet tanager is distinguished by his coal-black wings. The females are more easily confused—olive backs and yellowish breasts—but the darker color of the scarlet tanager's wings is the perceptible difference.

The rose-breasted grosbeak is slightly larger than the starling. The male has a big red "strawberry" on an otherwise all-white breast. His head and back are mostly black, making a striking contrast with the white underparts. His mate reminds you of the female red-wing, but the large seed-eating bill is very pronounced. The animal portion of the rose-breasted grosbeak's food is similar to that of the tanagers, but seeds, buds, and wild fruits make up approximately 50 percent of its diet.

Tanagers and rose-breasted grosbeaks are more plentiful than the novice birder realizes. Their songs are somewhat similar to those of the robin and the red-eyed vireo, and often they are not noticed by the untrained ear.

The great diversity of plant life in the deciduous forest

provides a multiplicity of nesting materials and home sites for birds. Just as certain species are adapted to feeding in definite niches within the forest, so are they inherently adapted to using specific materials and locations for their nests. Virtually every substance is used, and all forest levels occupied, by one species or another. But it is the understory trees—the dogwoods, the witch hazels, the hornbeams, and a variety of shrubs and saplings—that are most densely occupied. Here in this shaded layer, we find the homes of the woodlands' master architects: the vireos.

The red-eyed vireo builds a cuplike nest suspended from a forked branch of a horizontal tree limb. Watching a pair of red-eyes build their beautiful pensile home, a person is reminded of one of nature's great mysteries. How do a pair of young red-eyes (or the young of any species), returning to the forest for the first time, know what materials to use and what procedures to follow in order to build a model home singularly characteristic of its species? They do not serve an apprenticeship, nor do they have a supervisor to show them what to do. We credit them with an innate sense of perception, but this only adds to the mystery of their actions. Let us watch a pair of red-eyes build their nest so that you have a better understanding of what I mean.

If we are lucky enough to observe the nesting site from the very beginning, we will see considerable hopping back and forth across the selected fork. This is undoubtedly a period of determining whether that particular fork is satisfactory, especially as to size. (I believe that mistakes are made sometimes, because I do not know of another reason why red-eyes will occasionally dismantle a nearly completed nest and use the materials to start a new one nearby.) The actual nest building begins by suspending rather long fibers, usually the supple strands of grapevine bark, from both twigs of the fork. These are "sewed" fast with spider webs, webbing from canker worms and caterpillars, or the silk from various cocoons. More fibers are hung in the same way until there is enough to begin weaving them together to form the bottom. The nest now has a basketlike appearance. This miniature basket is strengthened by adding bits of bark (usually birch), rootlets, fine grasses,

paper from wasps' nests, and portions of dead leaves. All loose ends are woven in, and the whole nest is bound together with quantities of silk and webbing. The outside is usually decorated or camouflaged with bits of lichens.

Although our woodland warblers are quite similar in size and feeding habits (insect-eating), they are quite diverse in their choice of nesting sites. Every level of the forest is utilized, from the floor to high in the canopy. The ovenbird is not the only ground nester of this family. The worm-eating warbler builds a similar nest amid wind-drifted leaves next to an old log or stump, or against the base of a tree. The black and white warbler and the Kentucky warbler will nest on or very near the ground. We look for the nest of the hooded warbler in the densest of thickets, usually no more than 2 or 3 feet above the ground. It is quite partial to thick clumps of laurel and rhododendron. The redstart nests in the understory, but the cerulean secludes its home high in the taller trees.

The redstart is not only the most common warbler of our deciduous woodlands, it is also the most colorful. The male is a striking pattern of orange, black, and white. He is quite cognizant of his beauty and uses it extensively in courtship and territorial displays. He patrols his selected territory with vigor, flashing his orange-banded tail as a warning to all would-be intruders. When courting a female, he also spreads his wings and tail, displaying his brilliance in a most captivating manner.

The usual nesting site of the redstart is in an understory sapling or shrub. The nest is securely wedged into a vertical crotch with three or more branches. The female builds the nest of rootlets, grass, and fibers of bark. The interior is lined with whatever soft material can be found— animal hair, feathers, or fine plant fibers. The outside may be finished with bits of lichens, bud scales, or seed pods.

Still more niches within the forest provide home sites for additional species. The brown creeper tucks its nest behind some loosened bark on the trunk of a tree, the lone white pine may be the home of a long-eared owl, and the dancing shadows on a sparse section of the forest floor may camouflage a brooding whip-poor-will. The grosbeaks and tanagers add their numbers to the populous understory, and the phoebe seeks shelter under an overhanging ledge or against the base of an upturned tree.

As the lush growth of summer tightens the canopy over the forest, plants, too, become involved in the constant struggle for life-sustaining energy. Some must die so others may live. Those that reach the direct rays of the sun, or receive sufficient reflected skylight, will survive; others will succumb in the darkening shade. The natural processes of pruning and thinning begin. Many lower limbs and young trees will die from overcrowding and the lack of light; others will survive to reach ever higher toward the original source of all energy. But nature will continue to harvest the forest in many ways. Wind storms will damage limbs and trunks and uproot entire trees; insects and disease will follow, and the trees will die. Even fire sometimes exerts beneficial controls, for certain trees must have a barren seed bed to perpetuate their own kind. Without periodic fires, they cannot survive.

The mature forest soon heals its wounds, but the scars of broken limbs and trees remain. This is a part of nature's scheme, for now the woodpeckers and other cavity-nesting specialists forage and live among the dead and dying. The dead will be returned to the soil, keeping the energy cycle intact.

Through the ages, woodpeckers have evolved as specialists, and they fill a particular niche in the delicate balance of the outdoor community that is not covered by other species. Their bills are long, heavy, and chisel-shaped for drilling through bark and wood. The woodpecker's tongue is exceptionally long and barbed; it can be extended far into drilled holes and the cavities of wood-boring larvae or grubs—its favorite food. When recessed, the long tongue is curved upward and forward following the contour of the skull. The bird's skull is unusually heavy, protecting the brain from the shock of drilling. The feet of most woodpeckers have two toes forward and two toes rearward to give them better grip and balance when climbing trees. (The three-toed species are exceptions.) Tails are stiff and spine-tipped; they serve as props when the woodpeckers are climbing or drilling.

As you sit quietly on your log seat in the woods, you will undoubtedly be treated to the entertaining antics of the downy woodpecker. First you will hear it tapping on some distant tree. You will be tempted to get up and go searching for this familiar woodland sound. But there is no need to move; the downy has probably spotted you already; sooner or later, its inquisitive nature will prevail, and it will move close enough for you to observe each other. The approach will be gradual, first to one tree and then to another, each move bringing it closer to you. Finally, it will settle on the trunk of a tree and pretend to feed. Notice how it hitches up, down, and sideways on the trunk, and how it weaves its head from side to side at each stop. As you observe these actions, you will also notice that the downy is busy all the time and, seemingly, is not a bit interested in your presence. The downy never looks you straight in the eye.

Now watch closely, and you will see how a woodpecker leaves a tree. Using its feet (and sometimes its tail as well), the downy springs backward, turns, and dives to pick up immediate flying speed, all within the fraction of a second.

The hairy woodpecker is not as easily observed as the downy. Although the range and the type of territory inhabited by each species are nearly identical, the hairy is considerably rarer and much more seclusive than the downy. Many smaller woodlots may not harbor a single hairy, but still provide homes for several pairs of downy woodpeckers. Look for the hairy in the deeper woods, and listen for its loud kingfisherlike call, or its loud distinctive drumming. At first the downy may fool you, but once you see and hear the hairy, you are not likely to be mistaken again.

The hairy's tree-climbing techniques are similar to those of the downy, yet somewhat individualistic. It will sometimes use a creeping motion and spiral about a tree in a manner reminiscent of the brown creeper or the black and white warbler. When it is being observed, it will work mostly on the far side of the tree, hiding much as a squirrel would do.

The feeding and nesting habits of both species are

comparable. The largest single item in their diet is the larvae of wood-boring beetles, often as much as 75 percent; ants comprise about another 20 percent. The waxy fruits of such plants as sumac, poison ivy, and bayberry supplement this diet, particularly in the winter. Both are cavity nesters, and they usually drill their holes in a dead limb or in the trunk of a dead tree. The cavities are gourd-shaped and up to 12 inches in depth. A few fine chips are left in the bottom as nesting material. The hairy will often return to the same nesting tree year after year, as long as the structure is sturdy enough to support another family.

The most wondrous of all our woodland woodpeckers is surely the pileated. Big and handsome, it works in the larger timbered areas with the skill of a lumberjack. It is really an exciting experience for the birder who sees this crow-sized woodpecker for the first time. The contrasting black and white coloration and the conspicuous red crest make identification unmistakable. (The nearly extinct ivory-billed is the only other woodpecker with a crest.) Its behavior is equally distinctive. I think I can describe it best by telling about my luckiest observation of this species.

I was in a remote section of Maine, some 10 miles or so north of Lake Kenebago, following a woodland trail en route to a small lake to do some trout fishing. A pileated woodpecker soared across the trail several yards in front of me and, with a few rather slow, rhythmic wing beats, lifted itself up about 30 feet onto the trunk of a decaying sugar maple. There was an immediate call, loud and strong, that sounded like a continuous run of the syllables "wuck-wuck-wuck-a-wuck." It disappeared on the far side of the tree, and I seated myself amid the low branches of a small beech tree to watch the proceedings; the trout fishing could wait. The maple was obviously a current feeding tree, for there was one vertical trench about 2 feet long already dug, and the interior wood seemed bright and fresh. At first the pileated was a bit reluctant to resume its drilling. It would hitch around the tree, weave its head from side to side in typical woodpecker fashion, and then seclude itself on the far side again. After repeating this act a few times, it started to chisel a new trench a foot or so below the first one. The outer layer flaked off quite easily, and the big woodpecker was soon working on the hard interior wood, obviously cutting its way into a colony of large black timber ants—the main item of the pileated's diet. I was amazed at the size of the chips that fell to the ground. (Later checking proved some of them to be 3 and 4 inches long.) Actually, some were more like long splinters, and considerable chiseling took place before they fell.

I watched this woodpecker for 10 minutes or more from a distance of about 200 feet, but I never did get to see it feed. It left the tree suddenly with an alarming cackle of "ka-ka-ka-ka." Later in the day when I was fishing on the lake, I could hear the loud drumming roll of the pileated. It may have been the same bird, but I was more than a mile from where I had seen it.

The range of the pileated woodpecker extends from southern Canada southward through Florida and the Gulf states, but it cannot be considered a common bird. It undoubtedly suffered a depletion in population after the harvesting of our virgin forests. Now there are indications that its numbers are on the increase once again. Many second-growth hardwood and mixed forests have increased sufficiently in size and extent to support this rather exacting woodpecker.

The typical nesting site of the pileated is a large, dead tree stub, usually in a remote section of the forest's bottomlands. The pileated will return to the same nesting tree for succeeding years, but it will always excavate a new cavity. I have known abandoned cavities to be occupied by screech owls and by wood ducks.

Although the red-headed woodpecker, the red-bellied woodpecker, and the flicker are often found in open woodlands, they can hardly be considered true forest birds. Today, these species are more at home in gardens, orchards, groves, parks, and similar open areas. For this reason they will be considered elsewhere in this book (see the Index).

Woodpeckers' importance as destroyers of insects is quickly recognized, but they make additional contributions to the functioning of the outdoor community that are not noticed so readily. Their drillings and excavations hasten the return of decaying trees to the forest floor.

Also, the vacated cavities provide homes for many woodland creatures.

As you wander through the woods, you will notice numerous old woodpecker holes in dead stubs and trees. These are the abandoned homes from previous years, but now many of them have new tenants. The most common hole nesters which follow the woodpeckers in our eastern hardwoods include the black-capped chickadee, Carolina chickadee, tufted titmouse, white-breasted nuthatch, and great crested flycatcher.

Chickadees have long been known as the most sprightly and the most cheerful of our woodland birds. And rightly so, for their familiar "dee-dee-dee" welcomes you to the forest at any time of the year. They are so trustful of man that they will often accompany you along the trail, flitting from tree to tree so close that there is usually no need to use binoculars. As you watch them, you will often find their actions quite entertaining, for they seem to delight in showing off for a captive audience. Their flight from branch to branch is almost instantaneous—so quick that it is often difficult to follow, especially with binoculars. They are constantly on the move, searching for plant lice, insect eggs, spiders, caterpillars, ants, and other bits of food. They will often cling to the outermost bud on the tip of a swaying branch in an inverted position. At times, they will turn completely over in somersault fashion as they search for tiny morsels in a place not easily accessible to other species.

Both species of chickadees will nest in abandoned woodpecker sites, but more often than not, they will excavate their own nesting cavities. Frequently they will finish a site that was started previously by an exploratory woodpecker. Chickadees do not have strong powerful beaks like the woodpeckers, so they select a low, rotting stub of softer wood. They prefer a stub with a wraparound type of bark, such as gray birch or poplar. Often, this strong wrapping of bark is all that holds the stub together at the cavity area.

Considering their diminutive size, chickadees rear large families. The average clutch of eggs will number from six to eight, although ornithologists have recorded as many as thirteen in a single set. The young are heavily feathered when they leave the nest, but they have a decidedly disheveled appearance. It is an interesting sight to see them all lined up on a branch waiting for food. They look like a line of unkempt forest urchins waiting for a handout.

The impelling forces within a maturing forest provide homes for cavity-nesting birds in different ways. In addition to holes drilled by woodpeckers, there are many knotholes scattered throughout the forest as a result of the natural processes of pruning—overcrowding, storms, and insufficient light. When a weakened limb falls to the ground, the remaining scar is subject to moisture, insects, and disease. Gradually a cavity is formed, resulting in a favorite nesting site for the titmouse or the great crested flycatcher. Lightning will split a tree, and the deep cracks provide nesting crevices for the nuthatch. Each force within the forest produces a characteristic change that benefits certain members of the community.

Nature's most violent methods of harvesting the forest —hurricanes, tornadoes, and heavy ice storms—bring about the most radical changes within the hardwood community. Limbs are broken, and trees are snapped and uprooted. The protective canopy is thinned or eliminated, and a gradual ecological change begins within the open forest. The thrushes, tanagers, grosbeaks, certain warblers, and other species may no longer find this habitat to their liking. But they will be replaced by those that do: towhees, thrashers, chats, buntings, and many more. The abundance of damaged trees and shrubs will eventually bring about an influx of cavity-nesting species adapted to this more open type of environment. Red-headed woodpeckers and flickers will be at home here; house wrens, bluebirds, and tree swallows will compete for the smaller cavities; sparrow hawks and screech owls may vie for the larger openings. These species will thrive here until the forest once again closes its canopy, and the deepening shade invites the return of thrushes and the vireos.

No matter how enticing the environment may be, or how abundant any one species becomes, nothing is allowed to increase beyond reasonable bounds. Nature exerts her relentless forces of control. An abundance of nesting sites is of little value if the surrounding territory lacks sufficient food to support the ensuing families. As the increased population competes for food and cover, the weak and the exposed are prey for patrolling predators. Thus, nature retains the strongest and most alert individuals to propagate the species.

Predation within the bird community exists in many forms. Body lice or internal worms may weaken the individual, making it an easy capture for the sharp-shinned or the Cooper's hawk. The cowbird's parasitic habit of laying its eggs in the nests of other birds undoubtedly limits the number of the host species that will survive. The destruction of nests by reptiles and mammals restricts population numbers. Hawks and owls patrol wide areas and help harvest the excess crop.

Among our eastern hawks, three species of buteos—the red-tailed, the red-shouldered, and the broad-winged—are the most common residents of the deciduous hardwoods. The red-tailed is the most widely distributed, but in certain areas of its range it is outnumbered by the red-shouldered or the broad-winged. Two of the accipiters, the sharp-shinned and the Cooper's hawk, are present in limited numbers, although they have a preference for coniferous or mixed forests. They are seen most often darting through the understory in pursuit of some smaller bird.

The red-tailed hawk and the broad-winged hawk prefer the drier upland sections of the forest, while the red-shouldered hawk is more at home in moist bottomlands and timbered river valleys. All three species show a preference for areas of larger timber, not for reasons of protection, but because it is more open and better suited to their hunting techniques.

In the spring, the buteos announce their arrival by soaring above the woods and uttering their calls of defiance against possible intruders. The red-tailed circles and cries "keeer-r-r-r" on a descending scale. The call of the red-shouldered is a pronounced two-syllable whistle: "kee-yer, kee-yer." The broad-winged whistles a long-drawn-out "k-wee-e-e-e-e."

Buteos have similar requirements for nesting sites and food, and therefore are not particularly tolerant of each other. You are not likely to find a red-tailed and a red-shouldered occupying the same territory. However, either species will permit one of the accipiters to nest nearby without any noticeable difficulty. Both species nest high (usually 30 to 75 feet above ground) and build their nests in a sturdy crotch against the trunk of the tree. The nests, constructed of sticks and twigs, are lined with strips of pliable bark, dry leaves, moss, and down from their bodies. On occasion, they will rebuild their old nests or build upon the foundations of nests originally constructed by crows, squirrels, or owls. When rebuilding such a nest, they will stake claim to it by placing a fresh green twig on the nest. This is especially true of the red-tailed hawk.

The red-shouldered hawk and the barred owl are quite compatible. A. C. Bent, in his *Life Histories of North American Birds of Prey*, gives this account: "I have always considered the red-shouldered hawk and the barred owl as tolerant, complementary species, frequenting similar haunts and living on similar food, one hunting the territory by day and the other by night. We often find them in the same woods and using the same nests alternately, occasionally both laying eggs in the same nest the same season, resulting in a mixed set of eggs on which one or both species may incubate."

The broad-winged is considered to be the tamest of our hawks, yet it is chiefly a deep-woods bird. Like the red-tailed and the red-shouldered, it feeds on small mammals, an occasional bird, and the larger insects. It will also perch along the edge of a pond waiting for a chance to capture snakes, crayfish, toads, frogs, or even an unwary minnow. The nest of the broad-winged is a comparatively flimsy structure, especially when it lacks the base of some other old nest. Like most hawks, the broad-winged rears a small family, averaging two eggs per set.

The broad-winged is typical of the many hawks that have a habit of keeping the nest furnished with one or more twigs of fresh green leaves. Just why they do this has long been a debatable subject among ornithologists. Some believe it is done for sanitation purposes; others believe it is a simple matter of decoration or camouflage. And there are those of a more quixotic nature who believe it is a sign of devotion for the mate—a bouquet of roses for the expectant mother.

And so the forest survives. And so the creatures that it shelters survive, in a balance according to the food and cover it supplies. Trees, shrubs, and ground plants continue their role as basic builders of life, by capturing the energy from the sun and the elements from air, soil, and water. Insects increase in multitudinous numbers, and are preyed upon at every level within the forest. Most are destroyed, but some must survive to pollinate the forest, to help remove the dead, and to propagate their own kind. As the never-ending struggle for life's energy continues, the pyramid of surviving numbers grows higher and narrower with fewer and stronger species at each succeeding level. In the forest community, the hawk, the deer, or the bear may reach the pinnacle, for they have few enemies other than man. But even they must succumb to nature's ways, and eventually surrender their place to the young and the strong. And yet, even in death, the energy cycle continues, for now the scavengers—vultures, crows, and beetles—come to the fore to claim their share. And then the bacteria, fungi, and mites return the remaining bits to the soil. The cycle is complete, and the same atoms of energy once again surge through the veins of the forest.

4 Birds of the Evergreens

The evergreen forest is a land of legend and mystery that keeps challenging one's imagination. To walk into its green, shadowy depths of springtime is to enter a strange new world—a world characteristically unique with its own vastness of uniformity, its own life forms, and its own odors and sounds. On occasion, it is shrouded in an austere silence that seems to still time's passing. You learn patience here, for time will not be rushed; it proceeds with the same metronomic beat that built this green world over eons past. Your senses become keen and alert. The aroma of sun-baked spruce and fir fills the air, and there is a pleasant resiliency to the duff and moss beneath your feet. The ferns cast lacy shadows on the ground, and the bunchberries are clothed in white. A spruce grouse flies to a low limb along the trail to watch your passing. It shows no concern, just curiosity—you are but one of the forest. And from the distance, a white-throated sparrow sings the praises of his country, "sweet Canada, Canada, Canada." You stop and you listen. You realize it is quite probable that no other human has ever heard the sweet notes of this particular bird.

Yes, the great green forest is an enchanted land. "Come," it seems to say, "come, and I will share with you my beauty and my secrets. I will help you find solitude and peace."

You accept its challenge, and suddenly you are alone—alone in an emerald world that beckons you onward and onward.

Because of certain physical, biological, and geographical differences within the vast expanse of the coniferous forest community on our continent, ecologists have divided it into three subdivisions for purposes of closer identification and reference. The broad band of evergreens spanning our continent south of the tundra, and extending southward through Canada into the northern edge of the United States, is referred to as the Transcontinental Coniferous Forest. The eastern extension of this band, reaching southward through New England, and into the Appalachians at higher elevations, is known as the Eastern Montane Coniferous Forest. Similar extensions into the Rocky Mountains, and into the Sierra Nevada–Cascades in California, constitute the Western Montane Coniferous Forest. In this book, we are concerned primarily with the eastern half of the Transcontinental Coniferous Forest and the Eastern Montane Coniferous Forest. In addition to these main subdivisions, there are extensive areas of managed pine forests in the South to be considered.

Evergreen Forest Formations

The ecological relationships within the range of our coniferous forests are similar, although there is considerable variation in both plant and animal species, depending on temperature and other physical factors. In northern regions, white spruce and balsam fir are dominant species and represent climax conditions in isolated undisturbed areas. In the transition area between forest and tundra, balsam fir is noticeably absent and is often replaced by black spruce and tamarack. Jack pine and paper birch are close associates of the dominant species.

The southern edge of the transcontinental band contains extensive stands of white pine from New England westward to Minnesota. Jack pine and red pine may occupy the less desirable sites, particularly in the lake states. In the mountainous extension of the coniferous forest from New England into the Appalachians, red spruce and hemlock gradually replace the white spruce, and at the southern end, Fraser fir becomes the ecological equivalent of the balsam fir in northern areas.

The numerous deciduous trees, shrubs, and ground-cover plants vary greatly from northern to southern transitional zones. Many of these will be included as we study the individual species of birds and their relationships to the plant life in the various biological niches of the evergreen community.

Birds of the Evergreen Forests

Bird species and numbers are not uniformly distributed throughout the great span of evergreen timberlands. A particular species will be found in the forest area only where physical and biological factors meet its specific needs. Some birds, like the red-cockaded woodpecker of the southern pinelands, have definite habitat requirements and are, consequently, very limited in range. Others—the hermit thrush and brown creeper, for example—are considerably more tolerant of habitat conditions, and are more widely distributed. The following lists include those forest species most likely to be found in the three subdivisions with which we are mainly concerned. Widely distributed species may occur in all lists, while others with more specific requirements will occur in only one. Also, each list contains a few species that are limited to a comparatively small section of the subdivision. As with all lists, they are not intended to be all-inclusive. Undoubtedly, on any particular field trip, some listed species will not be found, and others may be added.

Birding in the Evergreens

The topography of our northern forest areas is largely the result of glaciation. The soil is comparatively thin, and underlying rock formations have been exposed in many places. Along the southern boundary of the forest, the soil is deeper because of extensive moraine deposits. Glacial movements left a rolling terrain with numerous lakes, bogs, streams, ridges, and rock outcroppings. These features often acted as barriers to the extension of climax vegetation, and resulted in a different habitat complex.

Uniformity within the evergreen forest is affected greatly also by the natural phenomenon of fire. In mature northern stands, the accumulated duff is sometimes so thick that reseeding is virtually impossible. Fire thins the

BIRDS OF THE EASTERN MONTANE CONIFEROUS FOREST

Creepers,
  Brown
Flycatchers,
  Olive-sided
  Yellow-bellied
Grosbeaks, Finches, Sparrows,
and Buntings,
  Crossbill, Red
  Finch, Purple
  Grosbeak, Evening
  Junco, Slate-colored
  Siskin, Pine
  Sparrow, Fox
  Sparrow, White-throated
Grouse,
  Spruce
Hawks,
  Goshawk

Kinglets,
  Golden-crowned
Nuthatches,
  Red-breasted
Owls,
  Barred
  Great Horned
  Long-eared
Thrushes,
  Hermit
  Swainson's
Vireos,
  Solitary
Warblers,
  Bay-breasted
  Blackburnian
  Blackpoll
  Black-throated Blue

Black-throated Green
Canada
Magnolia
Myrtle
Nashville
Palm
Parula
Pine
Woodpeckers,
  Northern Three-toed
Wrens,
  Winter

BIRDS OF THE TRANSCONTINENTAL CONIFEROUS FOREST

Chickadees,
  Boreal
Creepers,
  Brown
Flycatchers,
  Olive-sided
  Yellow-bellied
Grosbeaks, Finches, Sparrows,
and Buntings,
  Crossbill, Red
  Crossbill, White-winged
  Finch, Purple
  Grosbeak, Evening
  Grosbeak, Pine
  Junco, Slate-colored
  Siskin, Pine
  Sparrow, Fox
  Sparrow, White-throated
Grouse,
  Spruce
Hawks,
  Goshawk

Jays,
  Gray
Kinglets,
  Golden-crowned
  Ruby-crowned
Nuthatches,
  Red-breasted
Owls,
  Barred
  Great Horned
  Hawk-Owl
  Long-eared
Thrushes,
  Hermit
  Swainson's
Vireos,
  Solitary
Warblers,
  Bay-breasted
  Blackburnian
  Blackpoll
  Black-throated Blue

Black-throated Green
Canada
Cape May
Magnolia
Myrtle
Nashville
Palm
Parula
Pine
Tennessee
Woodpeckers,
  Black-backed Three-toed
  Northern Three-toed
Wrens,
  Winter

duff and exposes the soil, thus preparing a natural seed bed. In the coastal plains of our eastern states, fire is used as a deliberate ecological control in the maintenance of longleaf pine stands. Natural periodic fires in the jack pines of Michigan (the only known breeding habitat of the Kirtland's warbler) have contributed to the continuous growth of young trees essential to the species' nesting requirements.

But man, more than any other factor, has wrought the greatest changes in the evergreen forest. There was a time when the only man-made sound in the great northern woods was the rhythmic thumping of paddles against the sides of birch-bark canoes, but now scarcely an acre stands that has not heard the ring of an ax, or the whine of a chain saw. Man's disturbances have brought about drastic changes in plant succession. There is no doubt that these disturbances have also brought about corresponding changes in forest bird populations.

Your First Trip

Your first trip into the northern evergreen forest will be a memorable one. The moment you step from your car, you will be met by the welcoming committee: black flies and mosquitoes, but do not let them deter you. At this point there are two things to remember. First: Maintain a proper mental attitude. Look upon them as warbler food and not as myriad tiny vampires destined to drain the last drop of blood from all bird watchers. Second: Break out your Cutter's insect repellent. I prefer to use the cream style on my face and hands, and to spray my clothing from a pressurized can. This procedure will make you relatively immune and enable you to enjoy the trip without sacrificing your good red blood.

There is one other precaution that everyone entering the vastness of the evergreen forest should take: Don't get lost! This may seem like a superfluous bit of advice, but remember, even experienced hunters have been known to spend a sleepless night in the woods because they could not find their way out. The interior of an evergreen forest is somewhat like the middle of the ocean: everything looks the same in all directions. If you stay on or near trails, you can easily retrace your course. A compass can be helpful,

BIRDS OF THE SOUTHERN PINELANDS*

Chickadees,
  Carolina
Gnatcatchers,
  Blue-gray
Goatsuckers,
  Chuck-will's-widow
Grosbeaks, Finches, Sparrows,
and Buntings,
  Cardinal
  Sparrow, Bachman's
  Sparrow, Field
  Towhee, Rufous-sided
Hawks,
  Broad-winged
  Red-shouldered

Jays,
  Blue
Nuthatches,
  Brown-headed
Owls,
  Barred
  Screech
Quails,
  Bobwhite
Tanagers,
  Summer
Turkeys,
  Wild
Warblers,
  Hooded

Parula
Pine
  Yellow-throated
Woodpeckers,
  Downy
  Hairy
  Pileated
  Red-bellied
  Red-cockaded
Wrens,
  Carolina

* Includes pine forests of all ages, from young managed stands to natural mature stands with deciduous undergrowth.

especially when used in conjunction with a map. If you don't have a map, first check the direction of your base line (your point of entry—road, stream, railroad track, and so forth). If you enter the forest and travel on a course approximately 90 degrees from your base line, then a reciprocal course (one plus or minus 180 degrees from your traveled course) will return you to your base line.

Old lumber roads are often the only means of access to the interior sections of the forest. The secondary growth of fir and spruce is usually so thick that off-trail penetration is impossible. Lumber roads invariably lead to open work areas of some kind. Some will lead you to rivers or streams, and others will provide access to ridges and bogs.

Birding in evergreen areas will be more meaningful and rewarding if you have some knowledge of the species you may expect to find in the various biotic habitats. With few exceptions, the different ecological niches are not necessarily restrictive boundaries for a particular species. Generally speaking, each species within the evergreen forest, like the birds of any major biotic community, will

show a decided preference for a certain niche. The sub-
titles which follow represent an arbitrary grouping of the
more obvious niches, or habitats, that one is likely to find
within the evergreen forest. Birds most representative of
each area are included. No attempt has been made to
make the listings all-inclusive.

Mature
Evergreens

Warblers constitute a large percentage of the birds to be
found in northern coniferous forests. One or more members of the family are attracted to each type of habitat.
The black-throated green, Blackburnian, and pine warblers
prefer older stands of trees. The black-throated green is
partial to hemlocks and pines, but look for the Blackburnian in the sunlit tops of fir and spruce. The pine warbler,
as its name implies, is chiefly a bird of the pinelands.

The black-throated green warbler is a diminutive songster of the treetops. Its light, wheezy "trees, trees, mur-
muring trees" is heard repeatedly, but the bird itself is
often difficult to locate. It feeds actively in the high, dense
foliage, picking an assortment of insects and larvae from
twigs, limbs, needles, and bark. When observed through
binoculars, the black-throated green can be recognized by
its black throat, bright yellow cheeks, and olive-green back.

The Blackburnian warbler is the most brilliantly colored wood warbler. The flaming orange of its throat and
head flashes like a burnished jewel against the background
of forest greens and sky blues. It seems less nervous than
the black-throated green, and will sing repeatedly from
the same high perch. The song is thin and high-pitched.
The most distinctive form starts with four or five "zip"
notes, and ends with a slurred trill. Peterson describes it
as "zip zip zip zip titi tseeeeee."

By contrast to the gaudy Blackburnian, the pine warbler blends with the soft gray-greens of its pine tree background. A dimly streaked yellow breast and two white
wing bars are the pronounced features of an otherwise
nondescript gray-olive-green warbler. The pine warbler is
widely distributed, breeding in the pine forests from Canada southward into Florida. Its feeding habits are one of
the best aids to identification. It creeps over the limbs and
trunks of pines searching for insects in much the same

manner as the black and white warbler or the brown creeper. At times, it can be seen on the ground picking at seeds or insects. The song will remind you of a chipping sparrow's trill, but it will be slower and more musical.

The nesting habits of these three warblers are quite similar. Usually, the nests are located on a high horizontal branch of an evergreen tree, but there are exceptions; nests have been found close to the ground and at intermediate heights. The nests are formed with such materials as small twigs, rootlets, bits of grass and bark, evergreen needles, weed stems, and moss. These are bound together with webs of spiders, worms, or caterpillars. The cups are lined with fur, hairs, feathers, fern down, or other soft materials.

Although the spring songs of warblers fill the air, the mature stands of evergreens do not belong to them alone; a number of other species will also be found here. The number and variety of birds will fluctuate, because even climax areas are not completely stable. Natural forces bring about changes that may deter one species but benefit another. At times, dense mature stands bring about their own destruction. Too much shade and the deep accumulation of duff prevent the growth of seedlings. Lightning, wind, or ice may damage individual trees, opening the way for insects and diseases which, in turn, create a different biological niche capable of supporting certain species of birds. The black-backed three-toed woodpecker and the northern three-toed woodpecker, for example, are attracted to dead or damaged trees because they provide both food and nesting sites. These rather uncommon woodpeckers frequently drill their nesting cavities in live trees, but if these trees were to be examined closely, they would undoubtedly show some kind of previous damage. Broken limbs and borers or other creatures initiate the injury, permitting fungi to enter and eventually destroy the heartwood. Thus, the excavation of a cavity in a live tree is not as difficult as it may seem.

The males of both species of the three-toed woodpeckers have yellow crowns, but they can be distinguished readily by the black and white barred back of the northern, and the solidly colored back of the black-backed.

These factors of damage and the ensuing work of the woodpeckers help create conditions attractive to the red-breasted nuthatch and the boreal chickadee. The red-breasted nuthatch is slightly smaller than its white-breasted cousin. Many of its actions are quite similar, but they are executed with much greater rapidity. It seems to be in a hurry when feeding, flitting from limb to limb, or from one tree to another. At times it will remind you of a warbler, and at other times it will act more like a flycatcher. But its food does not consist entirely of insects; many seeds of spruce, fir, and pine are eaten, especially in the winter. The boreal chickadee is much like its more southern counterpart, the black-capped. It is the only member of the chickadee family with brown predominating on the cap, back, and sides.

Large conifers are also the home of the kinglets, both the golden-crowned and the ruby-throated. Kinglets are tiny birds (3½ to 4 inches in length) with short, stubby tails. They feed high in the thick branches of the conifers and are thus difficult to observe. They are chiefly insectivorous and sometimes will reveal their location by darting into the air in warblerlike fashion to capture a passing insect. Their nests are tiny, globular structures, usually located in the thick upper branches of a tall spruce or fir. Usnea lichens and moss are woven together and bound with the webbing of spiders or webworms. Bits of fur and feathers are used for the soft lining.

The golden-crowned kinglet has the more conspicuous crown of the two species. Its head is brightly striped, with orange predominating. The ruby-crowned has a single scarlet head patch that is difficult to discern in the field. A pronounced white eye ring is the best mark for distinguishing it from the golden-crowned. Kinglets can be told from warblers by their short, stubby features, and by their seemingly nervous habit of flicking their wings.

Mature stands of cone-bearing evergreens are also the places to look for red crossbills and white-winged crossbills. Both species are erratic as to the time and place of nesting, and in their postnesting wanderings. Apparently, their abundance in any one location is determined largely by the current crop of seed-bearing cones. Both species have been known to nest any time between late January and August, indicating that the time of rearing young is determined by the availability of food.

Crossbills are unique in their appearance and actions, and their identification is not difficult. As their name implies, the long thin mandibles are crossed in a scissorslike manner—a special adaptation for removing seeds from cones. Also, the beaks are used parrot-fashion as an aid in climbing. The red crossbill is a deep brick color with dark wings; the white-winged is more pinkish and has two wide white wing bars that are clearly visible, even in flight. Both species are approximately the size of a house sparrow. Despite their highly specialized beaks, crossbills do not feed on the seeds of evergreens exclusively. Other seeds, fruits, and insects supplement their diet.

A number of other birds are likely to be found amid the larger evergreens. The thrush that darts through the understory is apt to be a Swainson's; brown creepers may be seen spiraling up the trunks; and flocks of evening grosbeaks or pine siskins may pause during their erratic wanderings.

The forest changes, sometimes radically, in many ways. One lone damaged or dead tree may harbor enough bark beetles or other insects to infest its neighbors, and an epidemic may follow. Trees weaken and die; they are toppled by the heavy burden of ice and the power of strong winds. A single bolt of lightning may start a fire that consumes hundreds of acres of trees. The topsoil is exposed and erodes from its base of rock and gravel. A severe wind storm may flatten an entire mountainside with the same results. Man-cleared land may fare no better. A single episode within the forest can create vast openings that will change the character of the forest for decades to come. The cause and severity of the change will determine the type of growth and life that will follow.

The loss of deep shade has far-reaching effects. The deep snow of winter is no longer protected from the warming rays of the sun. Rather than melting slowly and seeping through the protective humus, it now melts rapidly, and the life-giving moisture is carried away from the forest in rapid runoffs. Erosion takes place, and soil is lost.

*Forest Edges
and Open Areas*

Where the soil has been thinned, a new struggle for dominance begins. Fireweed and grasses gain a foothold in the drier soil. They will consume most of the moisture and deter the seeding and growth of new trees. In spots where soil and moisture are sufficient, trees will grow and eventually shade out the surrounding grass and weeds. The long, slow process of restoring the forest will continue through many stages for indeterminate years.

The processes of restoration will make way for new temporary plant species regardless of the events that open the forest. Each of the new and varying habitats will attract a number of birds and other wildlife specially adapted for survival amid its peculiarities. Along the edges, parent trees will provide enough protection for the gradual reestablishment of their own kind. Birches and aspens will thrive in the abundance of light and furnish a protective canopy for seedling evergreens. Eventually, the evergreens will become dominant and destroy their own nursery with shade. The birches and aspens will have fulfilled their purpose. Shrubs such as mapleleaf viburnum, withe rod, elderberry, and snowberry will become established and produce an abundance of wildlife food. On the ground, bunchberry, bearberry, crowberry, and similar plants will provide more food and help retain the forest soil. This variety of plants and food makes the forest edges and open areas attractive to a great many birds.

Despite their names, the Tennessee and the Cape May are two warblers indigenous to the open edges of northern evergreens. The Tennessee warbler is the more common of the two, and is partial to a mixture of spruce, aspen, and thick understory growth adjacent to some open grassy areas. Your best chance of finding the Cape May is along the edges of mature stands of spruce or fir mixed with birches or aspens. There are some striking differences, yet noticeable similarities, between these two warblers. As noted, their preferred habitats are much the same, often overlapping, but there is little competition. The Tennessee nests on the ground in a mat of sphagnum moss. The nest is protected by an overhanging bough or shrub; it is built mostly of dried grasses. By contrast, the Cape May builds high in a spruce or fir. The nest is built of twigs, vines, grass, and sphagnum moss. It is lined with fine dry grass or hairs from any of the woodland animals. The feeding habits of the two species are quite similar; both are chiefly insectivorous, and peculiarly, both are known for their habit of piercing ripe grapes to drink the sweet juice.

The Tennessee warbler is not unlike the red-eyed vireo in appearance—olive-green above, light underneath, and a white line above the eye. It is smaller than a vireo and has the typical thinly pointed bill of a warbler. By comparison, the Cape May is one of the most colorful warblers of the northern woods. A yellow rump, yellow underparts finely streaked with black, chestnut cheeks, and a large white wing patch are all distinguishing features.

During the winter, the white-throated sparrow, slate-colored junco, and purple finch are widely scattered throughout the East. Then they are among the most common birds about our feeding stations, but during the spring and summer, we find them in the open areas of cool evergreen forests. The junco, the slate-colored "snowbird" of winter, breeds from the tree limits in northern Canada southward through the mountains to northern Georgia. The white-throated sparrow breeds as far south as the Pocono Mountains of Pennsylvania, but the purple finch extends its breeding range southward into the mountains of Maryland.

The soft, musical trill of the slate-colored junco is one of the most pleasant sounds of the woodlands. The song seems to flow forth from every opening—along trails, roadsides, windfalls, bogs, and shrubby areas. The white-throated sparrow extends its melancholy welcome from a low spruce bough. The purple finch expresses its enthusiastic love of spring from the top of the highest tree. At times, with the sun accenting its rosy brilliance, it will fly into the air and perform a gliding, spiraling, fluttering, aerial dance as it sings to its mate. All three species feed on the seeds, insects, and wild fruits that are abundant in forest openings. In addition, the purple finch is partial to the tender buds of new growth. The junco and white-throat are ground nesters, but the purple finch nests in the evergreens.

If, in your wanderings along the edge of tall evergreens, you should hear the loud and boisterous call of "quick, three beers," don't credit it to a recent visit to your local

pub. Instead, look to the top of the tallest dead tree. Chances are, there you will find the "thirsty" olive-sided flycatcher. It will be a stocky bird compared to other flycatchers, and will have a heavy bill and a seemingly large head. The dark breast will be divided by a vertical strip of white.

This evergreen edge may be the place to find the long-eared owl or, perchance, the great horned or the saw-whet. Look for their splashings and pellets beneath the trees. (Pellets are the undigested parts of an owl's diet—bits of fur and bones that are regurgitated in small oblong wads. By soaking them apart in water and examining the contents, it is possible to determine exactly what the owl has been eating.)

Immature or Stunted Evergreens

Stands of young evergreens and those stunted by lack of soil and moisture add a low-level type of habitat to the complexity of the evergreen forest. Perhaps we should also include the scattered stands of the comparatively smaller jack pine. The jack pine spreads profusely after a fire. In fact, the intense heat of fire is needed to pop open the cones and release the seeds; otherwise, the unopened cones cling to the trees for years.

This low-level evergreen habitat attracts a number of woodland birds. The magnolia warbler and the myrtle warbler are often the most abundant species.

Of all the warblers common to the evergreens, the magnolia is one of the easiest to identify. It is seen most often near eye level and is unusually tame. The predominant colors are black and yellow—yellow underneath with black streakings, and blackish above. The broad horizontal band of white dividing the dark tail is the most diagnostic feature. The black and white cheek and the large white wing patch are quite pronounced also.

The myrtle warbler has several distinctive characteristics that help to identify it. Also, it may be the most abundant (at least, the most often seen) warbler in the East, especially in the winter and during migrations. When the myrtle is flushed, its flight is quick and erratic, and is invariably accompanied by a number of "chep" notes. A bright yellow rump is quite obvious, especially in flight.

Many warblers build dainty, intricately constructed nests, but not the magnolia or the myrtle; their nests are loose and bulky. Twigs, weed stems, grass, and rootlets are used. The nest of the magnolia often can be identified by the binding of cinquefoil runners and the lining of fine black rootlets. Both species help keep the young trees free of plant lice, weevils, beetles, sawfly larvae, and other insects. The diet of the myrtle warbler also includes a variety of seeds and berries. This flexibility in diet enables it to arrive early on the nesting grounds, and to be the latest to leave.

Nearly every coniferous forest has its cool, moist glades where the ground is carpeted with varying shades of green mosses. Here we find ferns, clumps of bunchberries, beds of twinflowers, creeping snowberries, and many other wild flowers, intermingled with young evergreens, shrubs, vines, and briers. This thick undergrowth furnishes protection for those species that nest on or near the ground, such as the Canada warbler, yellow-bellied flycatcher, winter wren, and fox sparrow. But the heavy vegetation often makes travel and observation difficult for human beings. Stream beds or old tote roads provide the best means of access. *Brushy Undergrowth*

Listen for the fox sparrow. Listen not only for its clear whistled song but for the sounds of its scratchings in the patches of dead litter on the forest floor. Like the towhee, the fox sparrow scratches with both feet simultaneously, turning over leaves and other matter as it searches for beetles, millipedes, grubs, other insects, dried fruits, and seeds. It is the largest sparrow in the East, and has a rusty, fox colored overall appearance. It is notorious for singing on stormy days.

The Canada is a fly-catching warbler. It prefers the dense undergrowth of the wetter areas for both feeding and nesting. A black pendant-type necklace against its bright yellow throat and breast is the best identifying field mark. The yellow-bellied flycatcher also favors the damper sections of the evergreen woods. It, too, feeds low, and unlike other flycatchers, it nests on the ground. The plaintive two-note call of "per-wee" with a rising inflection is often heard in the underbrush before the bird is seen. Notice the light yellowish wash underneath from throat to tail.

Look for the winter wren amid piles of brush, the roots of fallen trees, tangled limbs, and similar forest debris. This tiny brown wren is sometimes referred to as being "mouse-like" in its actions. This is understandable when we see it scurrying through a brush pile, searching it thoroughly for insects and their larvae. Its actions are quick, and often we see little more than a flash of brown. The heavily barred breast and short, stubby tail are reassuring field marks.

The winter wren has one of the loveliest songs to be heard in the coniferous woodlands. This ecstatic song bubbles forth in a long series of high, clear warbles and vibrant trills. Once heard, it will not be forgotten.

Northern Bogs

The bogs of northern forests are among the most botanically rich habitats to be found anywhere. The plant life is abundant, greatly varied, and often specifically indigenous to a small ecological niche. The vegetation will vary according to formation and location, but generally, northern bogs are areas dominated by such plants as tamarack, black spruce, bog rosemary, dwarf birch, leatherleaf, Labrador tea, alders, and willows. The ground is covered with sphagnum and other varieties of water-tolerant mosses.

Bogs may be formed by stream dispersion into low-lying areas, by beaver workings, or by natural succession from lakes and ponds. Natural bog succession is very apparent around many of the smaller bodies of water. Submerged and floating plants give way to grasses and sedges. These often form a thick floating mat capable of supporting seedling shrubs such as leatherleaf, Labrador tea, and bog rosemary. Other plants, including speckled alder, horsetail, marsh cinquefoil, and goldenrods, help form a binding root system which eventually anchors the mat. Tamarack and then black spruce follow the shrubs. Finally, the balsam fir-spruce climax may claim the area.

Typical breeding birds of northern bog areas, and the particular niche where they are most likely to be seen, include those given in the list on the facing page.

The northern edge of the Transcontinental Coniferous Forest gradually gives way to the vast stretches of tundra. This ecotone, or intermixing of two distinct biotic communities,

BIRDS OF NORTHERN BOGS

Bittern, American:	*Sedges and cattails along water's edge.*
Flycatcher, Trail's:	*Alder thickets.*
Sparrow, Lincoln's:	*Dense shrubby thickets. Secretive, but curious. Try calling by squeaking on back of hand.*
Sparrow, Swamp:	*Open marshy areas. Ground feeder. Most often seen while singing from perch.*
Swallow, Tree:	*Dead tree stubs, or in flight above the bog.*
Warbler, Nashville:	*Dwarf birches and spruce bogs.*
Warbler, Palm:	*Tamarack-spruce complex. Flips tail constantly.*
Warbler, Wilson's:	*Willows and alders. Active fly-catching warbler.*
Waterthrush, Northern:	*Shrubby areas along water. Walks with teetering motion like spotted sandpiper.*
Yellowthroat:	*Thick tangles along ditches and water edges. Wrenlike in its actions.*

does not follow a definite latitudinal line. Often the borders are abrupt, but black spruce and tamarack extend northward in the valleys, and fingers of tundra reach southward on higher ridges. The bird life overlaps, also, and we find species peculiar to both habitats. In addition, there are certain species closely allied with the intricate relationships of this ecotone.

Tundra-Coniferous Ecotone

This northern transitional zone is the home of the hawk-owl—a true owl that looks and acts like an accipiter. It hunts in the daytime, flying low over the muskeg and shrubs, or from its favorite perch on the top of a dead tree. When the hawk-owl is perched, its long tail is often raised and lowered repeatedly, and sometimes it is cocked upward at a jaunty angle.

Other species which are confined mainly to this zone include the northern shrike, gray-cheeked thrush, tree sparrow, common redpoll, and blackpoll warbler. These species are most abundant in areas where paper birch, alders, and dwarf willows are intermixed with stunted black spruce and tamarack.

Along the edges of the forest, where the conifers gradually give way to deciduous stands, we find numerous birds from each type of habitat. (Both habitats, and the birds indigenous to them, have been covered elsewhere in this book.) Again, the latitudinal line is irregular with extensions of both the coniferous and the deciduous forests intermixing. Representative species of this mixed growth include the hermit thrush, black-throated blue warbler, and solitary vireo. The hermit thrush is distinguished by its clear flute-like song, and rusty-red tail (especially noticeable in flight) and, when perched, by the habit of cocking its tail and then lowering it slowly. The black throat and sides and the conspicuous white wing patch identify the black-throated blue warbler. Its song is one of the easiest to remember: an ascending "zur, zur, zur, zree" or "I am la-zy" (Peterson). The solitary vireo sports a white throat, white spectacles, and white wing bars.

Coniferous-Deciduous Ecotone

Of all the species listed under Birds of the Southern Pinelands on page 51, the ones most closely confined to this particular habitat are the red-cockaded woodpecker, brown-headed nuthatch, and a subspecies of the Bachman's sparrow.

Southern Pinelands

The red-cockaded woodpecker is on the U.S. Fish and Wildlife Service list of endangered species. The question of survival is associated closely with the bird's specific nesting requirements. "It builds a unique nest deep in the pine forests of the South, selecting for its drilling a live tree, which has been attacked by a fungus termed 'red heart.' The fungus is just as selective as the bird. It can be found only in mature trees, some approaching a century of age, looming high above the forest floor. The fungus softens the core of the tree, apparently making the woodpecker's job much easier. After drilling a hole several inches deep and slightly smaller than a tennis ball in circumference, the woodpecker then proceeds to puncture a large area of bark around the hole until sap or resin begins oozing out. The red-cockaded is the only bird known to perform this puncturing act, and reasons for it are not clear to ornithologists. They assume, however, that it is a measure designed to protect the nest against predators."*

Fortunately, some lumber companies are now cooper-

* "There's Hope for the Red Cockaded Woodpecker," *Florida Naturalist*, Vol. 44, No. 1A (Feb.–March, 1971), p. 4.

GENERALLY SCATTERED BIRDS OF THE NORTHERN CONIFEROUS FORESTS

Creepers,
    Brown
Grosbeaks and Finches,
    Grosbeak, Evening
    Grosbeak, Pine
    Siskin, Pine
Grouse,
    Spruce

Hawks,
    Goshawk
Jays,
    Gray
Nuthatches,
    Red-breasted
Owls,
    Saw-whet

Warblers,
    Blackpoll
    Parula
Waxwings,
    Cedar
Wrens,
    Winter

ating in an effort to save this endangered woodpecker; nesting trees are left standing. Perhaps such efforts will save the red-cockaded from going the way of the Carolina parakeet and the passenger pigeon.

The brown-headed nuthatch is common in open pine woods, especially previously burned areas that have a number of dead stubs and trees remaining. It is easily recognized by the distinctive brown cap, the only eastern nuthatch so marked. It is a thorough hunter, searching the trunk and limbs of a tree from bottom to top, often hanging from the tips of branches or from cones in chickadee fashion. The brown-headed is the most sociable of nuthatches. After nesting, small flocks join with chickadees, titmice, and woodpeckers. Constant chattering often reveals the presence of a roaming flock.

The Bachman's sparrow is quite secretive and often overlooked. It is a ground nester and prefers open pinelands with an undercover of grass and shrubs. Its song, perhaps the most beautiful of all the sparrows, is often being compared in quality and pattern to the song of the hermit thrush, and is the best means of locating and identifying this elusive sparrow.

Numerous birds of the evergreens are not restricted to any particular niche, but may be generally scattered throughout vast areas. Your check list for the northern coniferous forests should include those given in the table above.

The nesting season is short in the north country. By

late August there is a cold nip in the nighttime air, and in the mornings lakes "steam" in the brilliance of a rising sun. September days are cool, and preparations for the approaching winter are in evidence throughout the forest. Red squirrels gather cones and defend their cache with a vengeance. Beavers are cutting young poplars and alders, and storing them in the mud near the underwater entrance to their lodge. The deer appear grayer and darker as they put on their winter coats. Bears are gorging themselves on berries, nuts, and grubs; they will den up with the first sustained blast of winter.

Birds, too, recognize the impending cold. On days when the wind swings to the north, the honking of geese is heard overhead as V after V pierces the southern horizon. Most species have discarded their bright nuptial plumage and now wear a sedately colored suit of strong new feathers. The warblers, swallows, flycatchers, and other insect eaters have gone, but there is still a harvest of seeds and fruits for the siskins, finches, waxwings, and grosbeaks. Their movements will fluctuate with the severity of the weather and the abundance of food. Only a few species will remain to challenge winter's severity.

The old fields have not felt the cut of a plow for the past ten years, and the adjoining meadow is no longer trampled by grazing livestock. The farm was carved from the wilderness nearly two centuries ago, but now it lies abandoned, a victim of man's changing patterns of life.

Nature seized the interim to start the long process of returning the land to its original stability. At first, the fields resisted any intrusion from the forest. The heavily matted sod made it difficult for new seeds to reach the soil, and most of those that sprouted were shaded out by the thick, undisturbed grass. But nature would not be denied. Weeds, no longer held in abeyance by repeated disturbances, reached maturity. Bull thistle, pokeweed, milkweed, steeplebush, mullen, yarrow, and similar plants gained a foothold and started to shade out the grasses. Winged seeds of maples and elms fluttered from mature trees along the fencerows; a few reached bare soil and began to grow. Birds scattered the seeds of multiflora rose, sumac, and berries. Thus, in many ways, the process of reclaiming the land gained increasing momentum with the passing of time.

Now the fields show obvious proof of the inevitability of nature's persistent pattern; eventually the forest will dominate the land again. But at this stage of transition, the struggle continues. In the center of the fields, timothy, bluegrass, orchard grass, and wild barley still dominate. On the higher ridges where the soil has been thinned by

5 Birds of Fields and Meadows

wind and water erosion, the cover is still sparse and scattered; wild strawberry, dewberry, cinquefoil, and white daisy are mixed with the stunted grasses. Along the fence-rows and the forest's edge, young trees extend outward, claiming a little more land each year. Black cherry, elm, and maple are the most prevalent pioneering species. In the corner of one field, next to a stand of black locusts, red cedars are spreading and growing rapidly. Here they have a symbiotic relationship with the nitrogen-fixing locust trees.

All across the old farm, the mosaic pattern of field greens is broken by the grays and browns of dead plants from previous years, and by the whites of daisies, yarrow, and Queen Anne's lace, by the yellow of buttercups, the burnt orange of black-eyed Susans, and the lavender of steeplebush and bull thistles.

The story of the meadow is quite similar—time has healed its wounds. The winding cow paths still converge on the old barway, but they are no longer just clay and mud; the creeping grasses and vines have closed the injuries, and only the scars remain. The lower meadow is lush with thick stands of purple loosestrife, elderberries, cattails, alders, and young willows. The big willow that used to shade the cows as they rested and chewed their cuds waiting for the evening milk call is partially dead. Flickers and starlings squabble over the nesting cavities. Portions of the meadow have resisted change successfully; overgrazing and soil compaction deterred the germination of new plants.

As the panorama of the old farm changed, the bird life also changed. New cover and new food attracted new birds and eliminated others. But always there existed one or more species adapted to fill every biological niche within its boundaries.

The fields and meadows of our eastern countryside are, for the most part, rapidly changing, unstable habitats. The type of vegetation and wildlife they attract depends upon such factors as location, soil structure, moisture, and man's activities. Fields may vary in form from plowed or

NESTING BIRDS OF FIELDS AND MEADOWS

Blackbirds,
   Blackbird, Red-winged
   Bobolink
   Meadowlark, Eastern
Larks,
   Horned
Plovers,
   Killdeer

Quails and Pheasants,
   Pheasant, Ring-necked
   Quail, Bobwhite
Sandpipers,
   Plover, Upland
Sparrows,
   Field
   Grasshopper

Henslow's
Song
Vesper
Warblers,
   Myrtle (in growths
   of bayberry)
Yellow

SUMMER BIRDS OF FIELDS AND MEADOWS

SUMMER FEEDERS

Barn Owls,
   Owl, Barn
Blackbirds,
   Blackbird, Red-winged
   Grackle, Common
Crows,
   Common
Doves,
   Mourning
Falcons,
   Sparrow Hawk
Finches,
   Goldfinch, American

Hawks,
   Broad-winged
   Marsh
   Red-shouldered
   Red-tailed
Owls,
   Great Horned
   Long-eared
   Screech
Starlings,
   Starling
Thrushes,
   Robin
Woodcocks,
   American

IN THE AIR

Goatsuckers,
   Nighthawk, Common
Swallows,
   Bank
   Barn
   Cliff
   Martin, Purple
   Tree
Swifts,
   Chimney

WINTER BIRDS OF FIELDS AND MEADOWS

WINTER FEEDERS

Barn Owls,
   Owl, Barn
Blackbirds,
   Meadowlark, Eastern
Crows,
   Common
Doves,
   Mourning
Grosbeaks, Finches, Sparrows,
and Buntings,
   Bunting, Snow
   Goldfinch, American

Junco, Slate-colored
Redpoll, Common
Sparrow, Song
Sparrow, Tree
Sparrow, White-throated
Hawks,
   Marsh,
   Red-shouldered
   Red-tailed
   Rough-legged
Larks,
   Horned
Owls,
   Great Horned

Long-eared
Saw-Whet
Screech
Snowy
Quails and Pheasants,
   Pheasant, Ring-necked
   Quail, Bobwhite
Starlings,
   Starling

Birding in Fields and Meadows

barren areas to those dominated by shrubs and young trees. We think of meadows as being lower and damper areas, usually fenced and used as pastures. As such, the vegetation and corresponding bird life will vary according to use and care.

As already indicated, bird life within any habitat changes somewhat with each transitional stage. The lists on the preceding page include those species which may be expected to be found nesting or feeding in fields and meadows with a cover of grass and weed mixtures. A few encroaching shrubs and small trees are incidental. Birds of shrubby areas and wooded margins will be included in the next chapter, "Birds of Brushy Borders." No attempt has been made to include the numerous migrants which often pass over such open areas.

Nesting Species

In the spring, the land is moist and warm, and a new growth of plants carpets the fields and meadows with vibrant hues of green. But if we examine this verdant cover closely with the eye of an artist, we find the massive greens broken by striations of grays, tans, and deep browns. The flat mats of undercover grasses and the bolder strokes of standing weed stems add a disruptive pattern to the dominant wash of greens. Light reaches the ground with varying degrees of intensity; the resulting shadows help soften and diffuse any uniformity of color. The birds of this grassland habitat nest on or near the ground, and are subject to easy predation. However, in most cases their body markings duplicate the broken designs of their background (this is especially true of the females), and the blending of disruptive shadowy patterns is the ground nesters' principal means of protection.

If there is one bird truly symbolic of eastern fields and meadows, it is surely the meadowlark. It is the clairvoyant of springtime, whistling a cheerful "spring-o'-the-yeeerr" from atop a fence post, often before the ground is free of its frosty hardness. The meadowlark's bright yellow breast with a contrasting black crescent presents an unusual color pattern, considering its habits and the family to which it belongs. At times, the bird seems conscious of being so conspicuous and will turn away from the observer. This habit often is noticeable when one is approaching a singing male. When aware of being observed, he will turn aside, hide the bright breast, and expose the subdued patterns of his side and back. His fluttering flight on stiffened wings reveals the white outer feathers of his broad tail. They are also noticeable as he walks along the ground flicking his tail open in a rather nervous manner.

The practice of deception is also used by meadowlarks during nesting activities. The nest is a grass-domed structure hidden in a slight ground depression amid withered stands of last year's grasses. On one occasion, I watched most of the nest-building process. When first observed, the female was carrying pieces of grass to several different locations. I had the feeling that she was employing such deceptive moves purposely to distract my attention from the real nesting site. However, on my second day of observation, she was concentrating on just one location. But she was still cautious. She never flew directly to the nesting site, but would land 20 to 50 feet away and walk to the site, occasionally picking up another piece of grass or two on the way. She would depart from the nesting site in the same manner. Only twice, during my observations, did the male make an appearance, and then only long enough to perform his manly duties. Knowing that meadowlarks often are polygamous, I assumed he had similar obligations elsewhere.

Barren fields and fields which have been freshly plowed also attract early harbingers of spring killdeers, horned larks, and upland plovers. There is nothing secretive about the killdeer's arrival; the loud repeated cry of "kill-deer, kill-deer," or "kill-dee, kill-dee," is heard as the bird passes high overhead or runs about the open fields in search of food. For some reason, I associate the killdeer's arrival with cool, misty, or foggy mornings. If this association is more than coincidental, the killdeers probably arrived with a flow of warm air from the south. Warm air flowing over cooler land and water would produce the foggy conditions—conditions which may stimulate excessive calls as an assurance of flock orientation. The horned lark and the

upland plover usually are seen before they are heard, as they are not as vociferous as the killdeer during their migratory movements. However, they have beautiful songs once their nesting territories are established. Both species have the habit of surveying their feeding areas from a low perch. Look for them atop a fence post.

The killdeer is seldom still. It runs rapidly across the ground, pausing only momentarily in typical plover fashion to look and listen, or to capture some morsel of food. Freshly plowed fields are attractive because they expose a variety of favorite foods, including earthworms, ants, beetles, centipedes, billbugs, wireworms, and numerous larvae. Grasshoppers, caterpillars, and flies are also eaten in quantity. Nesting requirements are rather specific, yet simple; open barren ground is essential. The nest, a slight depression in the ground lined with grass, usually is placed where the brooding female has a view in all directions. Bare spots in fields, exposed gravel areas, and closely grazed meadows are favored locations. The four eggs are tan and heavily blotched to match the barren soil.

The killdeer is a master at the "broken-wing" ruse, a sure sign that a nest or young are in the vicinity. The female will flutter away from the nest, dragging and flapping her wings as though one or both were broken. She will gasp, scream, roll on her side, and employ other antics that will entice you to follow her, thus protecting the eggs or the young.

My experiences with the horned lark have been rather limited, with most observations taking place during the winter months. I recall observing nesting pairs on two occasions, one on a comparatively small country airport with grass runways, and the other amid the closely mowed stubble in the outer fringes of a large municipal airport. Both instances seemed to verify the horned lark's preference for large expanses of open areas.

You will find the horned lark walking across the ground (not running like a killdeer, or hopping like a sparrow), or perched on a low post, rock, or clod of dirt. It is slightly larger than a sparrow, and has black "sideburns" extending downward from the eye, a black chest band, and two tiny black "horns" (not always visible) as the outstanding

Field Sparrow: *pink bill.*
Grasshopper Sparrow: *unstreaked buff-colored breast.*
Henslow's Sparrow: *the two-syllable song of "flee-sic." Often heard at night.*
Song Sparrow: *central breast spot.*
Vesper Sparrow: *white outer tail feathers.*

field marks. Like the killdeer, it nests in a slight depression, but the nest is more carefully lined with fine grass, hair, or feathers. Seeds are its chief source of food, except during the nesting season, when various insects are consumed. The song of the horned lark has been described as light, airy, tinkling, wild, and joyous. All of these superlatives, and more, are readily recognized as the bird ascends to great heights while it sings. Also, it causes one to wonder about the heralded flight song of the European skylark. Could it be even more beautiful?

In ornithological systematics, the upland plover is classified as a sandpiper. It was once known as the Bartramian sandpiper, a name based on structure and evolutionary relationships, but its ploverlike habits and attraction to upland fields and prairies make the new name more appropriate. It is a comparatively large bird, measuring 10 to 12 inches in length and more than 20 inches in wingspan, yet it weighs less than half a pound. Long yellow legs, a long thin neck, and a small pigeonlike head are the most diagnostic features. Its heavily streaked tan body blends into the broken pattern of tan soils and dry grasses.

Fields and meadowlands that have not been cultivated, mowed, or grazed for a year or more soon become enveloped in a growth of maturing plants. The taller grasses and weeds become dominant, and the bird life changes. Horned larks and upland plover disappear, and killdeers seek the last barren exposures. But this new growth, with its increased variety of insects and abundance of ripening

*Watching
the Grassland
Sparrows*

seeds, now becomes attractive to a number of grassland sparrows. The grasshopper, Henslow's, and vesper sparrows will be found here. The field sparrow and the song sparrow will be most common where there is a beginning growth of briers, shrubs, and saplings.

In general terms, we can say that sparrows are small brown birds with streaked backs and short, seed-eating beaks. There is considerable similarity in body patterns, and the inexperienced birder should use a field guide to establish distinguishing field marks and habits. The sparrows of open fields feed and nest on or near the ground; they are quite secretive, and sightings often have to be made quickly. One field mark or one habit is individually characteristic of most species, as indicated in the list on the preceding page. Consult your field guide for additional field marks, flight characteristics, and songs.

Watching Other Nesting Species

To me, the bobolink is the most exciting bird of our fields and meadows. The male is a gay impresario, a formal dresser, a renowned songster, and an international traveler. He is handsome, ebullient, and at times provocative. Undoubtedly, my enthusiasm for this bird dates back to grade-school days when we had to memorize William Cullen Bryant's "Robert of Lincoln." We not only learned the poem, and that the word "bobolink" was an abbreviation of its title, but during the last school days of May we could see and hear this gay songster singing from the fields as we walked the country road to school. The lines "Bob-o'-link, bob-o'-link/spink, spank, spink," would be remembered each time the song was heard.

The male bobolink is easily recognized in his formal nesting plumage—black below and mostly white above, the only American songbird to be so marked. This reverse pattern accounts for the rather unflattering, but descriptive, colloquial name of "skunk bird."

The song of the bobolink is so individually characteristic that it defies imitation or meaningful description. Numerous writers and ornithologists have endeavored to interpret the explosive bubbling notes. Thoreau wrote, "This flashing, tinkling meteor bursts through the expectant meadow air, leaving a trail of tinkling notes be-

SUMMER BIRDS OF FIELDS AND MEADOWS AND THEIR FOODS

Crow, Common:	Cultivated grains, wild fruits, cowpeas, chufa, sumac, bird eggs, grasshoppers, beetles, caterpillars, and other insects.
Dove, Mourning:	Bristlegrass, ragweed, knotweed, crabgrass, panicgrass, and cultivated grains.
Goldfinch, American:	Ragweed, goosefoot, thistle, shepherd's-purse, dandelion, goldenrod, milkweed, plus a few aphids and small larvae.
Grackle, Common:	Grasshoppers, crickets, bees, earthworms, snails, bristlegrass, ragweed, wild fruits, and grain.
Hawks and Owls:	Mice, rats, shrews, rabbits, squirrels, snakes, frogs, crayfish, birds, grasshoppers, beetles, and other insects.
Nighthawk, Common, Chimney Swift, Swallows, and Purple Martin:	Flying insects.
Robin:	Earthworms, beetles, weevils, caterpillars, blackberries, strawberries, blueberries, and other fruits.
Starling:	Grasshoppers, beetles, caterpillars, millipedes, and wild fruits.
Woodcock, American:	Earthworms, grubs, insects, and larvae.

WINTER BIRDS OF FIELDS AND MEADOWS AND THEIR FOODS

Bunting, Snow:	Bristlegrass, ragweed, goosefoot, sandgrass, pigweed, beachgrass, knotweed, panicgrass, and bulrush.
Crow and Starling:	Cultivated grains, sumac, bayberry, poison ivy, greenbrier, sunflower, grass and weed seeds.
Dove, Mourning:	Bristlegrass, pokeweed, ragweed, crabgrass, knotweed, cowpea, doveweed, chickweed, panicgrass, and cultivated grains.
Hawks and Owls*:	Rabbits, squirrels, rodents, and birds.
Junco, Slate-colored, Tree Sparrow, and White-throated Sparrow:	Greenbrier, ragweed, bristlegrass, dropseedgrass, crabgrass, goosefoot, knotweed, pigweed, goldenrod, broomsedge, and seeds of other weeds and grasses.
Lark, Horned:	Bristlegrass, ragweed, knotweed, pigweed, goosefoot, sunflower, crabgrass, timothy, and some grain.
Meadowlark, Eastern, American Goldfinch, and Song Sparrow:	Ragweed, bristlegrass, pigweed, timothy, panicgrass, knotweed, sunflower, and some grain.
Pheasant, Ring-necked, and Bobwhite:	Smartweed, bristlegrass, ragweed, multiflora rose, sumac, berries, and grain.
Redpoll, Common:	Alder, birch, ragweed, smartweed, pigweed, bristlegrass, goosefoot, thistle, and sedge.

* A few of the previously mentioned hawks will winter over.

hind." F. Schuyler Mathews referred to the song as "a mad, reckless song-fantasia, an outbreak of pent-up, irrepressible glee." Other writers have likened the song to "a runaway music box" and "tin cans tumbling down the stairs." These descriptions imply quality, but lack recognizable detail. Once you hear the bobolink sing, you will understand the inadequacies of these literary endeavors, and the song will not be forgotten, for as T. Gilbert Pearson once wrote, "In its invariable and infectious spontaneity, and the fine frenzy of its delivery, his song stands alone in the musical utterances of American birds."

Unfortunately, the bobolink is not as plentiful as it was years ago, especially in the East. The lessening demand for hay and the modern methods of quick harvesting have helped to deplete its numbers. Also, migrating birds suffered the wrath of southern rice growers as feeding flocks blackened their rice fields. The bobolink's expansion westward into more extensive grasslands provides hope for its continued survival.

The red-winged blackbird can no longer be considered a bird exclusively bound to a habitat of cattails and rushes. It is now abundant in upland fields and meadows. Usually, the grassy nest is lashed to a clump of sturdy weed stems a foot or two above the ground. This adaptability to a new environment has enabled the red-wing to expand its numbers greatly. Tremendous flocks migrate and winter together, often incurring the wrath of farmers because of extensive damage to maturing corn and other crops. Drastic control measures have been sanctioned in some areas.

The ring-necked pheasant and the bobwhite are familiar game birds around most farms. Despite yearly hunting pressure, these two species continue to maintain balanced populations in areas where adequate cover remains. The elimination of fencerows and hedges, and other clean farming methods, are the main threats to the survival of these two popular game birds.

In Oregon, where the ring-necked pheasant was first introduced into the United States, its numbers have declined rapidly. Urbanization and uniformity of crop production continue to reduce pheasant habitats throughout the state's farming valleys.

The main wildlife foods of fields and meadows are insects and seeds. In addition to the nesting species, other birds are attracted to these bountiful feeding grounds. Mammals are there, too, including mice, shrews, and rabbits. These, in turn, attract the predatory hawks and owls.

The hawks which you are most likely to see over our eastern grasslands are the sparrow hawk, marsh hawk, red-tailed hawk, and red-shouldered hawk. The numbers present will be in direct proportion to the available food supply. The sparrow hawk is frequently the most common and the easiest to recognize. It is a small, robin-sized falcon (pointed wings and narrow tail) with a rusty back and pronounced side whiskers. Utility poles and wires are favorite perches, or it will hunt over open areas by hovering. The sparrow hawk comes to the field in search of grasshoppers, crickets, beetles, lizards, small snakes, frogs, and mice. An occasional small bird (usually a sparrow, as the name implies) is also captured.

The red-tailed and the red-shouldered hawks are buteos (broad rounded wings and tail) similar in size and flight patterns, often making positive identification difficult for beginning students. Varying color phases (check your field guide) also add to the confusion. Comparisons through experience will show the red-tailed hawk to be the chunkier of the two. Also, the rust-colored upper surface of its broad open-fanlike tail often is visible as the bird banks in soaring flight. The red-shouldered hawk's name implies a means of easy recognition, but the rust color on the shoulders is quite inconspicuous. The best field marks are the banded tail and the uniformly reddish underparts. In addition to soaring, both species will hunt patiently from a perch. The top of a dead tree is a favorite perch of the red-tail. Normally, the red-shouldered perches lower, where it can drop easily on unsuspecting prey. Both species feed mainly on rodents, large insects, reptiles, and small amphibians.

The marsh hawk is a large harrier with long, narrow wings and a prominent white rump. You will find it flying low over fields, meadows, and marshes, dipping and turning to maintain flying speed as it searches for rodents.

Man has the knowledge and tools to manage the land

Summer Feeders

to satisfy his own needs, and as long as he does so, natural succession is deterred and a relative degree of stability is maintained. But once man relinquishes his control, the laws of reclamation become the ruling force; the initial processes of returning the land to the forest, from which it was carved, begin. The forest's edge tapers farther and farther into fields and meadows; fencerows widen; and the first canopy of leaves shades the ground. The rains of repeated seasons leach minerals from the soil; this does not deter the woody plants, but the grasses and weeds can no longer survive. The food products—leaves, buds, bark, wood, seeds, and fruits—are not abundantly rich in minerals, but they appeal to active insects, birds, and mammals that can gather them in quantity. Most birds of the mineral-rich grassland have disappeared, but they are being replaced by those species adapted to the food and cover of young woodland plants.

Old fencerows and the woodlands' brushy borders reveal, in part, the history of the land and its people. The early settlers farmed mainly to sustain their own families. Farms were small, limited by the difficulties of clearing the land, family labor, and the efficiency of available tools and power. But the land was rich, and families survived for generation after generation. Today, the old stone walls of New England, the patchwork hillsides of Pennsylvania, and the wide, mature fencerows that cut across southern farmlands still tell the story of these early pioneering endeavors.

The changing of forest to fields and meadows enabled many birds to extend their range and increase their numbers; conversely, the true woodland birds suffered from a loss of habitat. The various "field" sparrows, meadowlarks, bobolinks, and other grass loving species filled these open niches as they developed, but a greater number of species found supporting cover and food in the ensuing growth of borders and brushlands.

Brushy borders, such as those between deciduous woodlands and adjacent fields, invariably contain great diversification in both food and cover. Here we find a continuing struggle for dominance among the grasses, weeds, briers, vines, shrubs, and trees. Certain species of birds and other wildlife reach their greatest abundance in this marginal habitat. Similar stands of mixed vegetation often develop along fencerows, ditches, ravines, rocky outcroppings, and other areas not suitable for cultivation. This

6 Birds of Brushy Borders

interspersion of habitats results in numerous and varied relationships that involve certain species of birds. The mourning dove, goldfinch, and bobwhite, for example, may feed mainly in one type of habitat, but resort to a different one for nesting or protection.

The number and variety of birds to be found along any one particular brushy border will depend on several factors: location, time of year, stage of development, and nature of adjoining communities. These factors were considered in the preparation of the bird list on the facing page, and as a result, the list includes only those species closely allied with brushy, or shrubby, borders as breeding areas. Abundant seasonal seeds and fruits attract many migratory and wintering species. (See Chapter 14, "Watching Songbirds in Winter.")

If larger trees are present, you may also find such species as the blue jay, orchard oriole, Baltimore oriole, cedar waxwing, yellow-throated vireo, warbling vireo, and common grackle.

Birding along Field and Woodland Borders

When the blustery winds of March are stilled by the warm days of spring, the gentle flow of life becomes an increasing surge as species vie for survival and dominance. Perhaps in no other outdoor community is this competition so obviously keen and so clearly visible as among the multitudinous forms of plant and animal life along the brushy borders of fields and woodlands. The competition takes place in many ways: for light, moisture, nutrients, living space, and food, but above all else, for the survival of individual species. To know the birds of these marginal lands, one must know something of the dynamic relationships that bind the community into a life-supporting unit. Many of the plants and birds involved can survive only at certain stages of the transitional struggle. Some are not so specific in their needs and can tolerate a longer period of change.

Let us take an early summer walk along a typical woodland border. What birds will we find, and why are they there? First, we notice that the wide band of mixed vegetation is multilayered, and that it extends from the old

BREEDING BIRDS OF BRUSHY BORDERS

Blackbirds,
  Cowbird, Brown-headed
Cuckoos,
  Black-billed
  Yellow-billed
Doves,
  Mourning
Flycatchers,
  Kingbird, Eastern
Grosbeaks, Finches, Sparrows,
and Buntings,
  Bunting, Indigo
  Cardinal
  Goldfinch, American
  Grosbeak, Blue
  Sparrow, Field
  Sparrow, Song
  Towhee, Rufous-sided
Mockingbirds and Thrashers,
  Catbird

Mockingbird
Thrasher, Brown
Quails and Pheasants,
  Pheasant, Ring-necked
  Quail, Bobwhite
Vireos,
  White-eyed
Warblers,
  Blue-winged
  Chat, Yellow-breasted
  Chestnut-sided
  Prairie
  Yellow

CAVITY-NESTING SPECIES*

Chickadees and Titmice,
  Chickadee, Black-capped
  Chickadee, Carolina
  Titmouse, Tufted

Falcons,
  Hawk, Sparrow
Flycatchers,
  Great Crested
Owls,
  Screech
Starlings,
  Starling
Swallows,
  Tree
Thrushes,
  Bluebird, Eastern
Woodpeckers,
  Downy
  Flicker, Yellow-shafted
Wrens,
  Carolina
  House

* Depending upon available stubs, dead trees, posts, etc.

stone-wall boundary outward into the field for some 20 or 30 feet. There are a few tall trees, saplings, numerous shrubs, herbs, and grasses of varying heights, and many low ground cover plants. The struggle for light is immediately discernible. In places nearest the wall, the encroaching trees from the forest have matured sufficiently to form a partial canopy. On the shaded ground, there are still the green plants of bloodroots, wood anemones, windflowers, spring beauties, and violets, but these frail flowers bloomed and made their maximum growth in the full light of early spring. Outward from the wall, the various shrubs and briers are temporarily dominant. Virginia creeper, bittersweet, poison ivy, and other vines make their bid for light by climbing above the lower levels of shade. Grasses and herbs requiring greater amounts of light survive in the openings and along the outer edge.

At places, the wall abuts outcroppings of gneiss bedrock. Portions of the exposed rock surface are covered with lichens, mosses, and ferns. They tell us a story of soil formation—or of the beginning of life itself. The lichens are pioneering plants which cling to the rock's surface with tiny rootlike fibers. These fibers release an acid that etches into the rock, releasing minerals and providing minute openings for moisture and wind-blown particles. Expansion and contraction aid the soil-building process by loosening additional bits of the surface. Mosses gain a foothold and are nourished by the mineral solutions released by the initial work of the lichens. Ferns are often the third-stage plants in this pattern of succession. Even these pioneering plants fill a particular niche in the lives of numerous birds. The phoebe and tufted titmouse use quantities of moss in nest construction. The down of ferns (especially cinnamon fern) is used as nest lining by the ruby-throated hummingbird, wood pewee, and various warblers. Many birds, including the hummingbird, wood pewee, blue-gray gnatcatcher, and some vireos and wood warblers camouflage their nests with lichens, but these lichens are generally gathered from the bark of trees.

A slim, tawny bird flushes from a tangle just ahead of us and flies directly into the woods. It lands on the low, dead limb of an oak. Through our binoculars we determine it to be a cuckoo, but which one—the yellow-billed or the black-billed? The large white spots on the tips of its dark tail feathers and the fact that its wings showed a rufous coloring in flight help determine it to be the yellow-billed. The nest is found in a hawthorn tree partially covered by wild grapevines. It is a rather flimsy platform, built of twigs, grass, weed stems, and leaves—seemingly a hurried accumulation of assorted nearby debris. Its most interesting feature is the lining: dried catkins of birch trees. Two greenish blue eggs are in the nest, an indication that incubation has not started. Another two or three eggs will be laid. The young, when first hatched, will be coal-black and naked, but within a few days they will be covered with stiff quills and look more like miniature porcupines than young birds.

The cuckoos find an abundance of food along the woodland borders, for now the varnished rings of tent cater-pillar eggs around the stems of black cherries have hatched. So great are the caterpillar numbers that the trees are already being defoliated. To the cuckoos, it is a feast for the taking, for they are one of a few birds that relish these spiny creatures. They eat them whole, spines and all. The Baltimore oriole also takes advantage of this profuse supply of food, but its etiquette is quite different. The oriole captures the caterpillar, holds it against a tree limb, and extracts the body juices. A feeding limb will sometimes be lined with dried caterpillar skins.

Of all the songs that fill the air on a summer morning, one song ascends above all others along the brushy bor-ders—not in volume, but by the suffusion of sounds from here, there, and everywhere. The "sweer-sweet-sweet-swee-swee" of the indigo bunting is an incessant proclamation of its territorial defense. The all-blue male sings his warning song from a high perch and defends his territory with vigorous pursuit at the slightest intrusion or provocation by other males.

The indigo seeks the security of the border's mixed brambles and shrubs for its nest, a tightly woven cup of grass, weed stems, skeletonized leaves, and fine strips of grapevine or cedar bark. Quantities of webworms, canker-worms, weevils, grasshoppers, beetles, and other insects are consumed in the process of rearing two broods of three or four young each.

A number of the young trees and shrubs along the woodland's border are understory forest species, witch hazel, American hornbeam, and flowering dogwood are the most common. These species will survive in the en-veloping shade of maturing oaks and birches.

Witch hazel grows best in the low moist sections of the border. Unlike most shrubs, it flowers late in the fall. The nutlike capsules will take a full year to mature, and the following fall they will "explode," scattering their seeds across the ground. Ruffed grouse, chipmunks, and squirrels may feed on the seeds, and the younger shrubs may provide winter browse for the white-tailed deer, but otherwise, the witch hazel is of little direct value to wild-life. Indirectly (and this is probably its most important

contribution), the late blooms are a final seasonal attraction for many insects, which in turn attract migrating warblers and other insect-eating species. The leaves and twigs of this shrub are still used in the manufacturing of witch hazel extract.

Hornbeam is recognized by its smooth blue-gray bark and sinuous form of growth. A very hard wood when dried, it is sometimes referred to as ironwood, and early settlers used it for wheel hubs, ox yokes, and tool handles. Grouse, pheasants, and quail feed on the buds, catkins, and nutlets. In the forest, it is a favorite nesting tree of the red-eyed vireo.

Many birds are attracted to fencerows and woodland borders by the flowering dogwood. Cumulative records show that at least 94 species feed on the red berries in fall and winter. Dogwood berries are especially favored by ruffed grouse, bobwhites, robins, thrushes, catbirds, brown thrashers, and cedar waxwings. The dogwood's characteristic growth of evenly forked, horizontal limbs provides ideal nesting sites for robins, wood thrushes, and vireos.

As we follow the forest's edge, we are continuously conscious of the great quantities of available wildlife foods. Some fruits are mature, and many others are in various stages of ripening. There are wild strawberries, dewberries, raspberries, blackberries, and blueberries. The vines of wild grape, Virginia creeper, honeysuckle, greenbrier, poison ivy, and bittersweet climb over old fences, walls, and piles of brush. Aesthetically, to the human eye, this tangle of vegetation may appear to be little more than an impenetrable jungle, but to the birds it is a Mecca of food, cover, and protection.

Raspberry and blackberry brambles are favorite nesting sites of the indigo bunting, and the thick tangles of greenbrier protect the nests of cardinals, catbirds, brown thrashers, and mockingbirds. These are among the most common birds of brushy borders. The catbird, brown thrasher, and mockingbird are quite similar in their habits. Even their songs have a remarkable degree of sameness about them—full, rich, abrupt phrases—and they are easily confused by beginning students. Usually, the catbird will sing each note singly; the brown thrasher will double each note; and the mocker has a tendency to triple each one. This is not an infallible rule, but it is a definite aid in learning to distinguish the three songs.

At first glance, the brown thrasher seems somewhat thrushlike in appearance, but upon closer observation there are distinct features that separate it from the thrushes. It is a slim bird with a long tail and a long down-curved bill. The breast is striped, not spotted, and the wings show two pronounced bars. The bright yellow eyes are conspicuous at close range.

The brown thrasher arrives quietly and often unnoticed. The male may be around for a week or two before he announces the defense of his selected territory from atop a shrub or small tree. Thrashers nest low in the thickest of tangles; hawthorns, osage orange, and multiflora rose are favorite nesting sites. The thorny character of these plants and the obvious protection they provide also appeal to other species. The goldfinch shows a decided preference for hawthorns, and a hedge of osage orange is the best place to look for the loggerhead shrike. Tangles of multiflora rose attract cardinals, catbirds, song sparrows, and most other border-loving species.

Wild grapevines are established along the border; the seeds may have been carried there by birds or mammals. As we study the vines, we notice characteristic growth habits and adaptive qualities that help them survive in this and other types of environmental complexes. The habit of climbing over other plants and objects as a means of support enables the wild grape to obtain a maximum of light with a minimum of self-supporting tissues. The canopy of broad leaves limits the amount of light available to the plants underneath, including those that support the climbing vine. Yet this dense shade is of value in protecting fledglings from the direct rays of the sun. If we cut a section from the vine, we notice several things: the woody part is composed of vertical sinews that give the vine great flexibility; the xylem vessels are comparatively large, for they must carry moisture for the entire canopy through a small, singular stem. This can be seen by the moisture dripping from the cut stem. The loose, supple bark of the wild grape is used in the building of many

nests. It is used extensively by thrushes, catbirds, cardinals, and to a lesser degree by other birds of the forest and its borders.

Similar to the wild grape, each plant within the border community fills a particular niche that contributes to the support of bird life and to the total functioning of that community. Food, cover, and nesting sites are the obvious contributions, but there are other functions not so conspicuous but nonetheless equally important. Some plants provide nesting materials; others attract and support insects. Some act as soil conditioners, and others aid in temperature control. Each function is essential to the survival of all.

Continuing along the woodland border, we hear a towhee scratching in last year's leaves; we see a brown thrasher turning over leaves with its bill, searching for insects and grubs; brown-headed cowbirds dart in and out of the shrubbery, evidently looking for a ready-made nest in which to lay their eggs. When the woodland ends, we follow the old fencerow that separates two abandoned fields. Portions of the wire fence remain, an indication that the fields have been used within the past few years. There are other signs, too, that tell of the field's recent history. The field through which we are walking shows an abundance of red cedars and greenbrier tangles—plants avoided by cattle. There is a scarcity of other trees and shrubs, another sign that this field was last used as a pasture. Across the fence, the border is a massive tangle of trees, shrubs, vines, and briers. The adjoining field is a mixture of grasses, weeds, and the saplings of elms, gray birch, aspen, black cherry, and a few maples, as well as other pioneering trees of open areas. We conclude this to be an abandoned hayfield.

Four members of the warbler family are in evidence along the fencerow: yellow, blue-winged, and chestnut-sided warblers and the yellow-breasted chat. From a thicket of vines, briers, and shrubs comes a warning. We are trespassers, and we heed the halting whistles. We are scolded, jeered, laughed at, and admonished in most emphatic terms, but the lecturer remains hidden behind his briery pulpit. We wait and listen, and soon are rewarded.

From the topmost brier, the bright yellow breast of the chat gleams in the morning sun.

The yellow-breasted chat is a mimic, a clown, and a showman. He chatters incessantly from an elevated perch, pouring forth a multitude of ecstatic sounds. In a moment of extreme exultation, he will spring into the air, and with wings beating rapidly and legs dangling, he will continue his musical tirade until seemingly exhausted, and then flutter back to his perch. As though his repertoire were not versatile enough, he mimics the songs and calls of other birds; as though the day were not long enough to express his full exuberance, he sings throughout the night.

For physiological reasons, the chat is difficult to classify, but many of its features are more indicative of the warbler family than of any other. A bright yellow throat and breast and white spectacles are the best identifying field marks. It is larger than a sparrow and has a heavy bill.

The yellow warbler is as much at home along fence-rows as in the bottomlands of willows and alders. In fact, it is the most widely distributed of all the warblers, with its range extending from coast to coast in most of the United States and Canada. And it is easily recognized, for it is the only warbler that appears to be all yellow. At close range, some darker coloring in the wings and tail and faint red streaks on the breast are noticeable.

Even in nest building, the yellow warbler is less discriminatory than other members of its family. Nests have been observed in almost every type of shrub or tree at heights from 2 to 50 feet above the ground. A variety of material is used, with the choice depending upon what is available locally. Plant fibers and plant down are the basic materials used in most nests. The down of cinnamon fern is used extensively and is often bound together with the fibers from dead milkweed stems, geum plants, and wild grapevines. Other materials frequently used include cotton, wool, hair, leaves, lichens, moss, and spider webs. The finished nest is compact, with a feltlike texture. Unfortunately, since the yellow warbler is a common nester in a variety of locations, it is a frequent victim of the parasitic cowbird. The cowbird will lay one or more eggs in the warbler's nest and depend upon the foster parents

to hatch and rear its young. This yellow warblers sometimes will do, to the detriment of their own young, if incubation has started. But more often than not they will bury the cowbird's egg (occasionally with one of their own) by building an additional tier on top of the nest. Nests have been found which contained as many as six tiers, indicating the yellow warbler's persistence in attempting to discourage this parasitic intruder.

The blue-winged and the chestnut-sided warblers are closely allied with the young woody growth of the fence-row and its adjoining fields. Undoubtedly, both species have benefited from the gradual clearing of forests and the subsequent growth of secondary hardwoods. The chestnut-sided is bound closely to the seed-shrub-tree complex and will disappear as the trees become dominant enough to form a shading canopy. The blue-winged is somewhat more tolerant and will sometimes nest in thick undergrowth sections of the deep forest. Both species nest quite low in a clump of briers, weeds, or shrubs. Frequently, the blue-winged will nest on the ground.

As with most warblers, these two are usually heard before they are seen. The chestnut-sided makes an emphatic announcement: "I want to see Miss Beecher." The common song of the blue-winged is a short, light "beeee-bzzz." Distinct chestnut sides and a yellow crown distinguish the chestnut-sided. A plain yellow breast in conjunction with two white wing bars and a black streak through the eye are the most diagnostic features of the blue-winged.

A bluebird carols its soft contralto notes from an old apple tree by the barway. It drops to the ground, captures an insect, and immediately returns to its perch on a low dead limb. This is the typical feeding procedure of the eastern bluebird. While it feeds on many ground insects—grasshoppers, crickets, and beetles—the bluebird invariably returns to a fence post or limb to devour its prey.

The bluebird is distinguished from the indigo bunting by its larger size (slightly larger than a sparrow), by the brighter sky-blue of back and wings, and the rusty robin-colored breast. It is a cavity-nesting species, showing a preference for hollow posts, old knotholes, and broken tree stubs.

The field sparrow is a common bird of weedy fields and brushy borders; as you walk, you may find it singing from the top of a small red cedar. The song is a plaintive trill that starts with three or four long, whistled notes and increases in tempo as it ascends or descends the scale until it fades away. It is among the tamest of sparrows, and close observation reveals the distinguishing pink bill.

As we walk through the barway into the road, we reflect upon the sounds that fill the air on this early summer day. There is the distinct whistle of the bobwhite, the mellow caroling of the bluebird, the staccato hammering of a woodpecker, the mournful coo of a dove, and in the distance a cuckoo calls for rain.

The woodland borders, the old fencerows—each has its own story to tell. We have but to follow them to learn of the past, observe the present, and contemplate the future.

7 Roadside Bird Watching

The great expansion of our highway system has been a rather paradoxical phenomenon in terms of bird watching. Unquestionably, many ideal habitats have been devastated by the awesome power of the bulldozer, but on the other hand, many new birding areas have been made accessible to the traveling public. Also, the modern highway has made it possible for anyone to visit most of the greatest birding spots in our country. We can only hope that the expanding highway system does not envelop the very things it now makes possible for us to see.

Permissible speeds of 70 miles per hour or more on our superhighways are not conducive to bird watching. However, in certain areas it is possible to get a recognizable glimpse of herons or red-wings in the ditches from which the roadfill was taken. Flocks of starlings and crows can be seen, and an occasional meadowlark may flush from the grassy median. Other birds are there, too, but for the most part they go unobserved; one is kept busy enough just staying alive.

Despite the massive encroachment upon our land by freeways, turnpikes, beltways, and any other names you care to give these concrete tentacles, we are fortunate enough to live in an era when not all of our country has been engulfed in this "supermania." A maze of country roads still winds through the rich farmlands and forests of our eastern states. Some are paved, and others are dirt or gravel. Along these less-traveled byways, we find roadside birding at its best.

The country road is not a singular type of habitat. Rather, it traverses or adjoins varied combinations of other habitats—fields, meadows, streams, marshes, woodlands, etc. —and assumes a bit of character from each. This diversification makes the country road an intriguing route for a bird hike.

The Country Road

Birds are attracted to the roadside for a number of reasons:

- Utility wires, fences, and posts make good singing perches and resting places.
- They also make good hunting perches, from which field mice, frogs, and toads can be easily seen as they cross the open road.
- Heat radiated from a paved road often attracts swarms of insects, and insects attract birds.
- Spring and summer showers leave earthworms and insects stranded on the road, making hunting easy.
- The dirt road is a good place for dust baths, and a source of gravel for doves and other species.
- The roadside supplies a variety of weed seeds and wild fruits.
- Road kills attract the scavengers.

You will note from the list on page 91 that the birds normally seen sitting on roadside utility wires and fences are birds of the open country. You will not find flocks of woodland birds gathered in this manner.

Every country road has its own story to tell. We have but to follow its winding way to learn of history and of life by the side of the road. Let us follow a typical country road and see what mysteries it reveals. To be specific, let us follow the two-mile section that I hiked twice a day for seven years to attend a one-room country school. This piece of road happens to meander through the low rolling hills of Chester County, Pennsylvania, but it could be anywhere—your state, your road.

Usually I was accompanied by other children, but some years I hiked it alone. Each trip to and from school seemed to hold some new adventure. Along this road I learned to know the birds, butterflies, chipmunks, squirrels, raccoons, foxes, and other forms of wildlife. My interest in

such creatures often accounted for my tardiness at school. Fortunately, an understanding teacher would often turn my finds into a more detailed learning experience. At times, I would have to pay the penalty and stay after school.

First, there was the bridge across French Creek just beyond our house. We always approached this bridge with a rock in one hand, because water snakes often sunned themselves on the stone abutments of the bridge, and they made such good targets. Often, a kingfisher would be sitting on the phone wire watching my favorite fishing hole. Just upstream from the bridge were the remains of an old dam. Here we often saw the green heron and the great blue heron, and spotted sandpipers teetering on the rocks below the dam. Every spring a phoebe returned to nest on the same girder beneath the bridge. And the young willow shoots at the end of the bridge provided us with just the right wood for making whistles.

As we passed the Weaver farm, we looked under the great sycamore for owl pellets. Barn owls nested high up in the hollowed crotch, but we could see them only in the dusk of evening. Barn swallows darted in and out from underneath the overhang on the front of the barn. We could see their mud nests plastered against the big hand-hewn beams. The nests were always close to the ceiling and lined with white chicken feathers, which often hung out over the edges. The swallows were quite congenial, and several pairs nested beneath this overhang. There was always a lot of chattering and flying about as we passed. The dark blue backs and long forked tails were plainly visible. We got to know the barn swallows quite well.

On the high roadbank beyond the barn, the first dandelions of the season bloomed in yellow profusion. Weeks before the first bloom, we would search through the grass for the young, tender plants, and we would have our first meal of dandelion greens, so delicious with a hot bacon dressing. When the blossoms seeded into white fuzzy balls, we would break off the long stems, blow on the balls, and watch the individual seeds drift away on their tiny parachutes. We looped the hollow stems into circles and made dandelion chains on the way to school. Goldfinches fed on the seed heads every day. Their bodies were as yellow as

COMMON BIRDS OF COUNTRY ROADSIDES

WIRE SITTERS

Blackbirds,
*   Blackbird, Red-wing*
*   Grackle, Common*
Doves,
*   Ground*
*   Mourning*
Falcons,
*   Hawk, Sparrow*
Flycatchers,
*   Kingbird, Eastern*
*   Phoebe, Eastern*
Hummingbirds,
*   Ruby-throated*
Kingfishers,
*   Belted*
Mockingbirds,
*   Mockingbird*
Shrikes,
*   Loggerhead*
Starlings,
*   Starling*
Swallows,
*   Bank*
*   Barn*
*   Martin, Purple*
*   Rough-winged*
*   Tree*

Thrushes,
*   Robin*
Waxwings,
*   Cedar*
Weaver Finches,
*   Sparrow, House*

FENCE POST SITTERS

Blackbirds,
*   Blackbird, Red-winged*
*   Meadowlark, Eastern*
Goatsuckers,
*   Nighthawk*
Larks,
*   Horned*
Owls,
*   Burrowing (Florida*
*   and Louisiana)*
Quails,
*   Quail, Bobwhite*
Sandpipers,
*   Plover, Upland*

ROAD-KILL SCAVENGERS

Crows and Jays,
*   Crow, Common*
*   Jay, Blue*

Eagles,
*   Eagle, Bald*
Vultures,
*   Black*
*   Turkey*

OTHERS

Grosbeaks, Finches, Sparrows,
and Buntings,
*   Bunting, Indigo*
*   Cardinal*
*   Goldfinch*
*   Sparrow, Chipping*
*   Sparrow, Song*
Mockingbirds and Thrashers,
*   Catbird*
*   Thrasher, Brown*
Pheasants,
*   Pheasant, Ring-necked*
Woodpeckers,
*   Flicker, Yellow-shafted*

the dandelions themselves, but their wings were a contrasting coal-black. As we approached, they would bound away, accenting each undulation with a song of "ti-dee-di-di." We called them "wild canaries" or "salad birds."

Beyond Weaver's farm, the road continued uphill for the next mile. It was bordered by fields, orchards, and woodlands. The last mile traversed a plateau of open farmlands; it was known as "the level." By traveling this two-mile stretch every day, we came to know each foot of it quite intimately. We knew where to find the biggest and

most luscious strawberries; these we often shared with the box turtles. We knew when the watercress greened in the woodland spring, and when the wild asparagus put forth its tender shoots. In the summer, there were raspberries, blackberries, and wineberries. There were cherries and apples. And in the fall, we knew where to find the wild grapes, persimmons, black walnuts, and hickory nuts. Always, the road seemed to provide some provender for hungry schoolchildren.

In the spring, when we picked the first bouquet of violets, bloodroots, and hepaticas from along the woodland's edge for our teacher, we knew the wood thrush had returned. We could hear its morning call resounding through the forest. And closer by, the ovenbird sang; sometimes we were lucky and could see it walking across the forest floor. A patch of wild columbine attracted hummingbirds. We would watch the tiny ruby-throat go from flower to flower, but we could never find its nest. The bluebirds were back, too, and had already started their first nest in an old fence post at the corner of Rock's orchard.

Our interest in birds continued to grow and eventually was shared by our teacher and other students. We kept a school bird list, and adding a new bird to the list became quite a challenge. Our teacher was quite firm about keeping the list accurate, and would not add a new species unless identification was reasonably certain. We learned to observe markings and habits closely, even to the point of making sketches. This firmness kept our enthusiasm and imagination under control. Otherwise, I am sure the list would have known no bounds. I am also certain that many birds were seen that never made the list. Our reference material was limited mostly to Chester A. Reed's *Bird Guide* (published in 1910).

Rock's orchard not only kept us supplied with apples, but it helped add several new birds to the list. It was here that we first identified the kingbird and the crested flycatcher. The kingbird would sit on the power line, dart into the air to catch a passing insect, and then return to its original perch. The long dark tail with its end banded in white soon became our way of recognizing this bird. The kingbird became one of our favorites when we discovered that he was the one we saw frequently battling the crows. His aerial maneuvers were a delight to watch, especially the way he would dive on a crow from above and behind—like a fighter plane diving on a bomber. At least, we thought so, and often provided the "ack-ack-ack" for his machine guns. The kingbird usually nested on a horizontal branch of one of the old pear trees in the orchard. The crested flycatcher nested nearby in the end of a hollow apple limb. We had read that the crested flycatcher always put a piece of discarded snake skin in its nest. This gave us an opportunity to find out if this were true, for the nest could be reached easily by climbing. And sure enough, the piece of snake skin was there! From then on we vowed the crested flycatcher would not build a nest without this peculiar addition. (I have since learned that a piece of cellophane or similar material makes an acceptable substitute.) The crested flycatcher looked somewhat like the kingbird in size and shape, but it had a rusty tail and a yellow belly. These two birds were not great discoveries, of course, but they were rather momentous ones to us at the time.

The sparrow hawk often accompanied us partway to school, or so it seemed. It would be hunting from the roadside power lines, and as we approached, it would fly ahead of us for 50 yards or so and then land on the line again. Eventually tiring of the game, it would return to the original starting point or take off over the open field to hunt for grasshoppers. When hunting over the field, it would often hover in midair as it searched the ground below. One spring we were surprised to find the sparrow hawks nesting in a tree cavity that we had watched the flickers excavate. The cry of "killy, killy, killy" was a call that we soon learned. Also, we learned to recognize the sparrow hawk by its rusty back and tail, and by its double black sideburns.

Meadowlarks were common along the hayfields. Usually, they would sing from the top of a fence post or phone pole. They were easily remembered by the big black V on their yellow breasts. A Baltimore oriole always nested in the big elm at the entrance to Rock's lane. The old split-rail fence along one of the fields that belonged to the Smith

Farm was a good place to look for resting nighthawks. They would sit horizontally on the rail, and it was sometimes possible to get quite close before they would fly. Often, there were purple martins sitting on the power lines, and one spring we found a shrike nesting in the Osage orange hedge.

But it wasn't just the birds along this road that held our interest. A number of plants and shrubs had special values. The giant mullen, for example, had broad tobacco-like leaves, and when dried, they made a mild adventurous smoke—much better than corn silk. And the seed heads attracted goldfinches and chickadees. The tiny leaves of "Indian tobacco" (pussy's toes) were our source of chewing tobacco. The dark juice was rather acrid, but it provided us with a spitting good time on more than one occasion. The tender bark of young black birch was like a refreshing drink of real birch beer. And there were other shrubs and trees from which we made the tools so essential to boys in the country. Willows and young chestnut sprouts made the best whistles. The dogwood had the best forks for slingshots, because they were straight and strong. Elderberry wood was easily hollowed and made excellent popguns.

After warm spring showers, glistening mud puddles dotted the old country road. These, too, attracted our attention. Sometimes it was just an opportunity to see if our new overshoes were actually waterproof, but usually it was some form of wildlife attracted to the water's edge that intrigued us most. Cabbage and sulfur butterflies gathered there in large numbers. Mud daubers and barn swallows gathered mud for their nests. Flocks of starlings would use the puddles for bathing, and occasionally a killdeer would wade the puddles searching for trapped worms and insects.

We traveled this same road during the summer to visit our friends, but on these days the old road seemed to be enveloped in an atmosphere of laziness. Cicadas droned monotonously from the trees, and the big brown "grasshoppers" kept flying down the dusty road ahead of us (our teacher informed us they were really locusts). If we were lucky enough to catch one, it would immediately show its defense by spitting "tobacco juice" on our hands. Sections of the roadside were blue with chickory. It was prettiest on cloudy days. When it was bright and sunny, we noticed that the chickory closed its flowers early in the day. Along the ditches flourished bouncing bet, or soapwort. We would break off a piece of the plant and use it like a cake of soap. It would form suds just like soap and really help clean our hands. Thistle heads were in seed; the goldfinches ate the seeds and lined their nests with the silky down. They were late nesters, but they were assured of an abundance of seeds of many kinds.

When school opened in the early fall, the old road had a new and exciting look. Asters and goldenrod covered the banks, and monarch butterflies flocked about the milkweeds. Spanish needles, tick trefoil, and burdocks stuck to our clothing, and we helped distribute the seeds along the road. Flocks of migrating tree swallows sometimes lined the phone wires from pole to pole, but the barn swallows were no longer seen around Weaver's barn. The starlings had regrouped and now flew about in tremendous flocks.

As fall progressed, the roadside became a blaze of color, and preparations for winter were evident everywhere. Woodchucks were fattening on the last bit of clover before hibernating for the winter. Chipmunks scurried across the road, their cheek pouches filled with cherry seeds or other goodies for their winter pantry. The squirrels were hoarding acorns, walnuts, and hickory nuts. Crows gathered in noisy flocks and progressed from corn field to cornfield. The white-footed mice were building their nests of finely shredded bark and grasses. (These would make excellent tinder for starting fires with flint and steel at our Scout meetings.) The persimmon tree hung heavy with fruit; it would not be soft and edible until after the first heavy frost. But the Baldwin apples were ripe— cracking hard and filled with juice.

The old road was a pretty desolate place in the winter. Some days, no one traveled it except us school kids and the mailman. But still, it provided us with treasures and excitement. We picked bittersweet and ground pine for Christmas decorations, and gathered various stems and stalks for dry arrangements. We learned that the teasel

plant was brought to this country by the early settlers, and that they used the dried teasel head to raise the nap on cloth so the weave and threads would not show.

We saw many of the common winter birds, mostly woodpeckers, chickadees, slate-colored juncos, and white-throated sparrows. Occasionally, we would see a cardinal in the greenbrier patch, or a flock of waxwings in the red cedar trees. When the ground was covered with snow, we learned to identify the tracks of rabbits, squirrels, opossums, raccoons, foxes, and deer. Snowy days meant that we could take our sleds to school. The last mile coming home was all downhill, and the ride was fast and furious. It was great fun, unless we happened to leave a battered lunch box or school books spilled and scattered along the hillside. But even this had its reward—it gave us an excuse for one more ride.

The incidents along this road were singular and seemingly unrelated. Yet, when one recalls them collectively, it is quite obvious that the old road had an ecology of its own. The birds depended upon the plants for food, nesting materials, and home sites. Undoubtedly, birds of previous years scattered many of the seeds that produced the mature plants. The water, the dirt road, and the gravel banks, the stone walls and the fences, the utility wires and poles —all these helped form a roadside community that supported a variety of birds and other wildlife. And so it is with every country road; each has a story to tell. Find your road and follow it. You may even find an apple to cheer you on your way.

Birding from Your Automobile

The automobile's greatest contribution to birding is transporting you from one place to another—taking you where the birds are. In addition, there are certain methods of birding and certain places in which the automobile can be a definite asset. All of today's birds were hatched in the era of the automobile. Birds are so used to the shapes, sounds, and movements of cars that they accept them as part of their natural environment. Birders can exploit this fact by using their cars as observation blinds. Often, birds can be observed at close range from an automobile, but they will take off the minute someone steps into the open.

I have used my car as a blind to watch waterfowl rafted on the edge of a lake, and to observe shore birds from an oceanfront road. I have used it effectively to watch marsh birds, sandhill cranes, burrowing owls, perching hawks, and dozens of other species. Actually, in the country, there are some birds to be seen almost anywhere you can pull off the road. Your automobile provides a sturdy mount for a spotting scope. All you need is a car window attachment such as those described in Chapter 16. A scope is advantageous when viewing extensive spans of water, grasslands, or marshes.

The automobile is an indiscriminate predator. It kills whatever happens to get in its way—bird, beast, or man. Small mammals killed on the highway attract the scavengers. *Road Kills* Depending on the location, crows, turkey vultures, and black vultures will be the most common. Passing a road kill often provides an exceptionally close view of these larger birds. Usually, when feeding on the highway and approached by a car, they will fly to a nearby post or tree and wait for it to pass. At times, they will just circle and land again when the car has passed.

In an area where both species of vultures are present, they can be distinguished by size when perched. The turkey vulture is considerably larger than the black vulture. Also, mature birds have red heads, while the heads of black vultures are dark. In flight, the turkey vulture soars with its wings at an angle above the horizontal. It soars in sweeping circles, tilting frequently from side to side to take advantage of air currents and gain more lift. The black vulture soars for a short distance with its wings straight out, and then flaps rapidly to maintain altitude and flying speed. The tail of the turkey vulture is long and narrow; the tail of the black vulture is short and broad.

Bald eagles will also feed on road kills. I recall rounding a curve in the road just outside Cape Coral, Florida, and seeing three adult bald eagles feeding on a rabbit in the middle of the road. They lumbered into the air, circled behind the car, and resumed their feeding. Unfortunately, the number of bald eagles is decreasing steadily because of the indiscriminate use of DDT.

Roadside Silhouettes

Birding from an automobile is often a momentary thing: you get a passing glimpse of a bird, but time and lighting conditions do not permit you to make such mental notations as color combinations and field marks. All you see is a silhouette in varying degrees of intensity, and then identification depends on size, shape, and posture. Birds in flight or on the water often appear as silhouettes also. As you become experienced in field recognition, you will notice that many birds can be identified instantaneously quite easily by size, shape, and distinctive postures. Of course, these characteristics are most easily learned when the bird can be positively identified by the additional use of color and field marks.

If you are a beginning birder, you will do well to study the silhouettes on the end pages of Peterson's *Field Guide to the Birds*. Although the silhouettes are small, they are accurately drawn in comparative sizes. Each bird is presented in a typical pose or flight pattern. *Birds of North America*, by Robbins, Bruun, and Zim, uses a number of comparative silhouettes with the introduction of each family or group. These are precisely drawn by Arthur Singer and will help you distinguish birds by shape and pattern. (For additional information on identifying birds by size and shape, see Chapter 2.)

For many long days and nights the pond lay beneath a smothering blanket of ice and snow. But now the warm rays of a spring sun challenge the cold's indomitable reign over the land. The ice cracks and rumbles like distant thunder. The snow thaws, and water pours into the pond in tiny rivulets and surging streams. The cold makes one last effort to exert authority, but its grasp is short-lived, for all things must yield to the will of the sun.

The pond was formed thousands of years ago by the awesome power of a glacier. The creeping stream of ice gouged out the soil and pushed it along like a blade of a giant bulldozer. Eventually, the glacier's great power waned before the dominant forces of the sun. The ridge of soil and rock formed a dam across the small valley; the ice melted and filled the depression: a new pond was born. The pond was sterile then, but nature immediately began the long, slow process of reclaiming the land. Throughout succeeding years, soil and vegetation washed into the pond. Microscopic organisms became the pyramidal base for other forms of life that would find their way to this new environment. Year after year, the sediment accumulated; new and varied plants grew in the enriched water and from the muck along its shallow edges. Numerous forms of wildlife increased in great numbers. Unknowingly, and in an infinitesimal way, they contributed to the eventual destruction of their own environment. Through plant distribution, procreation, feeding, and death, they aided the

8 Pond and Streamside Bird Watching

processes that would turn the pond back to dry land. Now, after millennia, the progress of this transition is quite visible: pond—to marsh—to wooded swamp—to forest.

The sun's rays become warmer, and the last vestiges of winter disappear in the flood waters of springtime. The pond is suffused in a new supply of oxygen, and life therein, mostly dormant during the cold months of winter, responds to the reviving infusion. The time is one of awakening—the rejuvenation of myriad life forms that will make the pond one of the most populous and most active of all outdoor communities.

Life in one of its simplest forms, the plant plankton, floats in the lighted water near the surface. Countless billions of these tiny microscopic plants give a greenish cast to the water. Their function is twofold: through the process of photosynthesis, they provide the pond with a source of sugar and oxygen; also, they are a direct source of food for the animal plankton and for the larvae, nymphs, tadpoles, beetles, snails, and clams that are so abundant in the pond. Water striders, backswimmers, water boatmen, and whirligig beetles emerge from the rotting vegetation and debris on the bottom of the pond and find their way to the surface. The nymphs of mayflies, damselflies, and dragonflies forage along the bottom; eventually, they will leave the pond and, as winged adults, assume a new role in the life of the community. Diving beetles, salamanders, frogs, and turtles free themselves from an encasement of mud and seek the warmth and oxygen of the surface water.

Everywhere about the pond, life responds to the urgency of the season. Seeds and egg cases swell with the beginning of new life, and nymphs and larvae seek the sustenance to acquire adulthood. Along the pond's edge, large gray tadpoles seek the shallowest and warmest water, but it will take another summer to complete their transformation into bullfrogs. The crayfish have unplugged their winter burrows and feed upon sow bugs and other tiny pond creatures. The earthworms have untangled themselves from the massive balls of hibernation and tunnel toward the surface. The willows have an apple-green hue, and the swamp maples are tinged with red. From the cattails comes the first "konk-ka-ree" of the red-wing, and in the evening, the plaintive "peent" of the woodcock can be heard. These are the first arrivals of the many birds that will depend upon the pond throughout the spring and summer.

Each pond or small lake can be looked upon as a microcosm—an isolated habitat mostly self-contained and largely independent of outside influences. However, each body of water and the life that it supports are affected by such factors as temperature, soil content, and whether it is located in an open or wooded area. Regardless of its physical characteristics and biological contents (barring excess pollution), the lone fact that it contains water is sufficient to attract a large number of birds and other wildlife. Each pond or stream acts as an oasis, and it is probable that at one time or another every species of birds within the surrounding territory can be seen near the water. Recognizing this fact, the bird list on page 103 includes only those species that are especially attracted to, or in some way directly associated with, this type of fresh-water habitat. Because of the similarity and proximity of fresh-water marshes and swamps, the reader should consult the lists in Chapter 9 for possible additions to this one.

Land absorbs heat more rapidly than water. The sun warms the forest floor; the spring peepers and wood frogs awaken from hibernation beneath their leafy covering. They head toward the pond for courtship and breeding. The night sleighbell chorus of the spring peepers signals the return of other creatures to the pond, now astir with the sustenance of life.

A few male red-winged blackbirds settle in the sedges along the edge of the pond, but the majority of the great flock continues toward the marsh. Here they will rest and feed on insects and last year's seeds. Some will stay to claim nesting territories, but most of them will continue northward. The flock will thin as additional territories are claimed in marshes, meadows, and fields northward into Canada. Although the nesting locations are selected early,

Pond and Streamside Birds

another two weeks or so will pass before the females arrive.

Other birds follow the receding ice line. A family group of Canada geese break their V formation and descend toward the pond. As they land, their broad webbed feet plow the surface momentarily, acting as brakes to slow their forward speed; with an accompanying back motion of the wings, the geese settle gently upon the water. Canada geese mate for life, and their social ties are quite close. Family groups stay together except during the nesting season, when they spread out over a region with rather definite boundaries. The geese in the pond feed on the roots of various aquatic plants. But they are restless; the call of the northland must be answered. Amid much clattering and honking, the flock is airborne once again. There is considerable calling and shifting of positions as they gain altitude and direction. But, as the fading sun tinges the western sky, the long V lances the northern horizon.

Out in the middle of the pond, a large bird is silhouetted against the glimmering water. It sits low in the water like a heavily laden freighter; it is a common loon. And on the far side of the pond, a pair of pied-billed grebes bob on the wind-blown ripples like a couple of corks. The loon has been on the pond for two days. It must be sure the ice is out and the winter storms are past before it ventures too far north; it cannot take off from land. The grebes, too, will spend several days on the pond, for they are strictly aquatic, also.

Here are some helpful facts to note when watching loons and grebes:
- Loons are larger than ducks, but sit lower in the water. Grebes are smaller than ducks, but sit higher in the water.
- Loons have thick necks and heavy, pointed bills. The necks of grebes are long and thin; the bills are pointed, but are not so heavy.
- Loons and grebes are chiefly fish eaters, and both are expert divers. They both have the ability to gradually sink out of sight by expelling air from within their bodies and from beneath their feathers.
- Loons and grebes need long, running takeoffs across

Coots,
    American
Eagles,
    Bald
Flycatchers,
    Phoebe, Eastern
Grebes,
    Pied-billed
Gulls,
    Herring
    Ring-billed
Herons and Bitterns,
    Bittern, American
    Bittern, Least
    Heron, Great Blue
    Heron, Green
    Heron, Little Blue

Night Heron, Black-crowned
Night Heron, Yellow-crowned
Kingfishers,
    Belted
Loons,
    Common
Ospreys,
    Osprey
Plovers,
    Killdeer
Sandpipers,
    Semipalmated
    Solitary
    Spotted
Swallows,
    Bank
    Martin, Purple

Rough-winged
Tree
Swans, Geese, and Ducks,
    Ducks (see list, page 109)
    Goose, Canada
    Swan, Mute
Warblers,
    Prothonotary
    Waterthrush
    Yellow

the water to become airborne. When endangered, they dive rather than take flight. Either can swim at periscope depth with just their heads above the water.

• The feet of both families are placed far back on their bodies. The loons' feet are webbed and used as propellers when swimming; the grebes' toes are individually webbed, and they, too, are used for swimming. They flare open to give push to the backstroke and close to reduce resistance on the forward stroke.

• The common loon and the pied-billed grebe are the species of their respective families most likely to be seen on eastern fresh-water ponds.

• The common loon has a dark, glossy head and neck. It wears a necklace of white.

• The red-throated loon is seen occasionally on ponds, but is observed most often along the coast in winter.

• The pied-billed grebe has a chickenlike bill with a definite pied marking across it.

• The horned and the red-necked are the two other species of grebes likely to be found on eastern ponds.

With warmer and longer days, the pulse of life surges everywhere about the pond. The willows, alders, aspens, and birches are shrouded in a misty profusion of catkins, and the swamp maples are festooned in the reddest of reds. Pollen drifts through the air, consummating the wonder of pollination; it settles on the water and gathers in floating rafts along the pond's edge. The pond is encircled with the pale greens of the spring's new growth. This verdurous carpet is accented by the designs of deep-blue violets, the white of bloodroots, the pink of spring beauties, and the pale lavender shadings of mertensia.

Within the pond, the long period of dormancy has ended for all creatures. Even the lethargic bullfrog has wriggled free of the mud and has taken its place along the edge of the pond. Bugs, beetles, spiders, worms, crustacea, nymphs, larvae, and eggs are present in many forms and astounding numbers. The night chorus is now a mixture of loud, discordant croaks and trills. Frogs and toads by the hundreds have found their way to the pond to mate and lay their eggs. The pond is so full of life that if it all survived, the pond could not hold the massive bulk. But this will not happen, for the physical and biological factors involved in nature's plan of survival will assure that only a sufficient number of individuals necessary to maintain a balanced environment will survive.

Above the pond, grackles wend their way northward in noisy flocks. Turkey vultures circle, looking for the first casualties of spring, and from beyond the trees comes the "kee-yer, kee-yer" of the red-shouldered hawk. A flock of robins progresses through the trees and shrubbery in a constantly moving wave; they eat hurriedly as they travel. Tree swallows fly low over the pond in loosely scattered flocks. Their flight is so erratic one wonders how many miles they actually travel in reaching their northern destination. Each day and night brings additional species to the pond; some will stay, but for others, home is still far to the north. As the great northward movement wanes, birds about the pond are already busy with the activities necessary to propagate their own kind. The herons have returned and stalk along the shallow edges. Secretively, the bitterns thread their way through the reeds and cattails; the coots squabble and chase each other all over the pond. The ducks have paired and seek nesting sites. Sandpipers and killdeers patter along the shoreline, and overhead the osprey watches for surface-feeding fish. The yellow warbler has returned to the willows, and the loud "tweet tweet" of the prothonotary warbler resounds from the wet bottomlands. Now, the great surfeit of life and energy in the pond will be harvested. There is purpose in abundance.

Much of the life within the pond gathers in the warm, shallow water of the edges. Minnows, frogs, tadpoles, reptiles, shellfish, and aquatic insects are there in great numbers. It is the season of plenty, and for the wading herons, hunting is easy. Although several species of herons depend upon the same basic food supply, there is little competition. Each species is adapted to a slightly different niche in the pond habitat. The green heron is small and comparatively short-legged; it still-hunts in the shallowest water. The little blue heron is an active feeder with a preference for crayfish, frogs, and insects. The Louisiana heron is also quite active when feeding, but it has an exceptionally long neck and bill, and is an expert at spearing fish. The longer legs of the great blue heron permit it to hunt in the deeper waters. The herons have large, slightly webbed feet, which keep them from sinking in the soft mud.*

Masses of frog eggs cling to the submerged plant stems in gelatinous globs. Millions of tiny black specks swell with the expansion of life therein, but nature decrees that only enough shall survive to replace the casualties of the season. The pond ducks are the first check on this potential explosion of life; they consume quantities of this rich food. But thousands of eggs reach the intermediate tadpole stage only to be preyed upon by the herons, reptiles, raccoons, and other shoreline marauders. The long siege in the cold water has ended for the dragonfly nymphs. They climb from the water on the stems of plants, and the miracle of transformation into adulthood begins in the warm rays of the sun. Hundreds will succumb to the patiently watching shore birds and other pondside creatures;

* For additional information on the identification and habits of herons, see Chapter 10.

others will fly away on transparent wings. But even for them, the incessant pursuit has not ended: they must escape such dangers as the instantaneous flick of a frog's tongue or the sudden swoop of a hovering sparrow hawk.

Along the downwind shore of the pond, a pair of spotted sandpipers feed at the water's edge; the pond has trapped a variety of insects which float ashore on the crest of gentle waves. The sandpipers walk slowly and deliberately with a teetering motion, now in the water, now out, picking up insects as they go. A dead fish has floated ashore and attracted a great many flies. The "teeter-tails" now employ a new technique: the teetering is stopped; the head is lowered and pointed forward so that it blends with the mottled background of the body. They stalk their prey and stand motionless until the flies land. With one quick peck of the sandpiper's bill, an unsuspecting fly is captured. The spotteds will nest on the ground near the water, perhaps on the back edge of a gravel bar, or in the thin grass beyond the water's reach.

The eastern side of the pond is wooded. From the dry upland woods, the land slopes almost imperceptibly to the water line. During the time of high water, this area serves as a flood plain for the pond; when the water is low, wide mud flats are exposed. Black willows and alders are the dominant trees near the water. The ground is mud-caked and littered with flood debris. Along the back edge of the flood plain, the willows and alders give way to maples, gums, swamp white oaks, and finally to the mixed hardwoods of the dry upland. To this wet, shadowy, and singularly odoriferous niche within the pond's total environment comes the diminutive golden bird of the wetlands: the prothonotary warbler.

At first, the song is heard: a loud, clear "tweet tweet tweet" without any inflections. One might confuse the song with that of the solitary sandpiper, but the solitary departed the pond days ago and now sings along the lakes in the Canadian wilderness. The coloring of the prothonotary warbler is so distinctive that the bird is easily recognized: a deep yellow (almost orange) head and breast, and gray wings. It is the only cavity-nesting warbler in the East.

The male arrives first and claims his territory by stuffing tree cavities and old woodpecker holes with moss. When the female arrives, she selects the nesting site (frequently in a willow stub 5 or 10 feet above the water) and does most of the work, lining the nest with rootlets, strips of bark, leaves, or whatever soft material happens to be nearby. Like other warblers, the prothonotary is chiefly insectivorous. It feeds low among shrubs, fallen trees, driftwood, and other flood debris.

The yellow warbler also nests in the willows, but it is not so inherently bound to a specific type of habitat. Here it is reasonably free from its perennial nemesis, the cowbird, because the red-wings patrol the pond's edges with a vengeance against these parasitic intruders.

Swallows come to the pond each day. They fly low over the water, and occasionally they skim the surface for a drink on the wing. The tree swallow is recognized by its dark back that reflects glints of metallic green. A number of them nest in abandoned woodpecker holes near the pond. The bank swallow and the rough-winged swallow are both brown above. The bank swallow has a white throat and sports a brown breast band; the rough-winged is more modestly garbed with a dusky throat.

An osprey hovers above the pond. With partially folded wings, it dives into the water and seizes a spawning bluegill in its talons. The osprey shakes itself free of water, turns the fish head first to reduce wind drag, and flies to the great nest of sticks in a dead oak at the far end of the pond. The act has been one of frustration; the osprey's long vigil for a mate has gone unrewarded. Nor will it be rewarded. This lone bird is symbolic of the tragic ending of a great drama. Man has poisoned the land and the water —the final curtain is closing.

There are many plants that grow in and around the pond. Some are submerged varieties such as coontail, muskgrasses, watermilfoils, and pondweeds. The duckweeds float freely; the leafy plants of water lilies and cow lilies float, but are rooted in the mucky bottom. Many plants emerge above the water; these include pickerelweed, rice

cutgrass, wild rice, bulrushes, spikerushes, and reeds. Wild millet, chufa, and smartweeds abound on the previously flooded flats. These plants serve a number of purposes in the pond community. They protect the shoreline by breaking the eroding force of·waves; they provide various insects and small mammals with a means of getting in and out of the pond; they provide cover and shelter; and perhaps most important of all, they are the chief source of food for a variety of pond ducks.

The number and species of ducks attracted to any one pond, lake, or stream will be influenced by the geographical location and the physical characteristics of that particular body of water. Black ducks and mallards may be content to nest about a pond in the open, but the wood ducks, goldeneyes, and buffleheads prefer woodland ponds. The mergansers like the clear water of northern woodland streams and rivers.

The greatest concentrations of pond ducks are in the central part of our country, but most species can be found in considerable numbers throughout the East. True pond ducks feed on the surface. Their food is chiefly vegetable, but it does include some animal matter such as mollusks, insects, and frog eggs. They feed by skimming the surface with their broad bills, by reaching beneath the surface, and where the water is deep, by tipping up—head submerged, tail straight up, and feet paddling the water. Pond ducks float high in the water, and they can "jump" directly into the air without any preliminary takeoff run. They are a gregarious lot and travel about in flocks except when nesting.

The list on the facing page includes species other than those normally classified as pond ducks. It is composed of those species that can be observed about ponds or streams at one time of the year or another.

The cool clear-running water of a woodland stream has a special fascination for wildlife and man. A stream incorporates movement, sound, and beauty; it is a means of transportation and a source of food. It is difficult to classify as a special type of habitat, for it often supports many of the same plant and animal species that are found in

DUCKS OFTEN SEEN AROUND PONDS AND STREAMS

Bufflehead	*Mallard*	*Shoveler*
Duck, Black	*Merganser, Common*	*Teal, Blue-winged*
Duck, Ring-necked	*Merganser, Hooded*	*Teal, Green-winged*
Duck, Ruddy	*Merganser, Red-breasted*	*Widgeon, American*
Duck, Wood	*Pintail*	
Goldeneye, Common	*Redhead*	

other fresh-water communities. Also, the characteristics of each stream vary according to location, terrain, and source of water. But each stream has some features that make it especially attractive to certain species of birds.

Streamside Birding

Ecologists tend to classify a stream and its tributaries as an independent evolutionary unit. Through distribution by water, plants and animals occupy every suitable niche along the full length of the stream. For example, the black willow is one of the most common trees along our eastern streams. The cottony down, to which the seeds are attached, floats upon the water, and during the periods of ice-out and flooding, many stems and twigs are broken off and carried downstream to be replanted in mud, sand, and debris. You will find the willows most plentiful at bends in the stream and in the flooded lowlands—places where the seeds and twigs are washed from the main current and find a natural anchorage. These willow bottoms are attractive to the prothonotary warbler and the yellow warbler. Species such as the woodpeckers, tree swallows, and wood ducks will occupy cavities in the soft wood of mature trees.

There are two methods of watching birds along a stream: you can sit on a cushion of moss, lean back against a stalwart tree, and watch the activities within view; or you can follow the stream. Depending somewhat on the stream, one method may be just as rewarding as the other. Personally, I prefer to follow the stream, especially if I can supplement my birding equipment with a pair of boots or waders and a fly rod. Some of my most exciting birding has been while fishing. They are complementary activities that supplement each other beautifully, and I recommend the combination with fervor. The last duck hawk I saw was along a trout stream in Maine; it flashed around a bend and passed so close I could almost touch it with my fly rod. Streams have led me past great colonies of bank swallows, burrows of kingfishers, and nests of spotted sandpipers. Perhaps the most exciting discovery of all—a once-in-a-lifetime experience—happened while I was fishing French Creek near the little village of Knauertown, Pennsylvania. I was following the meandering stream through Lytle's meadow when I discovered a number of chimney swifts using a large, hollow tree stub as their nesting site. Your discoveries will undoubtedly be different, but around each bend, a new adventure awaits you— and perhaps a brook trout will rise to your drifting fly.

The loud, rattling call of the belted kingfisher is a common sound along our eastern streams and ponds. The metallic-sounding clatter is uttered often, as the bird flies low over the water, and just after landing on, or departing from, a favorite fishing perch. Mostly, the call is given as a warning against possible intrusion by other members of the species; the kingfisher will not tolerate poaching on its selected territory.

The belted kingfisher is the only member of its family to be found in the East. It hunts from a perch over the stream, or by hovering in midair. When a fish is sighted, the kingfisher dives into the water like a tern and captures the fish in its long, heavy beak. If you watch the kingfisher after such a capture, you will see it fly to a convenient perch and then rap the fish against the limb several times. This stuns or kills the fish so that it can be more easily maneuvered into a head-first position for swallowing. The nest of the kingfisher is placed at the end of a burrow, which it digs in the side of a steep, clean bank. The selected bank is usually quite sandy, but it must be compact enough to prevent the burrow from collapsing. The burrow is usually 4 or 5 feet long and about 4 inches in diameter. It is found most often along the bank of a stream, but if the stream banks are too low, or not of the right soil consistency, the kingfisher will nest inland.

The belted kingfisher is easily recognized. Slightly larger than a robin, it has a large, ragged, blue-gray crest and a heavy bill. Both sexes are blue-gray above and white underneath; the male has a single, blue-gray chest band, but the female is a bit more colorful with two chest bands, one blue-gray and the other rusty brown.

Bank swallows also nest in self-dug burrows, often along the bank of a stream, but their requirements for a suitable nesting site are more specific than those of the kingfisher. They are colony-nesting birds, and the bank selected must be large enough to hold a number of burrows. It must be quite high, vertical, and free of vegetation. Also, it must be of the right sand and gravel consistency to permit digging, yet avoid collapse. For these reasons, bank swallows are most abundant in areas of glacial moraine deposits.

Every stream has its spotted sandpipers. They flutter from rock to rock, or for short distances along the shorelines, on stiff, downcurved wings. The clear, loud call of "peet-weet, peet-weet" is very distinctive. One can easily see how this sandpiper gets its name; in breeding plumage, it is the only member of its family with a spotted (rather than streaked) breast.

Certain species of birds are attracted to streams with specific physical characteristics. Small, shaded, woodland streams attract the waterthrushes. Phoebes will nest on stone ledges and under bridges. Black ducks may be at home in slow, sluggish streams, but the mergansers prefer the cool, clear waters of northern trout and salmon streams, where they feed on the small fry, often to the consternation of fishermen.

Regardless of where your favorite stream may be, it is undoubtedly an ideal place to watch birds. In addition to the water birds, warblers and vireos sing from the tree-tops; the calls of thrushes and ovenbirds echo from the adjacent woodlands; ruby-throated hummingbirds feed amid the jewelweeds and cardinal flowers; and dozens of species come to the stream to drink and bathe. The lure of a stream attracts many birds and is specially rewarding for those who come to watch them.

9 Birds of Fresh-Water Marshes and Swamps

The marsh has been building imperceptibly year after year, century after century. Its acreage was once a part of the adjacent pond, but now it is green and lush with a variety of plants, and it supports many forms of life which are solely dependent upon this stage of the continuing transition.

The processes of change were slow. Decaying plant and animal matter settled to the bottom of the pond; algae were supported by the humus and, in turn, contributed to the enrichment of the soil and water. Wind-blown and floating seeds settled along the pond's edges—cattails, bur-reeds, pondweeds, rushes, and grasses began to grow. The spores of horsetails found root, and tiny duckweed plants were carried in on the feet of waterfowl; they floated free and multiplied. Muskrats found their way to this new source of food. They fed upon the roots; pieces floated free and were replanted. The marsh had its beginning at the pond's edge.

Other processes, too, were helping build the marsh. Heavy rains and floods over a period of many years carried tons of mineral-rich soil and debris into the upper reaches of the pond. The projecting vegetation slowed the water, settled the soil, and contained the debris. Even during drier periods, the protruding plants captured seeds, dust, leaves, and other wind-blown matter. In a less spectacular way, these events, too, contributed to the building of the marsh.

As the pond gave way to the encroaching marsh, animal life within this watery environment also changed. The burrowing nymphs disappeared and were replaced by those that climb on plants extending above the water. Caddisfly larvae no longer built their protective cases from grains of sand; a slightly different species used bits of vegetation instead. Gill-breathing snails could not survive in the smothering muck, and their niche was filled by a lung-breathing variety. As the dense vegetation lessened the amount of oxygen in the water, a pattern of survival evolved: completely aquatic species became fewer, and air-dependent species became more numerous.

This environmental transition brought about some significant changes in bird populations. To some species, such as certain ducks, herons, and sandpipers, the changes were of little consequence; their diet and habits were flexible enough to adjust to either habitat. Other species, including the common loon and American and red-breasted mergansers, were present only as long as deep open water existed. But others, like the sora and king rails, could survive only in the marsh. The abundance of food and cover in the marsh appealed to certain land birds. In comparatively recent evolutionary time, a number of species, including the kingfishers and the marsh wrens and sparrows, have become adapted to this watery environment.

The marsh is no more static than was the pond. Change is constant, and the features of a true swamp begin to emerge around its borders. Buttonbush, alders, willows, maples, cypress, cedars, and elms encroach upon the marsh in orderly ecological succession. The natural laws of land reclamation will be enforced until the area finds stability in a climax forest condition.

Marshes and succeeding swamps are formed in other ways. Many of our largest marsh areas are at the mouths of streams and rivers, where they empty into larger bodies of water. The land is often low and flat, and the flowing waters may cut a number of channels. Some will change course during times of flooding. Tremendous amounts of soil are washed in from the uplands, and new marshy deltas are formed. Severe storms, involving wind, water, ice, soil, and debris, often initiate new ponds or marshes by blocking off sections of a lake or river. If the barrier holds for a year or so, it is enlarged and becomes permanent through additional accumulations and through the growth of soil-holding plants. The isolated areas are usually low and, with existing vegetation, assume a marshy status in a comparatively short period of time.

Beavers, of course, are great builders of dams, which flood low-lying areas and bring about drastic changes in the vegetation complex. Trees and shrubs are killed by flooding, and water-tolerant plants become dominant. The dead trees provide an abundance of nesting cavities for woodpeckers, tree swallows, wood ducks, and other species.

And finally, there are man-made marshes. Sportsmen and conservationists have long recognized the value of wetlands in the preservation of wildlife. Through their interest, money, and guidance, many valuable contributions have been made, especially in the maintenance of waterfowl populations.

Since marshes and swamps are in a constant state of change, the bird populations in any one area will depend largely upon its stage of development and its physical and geographical location. The list on the facing page includes those species most likely to be found in the open marshes and partially wooded swamps. It includes transients as well as nesting species, and pertains to the eastern half of our country, excluding those species indigenous to the southernmost marshes and swamps. These species are covered in Chapter 12, "Watching Our Tropical Birds."

Birding in Marshes and Swamps

Time

Birding is best in the early morning. This is especially true in the wetlands, as any duck hunter can verify. The ducks are active, some returning from nighttime foraging and others flaring and wheeling from one feeding spot to another. Herons glide in from all directions; snipe zigzag by with incredible speed; flocks of red-wings rise momentarily and settle to resume their feeding; and swallows dart about, feeding on the wing. Rails call, coots cackle,

PROBABILITY LIST FOR BIRDS OF FRESH-WATER MARSHES AND SWAMPS

Blackbirds,
  Red-winged
Ducks and Geese,
  Duck, Black
  Duck, Ring-necked
  Duck, Wood
  Goose, Canada
  Goose, Snow
  Mallard
  Merganser, Hooded
  Pintail
  Shoveler
  Teal, Blue-winged
  Teal, Green-winged
Eagles and Hawks,
  Eagle, Bald
  Hawk, Marsh
  Hawk, Rough-legged
Grebes,
  Pied-billed
Gulls and Terns,
  Gull, Bonaparte's
  Gull, Ring-billed
  Tern, Caspian
  Tern, Forster's
Herons and Bitterns,
  Bittern, American
  Bittern, Least
  Egret, Common

Egret, Snowy
Heron, Great Blue
Heron, Green
Heron, Little Blue
Heron, Louisiana
Night Heron, Black-crowned
Night Heron, Yellow-crowned
Kingfishers,
  Belted
Ospreys,
  Osprey
Owls,
  Barred
  Short-eared
Plovers,
  Killdeer
Rails, Gallinules, and Coots
  Coot, American
  Gallinule, Common
  Rail, King
  Rail, Sora
  Rail, Virginia
Snipes, Woodcocks, and Sandpipers,
  Sandpiper, Pectoral
  Sandpiper, Semipalmated
  Sandpiper, Solitary
  Sandpiper, Spotted
  Snipe, Common
  Woodcock, American

Yellowlegs, Greater
Yellowlegs, Lesser
Sparrows,
  Savannah
  Sharp-tailed
  Swamp
Swallows,
  Rough-winged
  Tree
Warblers,
  Cerulean
  Hooded
  Kentucky
  Myrtle
  Palm
  Parula
  Prothonotary
  Swainson's
  Waterthrush
  Yellow
  Yellowthroat
Woodpeckers,
  Downy
  Pileated
  Red-bellied
Wrens,
  Carolina
  Long-billed Marsh
  Short-billed Marsh

gallinules laugh, and from the wooded areas comes the mixed chorus of morning songsters. The marsh is alive and active. By midmorning, the sounds and movements will lessen considerably, and birding will not be as rewarding.

Some marshes and swamps have access roads or trails; others are accessible only by canoe or boat. I have a decided preference for traveling on foot, whenever possible. *Travel* This puts one in physical contact with the environment.

Senses become keener and help develop an aura of appreciation for one's surroundings. If possible, when exploring a strange marsh area for the first time, have someone who knows the area accompany you. Don't go alone. Marshes and swamps can be treacherous, especially for those of us who are not as agile as we think we are.

The weather and mode of travel are general factors that should influence your selection of clothing.*

Clothing   *Footwear:* If walking, wear old shoes or sneakers that you do not mind getting wet and muddy, or boots that will keep your feet dry. Sneakers and moccasins are ideal for use in canoes or boats.

Trousers and jackets: Long trousers to protect the legs and a jacket or long-sleeved shirt to protect the arms are practical items. Do not wear shorts. Many marsh plants are sharp-edged and may cut or irritate the skin. Also, the less skin area exposed to mosquitoes, the better. If you plan to do any wading, long trousers will protect you from clinging leeches.

Headgear: A visored cap will help shade your eyes from the sun and glare off the water.

Binoculars, field guide, and notebook: Essential items on any field trip.

Equipment   *Insect repellent:* A precautionary item. The need for it depends on the time of year.

Snakebite kit: Another precautionary item that should be carried, especially in southern marshes and swamps where cottonmouths are prevalent.

Walking staff: I know a few birders who always carry a walking staff. I have seen them use a staff as a support in crossing areas of treacherous footing, as a probe to test the depth and safety of mucky bottoms, and as a steadying rest for binoculars and cameras. They tell me it gives them a sense of security against attack—from what, I cannot imagine. A lightweight, sturdy staff can be made from bamboo. The ground end should be taped.

* For additional information on clothing and equipment for field trips, see Chapter 17, "Techniques Afield."

BIRD SOUNDS OF MARSHES AND SWAMPS

Winnowing	*A distant, ethereal, hard-to-locate, somewhat eerie flight sound. Made by air rushing through the feathers during courtship displays*	*Common Snipe*
Pumping	*A guttural sound like that of an old wooden hand pump. Sometimes called "stake driver" or "thunder pumper"*	*American Bittern*
Cooing	*Soft, hollow, cooing notes, emanating from the marsh vegetation. Repeated rapidly five or six times*	*Least Bittern*
Bubbling	*A dry, ecstatic "tsap—tsap—tsap-tsap-tsap-tsap-ap-errrrr," on a declining scale, but increasing in tempo*	*Short-billed Marsh Wren*
Chattering	*A grating, unmusical chatter, ending in a rather harsh "ut-ut-turrrrr-ur." The last note has a soft whistle quality. Heard day or night*	*Long-billed Marsh Wren*
Rattling	*A loud, cutting rattle, sounded in flight or from a perch above the water*	*Belted Kingfisher*
Clamoring	*The loud, resonant clamoring of many birds. Heard most often in the early morning or evening, when flocks are arriving or departing*	*Canada Geese*
Quacking	*A distinct verbal "quack, quack" reminding one of the familiar domestic ducks*	*Mallard, Black Duck, Shoveler*
Cackling	*A spontaneous, henlike cackle often answered by other members of the species. Like a chicken yard in the marsh*	*Common Gallinule*
Squawking	*Repeated, harsh, guttural squawks, low and drawn out. Usually given when alarmed*	*Great Blue Heron*
Whinnying	*Clear, quavering whistles, uttered in rapid succession, descending the scale and decreasing in tempo*	*Sora Rail*
Grunting	*A slow-starting, stuttering grunt. "Bup——bup——bup—bup-bup-bup-bup-bup-bup" given on a single tone, but increasing to a rolling tempo*	*King Rail*
Tweeting	*A clearly enunciated "tweet, tweet, tweet, tweet, tweet" coming from the wooded edges*	*Prothonotary Warbler*
Hooting	*An emphatic, questioning hoot, with a southern drawl: "Who cooks for you? Who cooks for you all?"*	*Barred Owl*

Our fresh-water marshes and swamps constitute one of the richest wildlife habitats to be found anywhere in the world. Their location is such that they are structured by the continuous accumulation of topsoil and life-giving nutrients from the uplands. The combination of soil, humus, a surfeit of minerals, and an abundance of water produces a luxuriant growth of water-tolerant vegetation. Every ecological niche within these wetlands has its counterpart of

FLIGHT PATTERNS OVER THE MARSH

HOVERING

Belted Kingfisher: *Body motionless, wings beating. Over water, when surface-feeding fish are spotted.*

Sparrow Hawk: *Hovers in one spot while hunting over grassy areas.*

Rough-legged Hawk: *Only eastern buteo to hover habitually when hunting.*

Marsh Hawk: *Not habitually, but occasionally when movement of prey has been spotted.*

Osprey: *Hovers over surface-feeding fish. Often dives from this position.*

Terns: *A favorite means of hunting over open water.*

SOARING

Turkey Vulture: *Wingspan of 6 feet. Wings held at a dihedral angle. Often soars for comparatively long periods between intermittent flappings.*

Black Vulture: *Noticeably smaller than turkey vulture. Wingspan less than 5 feet. Wings are broad and held on a nearly flat plane.*

Bald Eagle: *Wingspan to over 7 feet. Soars with wings on the horizontal—like a flying board.*

Osprey: *Smaller than turkey vulture. Wings have slight dihedral angle next to the body, then horizontal.*

Hawks (buteos):   *Most of the buteos soar in circles high over open areas.*

Gulls: *Sometimes soar when circling over potential feeding areas.*

GLIDING

Owls: *Glide silently.*

Herons: *Often exceptionally long glides before landing.*

Hawks (accipiters):   *Short wings and long tail. Sails or glides for short distances after several rapid wing beats.*

Other Species: *Many birds glide for varying distances before landing. It is particularly noticeable with geese, certain ducks, egrets, bitterns, and gulls.*

FLAPPING*

Herons, Egrets, and Bitterns: *Slow, deliberate, rhythmic wing beat.*

Ducks: *Fast, continuous wing beat.*

FAST FLIGHT

Loons, Falcons, Waterfowl, Shore Birds, Swallows, Swifts, and Hummingbirds.

UNDULATING FLIGHT

Woodpeckers, Nuthatches, and Goldfinch.

ERRATIC COURSE

Common Snipe, American Woodcock, and Savannah Sparrow.

WEDGE FORMATIONS

Swans and Geese.

COMPACT FLARING FLOCKS

Green-winged Teal, Blue-winged Teal, Yellowlegs, and Red-winged Blackbirds.

---

* The smaller the bird, the faster the wing beat. The frequency may vary from less than 2 beats per second for the great blue heron to as many as 70 beats per second for the ruby-throated hummingbird.

NESTING SPECIES IN MARSHES AND SWAMPS

ON THE GROUND

Ducks,
    Duck, Black
    Mallard
    Teal, Blue-winged
    Widgeon, American
Hawks,
    Marsh
Owls,
    Short-eared
Plovers,
    Killdeer
Rails,
    King
Snipes, Woodcocks, and Sandpipers,
    Sandpiper, Spotted
    Snipe, Common
    Woodcock, American
Sparrows,
    Savannah
Warblers,
    Kentucky
    Yellowthroat

IN TREE CAVITIES

Ducks,
    Duck, Wood
    Merganser, Hooded
Owls,
    Barred

Swallows,
    Tree
Warblers,
    Prothonotary
Woodpeckers,
    Downy
    Pileated
    Red-bellied
Wrens,
    Carolina

ON PLATFORMS OR TUSSOCKS
JUST ABOVE THE WATER LINE

Bitterns,
    American
Coots,
    American
Grebes,
    Pied-billed
Loons,
    Common
Rails,
    Virginia
Sparrows,
    Sharp-tailed

IN VEGETATION JUST ABOVE THE MARSH

Bitterns,
    Least
Blackbirds,
    Red-winged

Rails and Gallinules,
    Gallinule, Common
    Rail, Sora
Sparrows,
    Swamp
Wrens,
    Long-billed Marsh
    Short-billed Marsh

IN SHRUBS OR TREES

Eagles,
    Bald
Herons,
    Egret, Cattle
    Egret, Common
    Egret, Snowy
    Heron, Great Blue
    Heron, Green
    Heron, Little Blue
    Heron, Louisiana
    Night Heron, Black-crowned
    Night Heron, Yellow-crowned
Ospreys,
    Osprey
Warblers,
    Parula
    Swainson's
    Yellow

---

animal life. From the soil beneath the water to the air above, life in multitudinous numbers survives in this richest of environments. And each niche attracts one or more species of birds especially adapted to survival in a microcosmic part of the wetland habitat. The relationships among the numerous life chains, including the birds adapted to each, provide the balance and stability that assure the survival of the total community.

10 Birds of the Mud Flats and Salt-Water Marshes

Time—the infinite reach of time—has molded our eastern seaboard into a vast and rich life-supporting area. From the inland mountains, this great coastal plain slopes gradually toward the sea. The closer to the sea, the less perceptible the gradient becomes; rolling hills give way to the more level fields and meadows, and finally to the salt marshes that slow and halt the encroaching tides.

Born of glaciation, alluvial deposits, sediments from the ever-moving tides, and the contributions of interdependent plant and animal life, salt marshes are among the most diversified and the most intricately balanced of all the habitats woven into nature's comprehensive plan for environmental survival. In a sense, they are individualistic. Each marsh has its own sounds—the varied intonations of the wind in the cordgrass, the moving water, the clatter of scurrying crabs, and the dissonant calls of the marsh birds. Each has its own characteristic odors—the sea, always the clean smell of the sea, the pungent odor of grasses, a trace of iodine from decaying seaweed, and on occasion, the lingering stench of death. Some marshes are stable, healthy, and continue to build; others are suffering a diabolical death from the effects of man's greed and ignorance.

The true salt marsh is treeless. Tough, leathery cordgrasses (*Spartina*) predominate. They have a deep, intertwining root system that holds the peaty soil in place. They are thick-growing, turf-building plants that preempt all suitable space from encroaching species. The cordgrasses are exceptionally salt-tolerant, and they will thrive in the most saline portions of the marsh. But there is considerable diversification in our Atlantic coastal marshes. There are sloughs, ditches, mud flats, sand bars, meandering fresh-water streams, and higher ground along the back edges. Certain sections may support such salt-tolerant plants as glasswort, eelgrass, and sago pondweed. Secondary plants may gain a temporary foothold on storm-damaged areas, or on the sand and debris deposited by unusually high tides. Here we may find the beautiful swamp rose mallow and the marsh mallow. Tidewater sagittaria, salt-marsh fleabane, asters, sea miltwort, and silverweed are also among the dominant secondary plants, but most of these are short-lived, for the far-reaching rhizomes of the spartinas inevitably reclaim the land.

The majority of Atlantic coastal marshes are protected from the direct assault of the sea by outer banks, sand dunes, islands, and inland channels. Most of them are adjacent to this "Intracoastal Waterway," but are, nevertheless, subject to the gentle flow of rising and falling tides twice each day. These tide-washed wetlands are extremely rich in nutrients, the basis of innumerable and highly complicated life chains. Buried in the mud flats are razor clams, hard clams, soft-shelled clams, burrowing shrimp, and a variety of allied worms. Snails cling to the sturdy stems of the cordgrass, which also provides homes for grasshoppers, crickets, spiders, and flies. Blue crabs, fid-dler crabs, beach fleas, and sandlings scurry along the grassy edges of the slough. The warm, shallow waters are teeming wtih mummichogs, killifish, and prawn. And there are birds, many birds, specifically adapted to fill their specialized roles in the living world of the salt-water marsh. There are birds with long legs for wading, and birds with large feet for walking on floating and submerged vegetation. There are divers and skimmers, and birds with pointed bills for spearing fish. There are birds with bills for sifting and straining, and birds with long bills for probing in the mud. Every life chain within this saline environment is in some way associated with birds —birds inherently adept at fulfilling a special niche in the complicated web of survival for all species.

Precautions for Birding in a Salt Marsh

Don't go alone. One or more companions can provide a helping hand when needed.

Know your tides. Don't get trapped or flooded by an incoming tide, or stranded (if in a boat or canoe) by an outgoing tide.

Watch your step. The thick mats of marsh grass cover holes, clumps, and ditches. Mud flats can be treacherously soft.

Avoid banks undercut by water. Your weight may cause them to break and crumble.

Wear protective clothing. Marsh grasses cut, the sun burns, and mosquitoes bite.

Carry insect repellent. The female marsh mosquito cannot produce eggs without a meal of high-protein blood, and bird watchers have high-protein blood.

Spring Comes to the Marsh

The pace of life in the marsh is slowed during the cold days of winter. Most marine life is dormant or has migrated to warmer waters. The marsh is blanketed with snow, and the tall grasses are broken down under its weight. The marsh freezes, and it thaws. Ice cracks, crunches, and moves with the ceaseless tides. Inadvertently, these harsh processes of winter prepare the marsh for an abundance of life in the ensuing spring. The vegetation is broken and ground up, and then mixed by the wash of the tides. By spring, the waters of the salt marsh and the surrounding bays are saturated with life-supporting nutrients. Now with the warming rays of the sun, it is here in the gentle flow of the enriching tides that life in its simplest form begins.

Each drop of the nutrient-enriched water may support thousands of unicellular plants (phytoplankton). These microscopic plants form the base for the pyramid of energy within this salt-water environment. Specifically, they oxygenate the water and provide the only source of food for the first-order consumers, zooplankton (animal).

Elsewhere across the marsh, life emerges from its dormancy. The female salt-marsh mosquitoes (*Aedes sollicitans*) lay their eggs singly on the dry land. Here the eggs await the flooding of the spring tides to start their

BIRDS OF THE EASTERN SALT MARSHES IN THE NESTING SEASON

Blackbirds,
  Meadowlark
  Red-winged
Crows,
  Fish
Ducks,
  Duck, Black
Gulls and Terns,
  Gull, Herring
  Gull, Laughing
  Tern, Common
  Tern, Gull-billed
Hawks,
  Marsh
Herons and Bitterns,
  Bittern, American

Egret, Common
Egret, Snowy
Heron, Great Blue
Heron, Green
Heron, Little Blue
Heron, Louisiana
Night Heron, Black-crowned
Night Heron, Yellow-crowned
Ibises,
  Glossy
Ospreys,
  Osprey
Owls,
  Short-eared
Rails and Coots,
  Coot, American

Rail, Clapper
Rail, Virginia
Sandpipers,
  Willet
Sparrows,
  Savannah
  Seaside
  Sharp-tailed
  Song
Wrens,
  Long-billed Marsh

development and wash them into remaining puddles and shallows. The wrigglers develop by countless thousands, but comparatively few survive, for they become the chief food item of the abundant killifish and the top minnows. Other insects emerge and, along with the numerous varieties of marine life, assume their innate roles in the miraculous life chains of the saline world. The brackish waters teem with life; they become the nursery of the sea. Fish, in great numbers and varieties, crowd into the estuaries to spawn, and the waters become richer still. It is to these bounteous waters that our marsh birds return in the spring to propagate their own kind.

The salt-water marsh can be considered as "home" for a great variety of birds. Some nest in the marsh; others nest in adjacent habitats and use the marsh as their main feeding area. Also, large numbers of spring and fall migrants will rest and feed about the marsh, the mud flats, and the surrounding waters.

The list of birds at the top of this page should be considered as a "probability" list—the species you are most likely to see about our eastern salt marshes during the nesting season. It includes both nesters and feeders. (The migrants will be added later.)

If there is one bird truly symbolic of the salt marshes, it is the clapper rail. Its range extends from southern New England southward along the Atlantic and Gulf coasts. This gray hen-size bird is often the enigma of bird watchers; it is secretive, evasive, and more often heard than seen. The voice, a rough "cac-cac-cac" cackling, has an elusive quality and is quite deceptive as to location.

Look for the clapper along the edges of marsh creeks, ditches, and sloughs. At low tide, it will venture onto the mud flats to feed. Note how it bobs its head and twitches its stubby tail when walking. When the clapper is disturbed, its flight is slow, with legs dangling, and is usually of short duration. On the ground, the clapper is fast. With head lowered and stretched forward, it can thread its way through the thick marsh grasses with incredible speed. Pursuit is pointless.

The clapper rail builds its nest on the marshy ground above the normal high-tide line. The nest is built of dry grasses and is usually partially shaded by overhanging vegetation. One or more noticeable runways often reveal its location. There seems to be considerable misjudgment in the choice of nesting sites. Frequently, many nests are inundated with high spring or storm tides. Such abnormally high tides take a heavy toll of eggs, young, and brooding females. The clapper compensates for these natural losses by rearing a large family of 9 to 12 chicks. During periods of flooding, the rails can be observed congregating on higher ground.

If you are ready to leave the marsh, and you have not had any success in seeing or hearing the clapper rail, try this: close your field guide with a sharp "bang." One disturbed clapper will often trigger an alarm that will excite every rail in the marsh. The resulting cackling may remind you of a chicken yard—one that has been disturbed by the sudden appearance of a fox.

In the upper reaches of the marsh, you may find the Virginia rail. This smaller, quail-size rail prefers the fresh or less brackish waters. Seemingly, it is even more secretive and more difficult to observe than the clapper rail. The repeated "tid-ick, tid-ick, tid-ick" call often reveals its presence. At times, it will also utter a series of grunts and similar noises that can be mistaken easily for those of a frog. Once you identify the call, and you are sure there are Virginia rails in the area, your best chance for observation is to seclude yourself in the vegetation and watch the more open edges and flats along the water.

The diet of the Virginia rail is varied. It will probe the mud flats for worms and larvae; it will eat small fish, snails, slugs, aquatic and land insects, and some seeds. It has also been known to feed in cranberry bogs and freshly mowed fields. Except for the preference for fresher water, its nesting habits are similar to those of the clapper.

The Virginia is distinguished from other rails by the combination of size and bill. It is the only small (quail-size) rail with a long, probing bill. Its rust color and gray cheeks are also decisive field marks.

One of the techniques of finding birds in marshes is to carefully scan the edges of ditches and narrow waterways as far ahead of you as possible with your binocular. At low tide, the ditch puddles and pools often trap or reveal an abundance of food. Rails will skitter from one side of the ditch to the other. Coots may be feeding on exposed water plants or algae, while the American bittern stalks the reedy edges. The salt-marsh ditch is home to the wary black ducks; they will flush the moment you are spotted. Black ducks "jump" into the air from the surface of the water, and they are easily recognized in flight by their all-dark bodies and the white linings of their wings. The coot, by contrast, must have a running, flapping start across the surface before it can get airborne. In flight, the white bills and the white borders on the trailing edge of the wings are distinctive.

Traveling the marsh's waterways by boat or canoe often provides the opportunity to see into, or underneath, the thick stands of cordgrass, cattails, or marsh elders. This is where you are likely to find the unique nest of the long-billed marsh wren. You will recognize it as a ball-shaped mass of tightly woven marsh grasses with an entrance hole on the side. The nest is lashed to a number of upright stems, usually 1 to 4 feet above the high-tide mark.

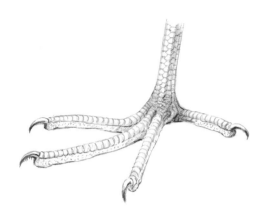

The long-billed marsh wren, like other members of its family, is extremely busy and boisterous during the nesting season. The male vents his energy and exuberance with chattering songs and by building a number of "dummy" nests. He is often polygamous, with two or more females nesting in adjacent territories. The male reigns over his domain with an air of authority and happiness, which he proclaims both day and night from his throne on the tip of a reed. His song is an accelerating rattle that ends in a single whistled note. At times, the song bubbles forth as the male flutters from one perch to another. The identity of the long-billed marsh wren can be established by habitat, and then by the combination of two field marks: a white eye stripe, and alternate stripes of white and dark brown on the back. Like other wrens, it is insectivorous.

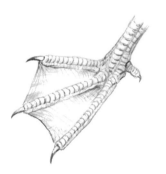

At the height of the nesting season, the shallow backwaters of our eastern estuaries are favorite feeding grounds of the long-legged waders, the fish-eating herons. In addition to the schools of killifish, mummichogs, or top minnows, there is an influx of fry from ocean species that have sought the sanctuary of these waters to spawn. Also, fingerlings born at sea, such as the prolific menhaden, instinctively seek the brackish waters in which to mature.

The herons are one of the most fascinating families to visit the salt-water marshes. They invite watching beyond the mere point of recognition. They are chiefly fish eaters, but not exclusively so. Other items in their diet include amphibians, crustaceans, small reptiles, and insects. Their long legs permit them to wade in water sufficiently deep to attract passing fish. Their necks are long and flexible, with vertebrae of unequal lengths. This feature helps them in feeding, and is probably the reason they tuck their necks into an S shape when in flight. Herons are sociable and mostly colony-nesting (often mixed). Their rookeries are usually on wooded islands or similar remote areas protected by surrounding waters.

During the breeding season, the egret members of this order—especially the common and the snowy—grow beautiful feathery plumes known as aigrettes. This added bit of beauty nearly caused their demise at the turn of the century, when countless thousands were slaughtered for the millinery trade. Through the persistent efforts of Audubon societies and other conservation organizations, laws were passed and enforced in time to save these two species from certain extinction. The most likely place to see this nuptial finery at its best is in the vicinity of a rookery during the courting and nest-building season.

Watching a heron rookery (through a binocular or scope, from a blind or other means of seclusion) also affords the opportunity to observe the courtship antics and other behavioral patterns of this interesting order. The simple task of preening, for example, may have more significance than merely straightening some disheveled feathers. Being chiefly aquatic feeders, the herons need to keep their feathers clean and reasonably waterproof. Special patches of feathers, known as powder down, are highly developed in the herons. These feathers are not molted, but continue to grow and powder away on the ends. Using their bills, herons apply this waxy powder to their feathers as a cleansing and dressing agent. It is believed to be used especially for removing fish slime and grease. Like most other birds, herons also dress their feathers with secretions from the oil glands.

The great blue heron is the largest, most widely distributed, and probably most adaptable member of its family to be found throughout our coastal marshes. It is equally at home in swamps and meadows, and along streams, ponds, and lakes. The great blue is a stealthy hunter. It will stalk slowly and silently through the shallows, spearing fish, aquatic insects, small reptiles, amphibians, and an occasional young bird. At times, it will stand motionless and wait patiently for its prey to pass within reach. The great blue nests in colonies and shows a preference for the higher trees. Depending on the vegetation available, it has been known to nest on the ground and upward to a height of 100 feet or more. Actually, this large heron is more gray than blue. Its large size—a height of approximately 4 feet and a wingspan of nearly 6 feet— makes it easily distinguishable from other herons.

The little blue heron is about half the size of the great blue, and it is a definite dark, slate-blue color. The immature little blue is all white and can be easily confused with the snowy egret. The best distinguishing field mark is the bright yellow feet of the snowy. The little blue seems to prefer inland ponds, but it is found frequently in the shallows of our bays and estuaries. In a mixed colony, it will nest in the lower strata, often at eye level or lower.

The Louisiana heron and the green heron are common feeders in the salt marsh. The Louisiana is a dark medium-size heron (slightly over 2 feet) with white underparts. Its long neck is thin and snakelike in appearance. In comparison to other herons, the Louisiana is a more determined feeder. It is not content to stand and wait, but actively stalks its prey, striking with extreme quickness and accuracy.

More often than not, the smaller green heron (18 inches) is flushed accidentally. Its startled cry of "t-yerk" is invariably accompanied by a white "chalk line" as it hastily departs for a more distant perch. The discovery of a dark "heron" with a long, decurved bill indicates you are watching the glossy ibis. At one time, this deeply bronzed bird was found primarily in the coastal marshes of Florida and the Gulf. Its range now extends through the Carolinas and northward.

The egrets have made a remarkable comeback since the days of the plume hunters. The common egret is the tall, white heron you often see standing in a statuesque manner along the edges of marshes, streams, and ponds. Like the great blue heron, it hunts by still-watching and by stalking slowly along the shores. Both the common and the snowy egrets often wander northward after the breeding season, sometimes as far as Canada.

A particular niche within the total functioning of the salt-marsh community is filled by two species of sparrows indigenous to this tidal zone. The seaside sparrow and the sharp-tailed sparrow lead rather secretive lives amid the thick marsh grasses and shrubs. Both species are often difficult to observe closely, as they spend most of their time on or near the ground. Flights are short and quick, and the songs are quite similar, leaving the observer confused with the sighting of just another "sparrow."

The seaside sparrow prefers the lower, wetter portions of the marsh, where tall cordgrasses emerge from the wet mud. Here it forages about for marine animals such as tiny crabs, snails, isopods, and aquatic insects. It nests on the ground just above the high-tide line, either directly in the tide drift or underneath clumps of grasses or shrubs. The seaside sparrow is not sharply colored. Rather, it has a dingy appearance as though there were a gray wash over its head and body. The yellow spot in *front* of the eye and the white line *below* the eye are the most pronounced field marks.

The sharp-tailed sparrow is not as exclusively bound to the salt marsh as the seaside sparrow. It is found most often in the upper reaches of the marsh adjacent to upland fields and meadows. This demarcative habitat—marsh to upland—also attracts the Savannah sparrow. The sharp-tail, as its name implies, has a pointed tail; the Savannah's tail is short and notched. The sharp-tail has a plain crown and a partially streaked breast; the Savannah will remind you of the song sparrow, but it lacks the central breast spot. The song sparrow often frequents the edges of the salt marsh, but this is by no means an exclusive habitat for it.

The great variety and abundance of food in the salt marsh make it a favorite feeding area of still other species. The willet feeds on the mud flats; the red-winged blackbird will nest in the sedges and cattails of the upper marsh; and the meadowlark can be seen fluttering over the drier grassy sections. In the air above the marsh, we may see the osprey, the marsh hawk, or the short eared owl. The common tern hovers and dives for fry and small fish; the herring gull and the laughing gull sally from one feeding spot to another. We recognize the willet in flight by its gaudy black and white wing pattern. The large marsh hawk soars low, dipping erratically over the marsh as it hunts. The white "cottontail" rump distinguishes it immediately.

Despite the tremendous demands of the nesting season, the marsh's food supply continues to increase. For if the rhythm of the seasons is to continue unabated in this salt-

Fall Migrants in the Salt Marsh

water environment, the marsh must produce an abundance of food to support the new families, the great flocks of southbound migrants, and the species that will winter there. By midsummer, the minute plankton have flooded all sections of this brackish world; the basis of life is everywhere. Tiny hydrobia snails abound in pools and ditches, while slightly larger melampus snails teem along the water's edge. Beach fleas are abundant in the muddy flats, and fiddler crabs scurry amid the grass in increasing hordes. Spartina stems are hosts to the lined periwinkles, and the tide drift swarms with green-headed flies and other insects. Fry and fingerlings have grown rapidly in the rich waters, and now seek protection in the shade of the lush growth of summer. Widgeongrass, eelgrass, and other aquatic plants are thick and green; the plants, seeds, and root stems will be the chief sustenance for many species of migrating waterfowl. The marsh is approaching its peak of abundance, and the early migrants have begun to arrive.

As the summer wanes, great flocks of migrating shore birds will rest and feed along the mud flats and beaches. The first list on page 133 (plus the birds already mentioned) will serve as a guide to the species you may expect to find about the salt marsh during late summer and fall.*

Observing the Fall Migrants

The cautions and techniques of birding in a salt marsh that were mentioned on page 122 are equally applicable during the fall. The grass still cuts; mosquitoes still bite; and the mud is still mud. However, there is one difference that may alter your approach somewhat. Many of the migrants are not as secretive as the nesting species, and you will find them flocked on the open mud flats, especially at low tide. Close observation is often difficult.

Most birding is done by groups that just walk along and observe whatever happens to come within range. Even this type of birding can be quite rewarding during the migration season. But if there is a particular point or flat

* Most of these species can be seen also during the spring migration. Additional references will be made to spring migrants (and plumages) in Chapter 11, "Birds of the Seashores and Beaches."

within the area that seems especially good, try watching it from the closest cover. Undoubtedly, you will be able to observe a greater number and variety of birds than you would by continuous walking. The sustained watching of one area makes it possible to set up and use your scope for really close viewing. The scope is also useful for observing waterfowl that have rafted far offshore. Remember: birding is best when the tide is low.

The majority of our shore birds are great travelers. Many nest in the northern tundra regions and then winter in South America. The tundra summer is short, and birds begin winging their way southward quite early. Some arrive along the New England coast in July, but it is during the month of August that the great, wheeling flocks of shore birds are most common over our beaches and marshes.

Among the earliest arrivals are the smallest species of sandpipers, referred to collectively as "peep." This collective term encompasses the least, semipalmated, Baird's, white-rumped, and western sandpipers. Differentiation in the field is often quite confusing, especially when the birds are in winter plumage. It is possible to see all five species along our eastern coasts, but the least and the semipalmated are usually the most common "peep" of the mud flats. If you were to see all five species together in winter dress, you would note these features:

• All are small—sparrow-sized.
• All are predominately brown and streaked.
• The least sandpiper, the smallest "peep," has a short, thin bill and yellowish legs.
• The semipalmated sandpiper is slightly larger than the least sandpiper. Its bill is short, but heavier, and its legs are blackish.
• The white-rumped sandpiper is gray-brown in color. Its full, white rump is noticeable in flight.
• The Baird's sandpiper has a buff-colored head and breast.
• The western sandpiper's bill is noticeably longer and downcurved slightly at the tip.

Flocks of bobolinks, tree swallows, and barn swallows are often among the earliest southbound migrants to gather about the salt marshes. I have seen tree swallows on Long Island in late July settle upon the dense stands of phragmites (a 7-foot marsh grass that grows in disturbed soil) in such numbers that this sturdy grass was weighted to the ground. When leaving such a resting area, tree swallows spend considerable time organizing themselves before continuing their southward journey. They depart in a swirling funnel that is often noticeable for a half-hour or more. Gradually, birds on the outer fringes of the circling mass begin breaking away and start south over the marsh in a loosely scattered flock, feeding on insects as they travel. The bobolinks must get an early start, for they will winter as far south as Argentina. The barn swallows, too, have a long journey since their winter homes range from Mexico to Brazil.

As the summer progresses, other species begin gathering about the marsh in increasing numbers. The dowitcher probes the mud flats with its long snipe bill in search of marine worms and insect larvae. Ornithologists invariably describe the dowitcher's feeding actions as "like a sewing machine." This is probably the best graphic description of their rapid up-and-down probings into the mud. Knots appear over the marsh in tightly knit flocks, wheeling and turning in unison as though they were but one bird. Even when feeding on the flats or beaches, they stay in compact groups and are rarely seen singly. They feed on tiny crustaceans, minute mollusks, marine worms, aquatic insects, and larvae. Despite their clannishness, they are quite congenial birds and are often seen feeding with other shore birds, particularly the black-bellied plover, the ruddy turnstone, and the dunlin. Knots have a habit of resting while waiting for the high tide to recede. As a group, they assume a characteristic pose that is a definite aid to identification. You see a group of chunky gray birds standing close together, with every bird facing into the wind. They are motionless; some are standing on just one foot; others have their bill tucked under a wing. When the receding tide again exposes the flats, the knots resume their feeding.

The semipalmated plover and the black-bellied plover are the two species of their family most likely to be found

BIRDS OF THE EASTERN SALT MARSHES IN LATE SUMMER AND EARLY FALL

Blackbirds,
    Bobolink
Falcons,
    Hawk, Pigeon
    Hawk, Sparrow
Plovers,
    Black-bellied
    Semipalmated
Skimmers,
    Black
Snipes and Sandpipers,
    Dowitcher, Short-billed
    Dunlin

Knot
Sandpiper, Least
Sandpiper, Pectoral
Sandpiper, Semipalmated
Snipe, Common
Whimbrel
Yellowlegs, Greater
Yellowlegs, Lesser
Swallows,
    Barn
    Tree
Swans, Geese, and Ducks,
    Brant

Ducks (see list below)
Goose, Canada
Goose, Snow
Swan, Mute
Swan, Whistling
Terns,
    Black
Warblers,
    Yellowthroat

DUCKS, GEESE, AND SWANS OF THE EASTERN SALT MARSHES IN FALL

Ducks,
    Bufflehead
    Canvasback
    Duck, Black
    Duck, Ring-necked
    Duck, Wood
    Gadwall
    Goldeneye, Barrow's
    Goldeneye, Common
    Mallard

Merganser, Common
Merganser, Hooded
Merganser, Red-breasted
Pintail
Redhead
Scaup, Greater
Scaup, Lesser
Shoveler
Teal, Blue-winged
Teal, Green-winged

Widgeon, American
Widgeon, European
Geese,
    Brant
    Goose, Canada
    Goose, Snow
Swans,
    Mute
    Whistling

BIRDS OF THE EASTERN SALT MARSHES IN WINTER

Blackbirds,
    Meadowlark
Crows,
    Common
    Fish
Falcons,
    Hawk, Sparrow
Gulls,
    Bonaparte's

Great Black-backed
Herring
Laughing
Ring-billed
Hawks,
    Marsh
    Rough-legged
Owls,
    Short-eared

Sandpipers,
    Willet
Sparrows,
    Song
Swans, Geese, and Ducks
    (see list above)

on the marshy flats. The plovers have a rather distinctive shape. Compared to the sandpipers, they are stockier, with thicker necks, and have heavier and shorter bills. The semipalmated will remind you of a small killdeer, but note that it has only *one chest band*. The black-bellied is our largest plover—robin-sized in length. It loses its black belly during the postnuptial molt, but the white rump, the white-banded tail, and the black axillar feathers (under the wing at the axis of wing and body) are distinctive field marks at any time of the year. Semipalmated plovers migrate in flocks but scatter about the flats to feed. They run rapidly, stop and feed, and then run several feet, stop, and feed again. By contrast, you will not see black-bellied plovers in large, compact flocks. You will find them scattered along the tidal flats, often feeding alone. Frequently, one or more of them can be seen accompanying a flock of knots.

Yellowlegs, both the greater and the lesser, are common migratory visitors in the low tidal areas of the salt marsh. When the two species are seen together, the obvious difference in size makes differentiation quite easy, but when a single bird is being observed, positive identification is often difficult. Both species, as their names imply, have yellow legs. The bill of the greater appears to be proportionately longer and heavier, and if you can get a good profile view, you will note that it is upturned ever so slightly. The bill of the lesser is slim and straight. The calls of both species are quite distinctive and often are the best means of identification. The greater yellowlegs is rather wary and somewhat of an alarmist when disturbed. Often it will flush with a series of loud cries—"wheu-wheu-wheu." The call of the lesser yellowlegs is softer, flatter, and shorter—"cu-cu."

The yellowlegs are not great probers. They wade in the shallows, where they catch a killifish, small crustaceans, and aquatic insects.

One of the more exciting birds to visit our coastal flats is the whimbrel. This bird has made a remarkable comeback from its severe depletion during the early days of market hunting. It is recognized by the long, downcurved bill. Sand fleas, small crustaceans and mollusks, marine worms, insects, and some berries are the chief items of the whimbrel's diet.

We have noted various adaptations of birds to fill a particular niche within the salt-water community, but perhaps none is so intriguing as that of the black skimmer. This bird cannot be classified with the more northern migrants, for it nests on sand and shell beaches (usually on islands) from Long Island south to Florida and Texas; it winters in the southern part of this range. But judging from my observations, it seems that after the nesting season is over, the skimmer will venture farther inland to feed. It is then that I have noticed it feeding most often in the backwaters of our estuaries.

Skimmers have a unique bill. They are the only birds with a lower mandible longer than the upper one—a physical adaptation peculiar to their unusual manner of feeding. The black skimmer feeds by feel rather than by sight. It flies low over the water, cutting the surface with just the lower mandible. When it strikes a surface-feeding fish, the upper mandible snaps shut to complete the capture. The skimmer feeds mostly in the early morning or late evening hours, when the surface-feeding fish are most active.

The black skimmer is nearly crow-sized and has a wing-span of nearly 4 feet. It is mostly dark above and contrasting white underneath. The red, 4-inch bill is tipped with black. The call of the skimmer is almost a bark—a loud, low "aup."

With the coming of cooler weather, bird life about the salt marsh continues to change. Many of the nesting species and early arrivals have gone, but now other species move in to fill the void. Even the warbler family is represented. The black-masked yellowthroat hunts amid the low shrubbery and grasses along the ditches. Its actions are noticeably wrenlike. If there are many bayberries in the area, myrtle warblers will surely be there. Some may stay all winter.

Our two smallest falcons, the sparrow hawk and the pigeon hawk, often follow the eastern coastline in loosely scattered flocks during fall migration. The falcons are recognized by their comparatively long tails and pointed wings. The sparrow hawk has a rufous or rust-colored back and tail; the tail is white-tipped, next to a broad, black band. The tail of the pigeon hawk is gray with alternate bands of black.

Cold days with biting winds bring flocks of waterfowl tumbling into the ponds and bay areas surrounding the salt marshes. With their arrival, a whole new dimension is added to the challenge of bird watching. Ducks arrive in great numbers and varieties. Occasionally, they are joined by a flock of Canada geese, snow geese, or brant. Many species will stay as long as there is open water, but others will continue southward. You will not find the great concentrations of surface-feeding ducks along the coast such as you would find in the central part of our country, but comparative figures surely would be equalized somewhat by the quantities of bay ducks and sea ducks.

There is no finite listing of waterfowl that would be applicable to all eastern salt marshes. Each species has a preference for a particular type of water (ditches, ponds, bays, or ocean), so the variety and number of birds in any one marsh will be determined largely by the type of water areas and the geographical location. Nevertheless, the salt marsh and its adjacent waters invariably hold elements of excitement and surprise for the fall observer. It's the time to be afield with your binocular, scope, and field guide. The second list on page 133 gives some possibilities that may help build your life list in a hurry.

The Salt Marsh in Winter

Winter brings a cold, white stillness to the northern salt marsh. The tall cordgrasses have bowed before the incessant winter winds and the drifting snow. Now the tip ends project through the whiteness in a mosaic of scattered tufts, uniformly angled by the prevailing winds. All but the most brackish waters are glazed with ice. The marsh is a flattened land; it has surrendered to the unyielding forces of winter. Still and dormant now, it awaits rebirth from the warming rays of a returning sun.

But dormancy within the marsh is only partial; the

processes of nature are never completely stilled. The pace of the tides has not changed; it continues with the same rhythmic certainty that has evolved through countless seasons past. On the coldest days and nights, waters of the flood tide freeze, leaving sheets of ice clinging to the mud banks and exposed root stems. The ice thickens until a slight thaw or another tide sends it tumbling into the water. Particles of vegetation are carried with the ice; soon they will be reduced to enriching nutrients that will support more phytoplankton. Portions of the frozen mud banks drop with the receding tides, often exposing bits of food for the foraging gulls or a wintering willet.

Puddles within the marsh, beyond the reach of the winter tides, may stay frozen for long periods of time. The oxygen supply cannot be renewed, and the fish trapped in these frozen puddles may suffocate. As the puddles thaw, the dead fish are scavenged quickly by gulls and crows.

Life in the grassy areas of the marsh continues also. The snow has been both a curse and a blessing. The search for food has become more difficult for most creatures of the marsh, but to some, snow has provided a certain degree of warmth and protection. The meadow mouse is warm and reasonably secure in its grassy nest beneath the snow. But when it scurries from one tuft to another in search of seeds, it must escape the searching eyes of the marsh patrol—the short-eared owl and the marsh hawk. The rough-legged hawk also hunts over the open marshes during the winter. We recognize it when we see a large buteo (broad, rounded tail and broad wings) hovering like the much smaller sparrow hawk.

Winter's indomitable forces may change the character of the marsh. In times of thawing and flooding, additional sand and loam are washed in from the uplands by the coursing fresh-water streams. Some will help build the marsh by settling in the thick vegetation, and quantities will accumulate to form new sandbars and sand flats. When the accumulations are extensive, new breeding grounds become available to certain beach-nesting species. The wind and the snow, freezing, thawing, and flooding—all these factors influence the physical character of the marsh and the lives of all the creatures that dwell therein. Most of

the inhabitants thrive and grow, but some succumb to suffocation, the intense cold, or the lack of available food. The marsh maintains an enduring balance.

Gulls patrol the winter marsh searching for any victims of winter's cruelties. The herring gull is there in the greatest numbers. We follow Peterson's advice and use it as a comparative basis to identify other members of the gull family. We note the gray mantle (back and folded wings) of the adult herring gull; its legs are flesh-colored. Young birds of the past season are uniformly brown; other immature birds are a mottled mixture of brown and white. The herring gull is quick to announce its annoyance at the intrusion of other species by a loud raucous "kee-ouch, kee-ouch, kee-ouch." Our largest gull, the great black-backed, is recognized by its size and slate-black mantle. The laughing gull is there, too, but it lacks the black head that is characteristic of its breeding plumage; now the head is white with a few black markings. It is smaller than the herring gull, and calls with a high-pitched laugh—"ha-ha-ha-ha-haah-haah." The ring-billed gull has returned from its northern breeding range. It looks like a small herring gull, but as the name suggests, there is a black ring around its bill; the legs are greenish yellow. The smallest gull we are likely to find over the winter marsh is the Bonaparte's gull—a ternlike gull in size and actions. It, too, lacks the black head plumage of the nesting season. Now its head is white, with a conspicuous black spot just back of the eye.

The scaup are rafted in the deep waters of the bay; mergansers feed in close along the edge of the rim ice. And a pair of talkative old-squaws drop into the bay with an ungraceful splash.

Birds that are most likely to be found about the salt marsh in winter include those given in the third list on page 133.

Birding in a salt marsh can be a rich and rewarding experience, but one cannot walk across the carpets of matted grass, or glide silently through its shifting waters, without sensing the feeling of impending doom. Must the cry of shore birds give way to the sounds of bulldozers and dredges? Must the aroma of salt hay and salt air be suffused in the stench of sulfur dioxide—the ominous odor of a dying land?

The salt marsh is still sheathed in mystery. We know that 80 percent of the sport fish and crustaceans native to our eastern seaboard spawn or grow in the brackish waters of our estuaries. But what other secrets are shrouded in the mystery of this saline habitat? Could it be that man is despoiling a vital link in his own chain of survival—the total ecology of the sea?

11 Birds of the Seashores and Beaches

Of all the plant and animal life forms spawned by the mother sea, more than four-fifths of them can still be found along the water's edge. The inland invasion by species was slow, even in geological terms, and although varying forms of life eventually reached across the land, innumerable species are still irrevocably bound to the vicinity of their origin. Surely no other habitat has such profusion of life, for survival depends upon sheer numbers. From the basic diatoms and plankton, upward through the pyramid of survival, the vicious pattern of "life eats life" prevails. To this bountiful, but cruel, environment comes a great variety of birds. Some come to nest and rear their young; others come just to feed. Some come to rest and winter in the relative security of its open waters, and for many it is a natural guideline for long migration journeys. Whatever the reason, each species fulfills a particular niche in the rhythm of life along the edge of the sea.

The eastern shoreline of our continent has two basic geologic formations: the rocky coast and the sandy beaches. Along New England and northward through the eastern provinces of Canada, the land masses drop abruptly into the sea. Cliffs, ledges, boulders, and scattered offshore islands protect the mainland from the incessant wash of the tides and the fury of ocean storms. Numerous bays extend inland, filling the valleys and lowlands, the paths of bygone glaciers. Southward from New England, the land slopes gradually into the sea. Actually, it can be looked upon as a huge delta extending from the mountains to the Atlantic, and then beyond to form the continental shelf. Here the mainland is protected by a series of outer beaches and long, narrow islands, built over the eons of mineral particles from the eroding mountains and carried there by the littoral current.

Birding along Our Eastern Shores

Over a period of years, I have had the opportunity to observe birds along much of our eastern coastline. I have seen the gannets dive in the Gulf of St. Lawrence. I have plied the foggy coast of Maine in the dory of a lobsterman, heard the fog horns growl, and seen the mirrored sun glow red on the morning's calm waters. I have roamed the beaches of Cape Cod, Long Island, Virginia, and the Carolinas. I have encircled Florida and the Keys, and felt the soothing warmth of Gulf waters on my aching feet. In the course of these ramblings, I reached some very positive conclusions concerning the watching of birds along the shore. I present them here, hoping they will temper your philosophy, enhance your enthusiasm, and make your seaside trips completely enjoyable.

• Most birding is more rewarding if done alone or with only a few companions. This is especially true along the beach. There are many other things to distract one's attention, and large groups have a tendency to string out along the way looking for shells, driftwood, etc. The area you want to watch becomes covered with people instead of birds.

• Early morning is best. The shore becomes "alive" as most creatures seek their first meal of the day.

• Expect the unexpected. Shore birding is unpredictable (one of its fascinations); the birds you expect to see may not be present, but they are often replaced by a rarity or two. The number and variety of birds present often depend upon the major movements of that particular day. This is especially true during spring migrations. Shore birds move north rapidly to take advantage of the short nesting season.

• Low tides expose larger feeding areas, and birds are

quick to take advantage of them. This is particularly noticeable in the North, where tide changes are greatest.

• Shore birds* often congregate around breakwaters, inlets, and brackish ponds. If birds are absent from the beach, these are the places to look for them.

• Late summer and early fall are the most rewarding times for watching shore birds. Cold weather comes early in the far North, and many species start south early.

• Fall plumages often are confusing. Carry a field guide, no matter how proficient in identification you may be. Often one or more birds will not conform to your memorized patterns.

• Colonies of ground-nesting birds should not be disturbed. Unprotected chicks are at the mercy of highly defensive and ruthless neighbors.

• Ocean storms frequently force rarities ashore. This is especially true during migration periods.

• A scope and tripod are an advantage at times, providing you have enough stamina to tote them. The scope is most useful in watching offshore birds, or for observing birds across bays and inlets.

• Dress warmly. The shore is usually cooler than you expect it to be. An unbroken ocean breeze can make the chill factor considerably cooler than inland temperatures.

• Carry your insect repellent. A fresh hatch of midges, or "no-see-ums," is like walking through a blizzard of tiny, hot ashes.

• The beach has more to offer than just birds. Observe its collections, life, and ecology. It will provide many excuses for additional trips.

• In summary: a low tide at dawn during August or September should be most rewarding.

There are differences between the rocky coasts and sandy beaches other than geological ones. Members of the marine phyla, and their relationships to one another, vary considerably. These ecological variances, in turn, attract those

---

* The term "shore birds," as used in this chapter, should not be interpreted in a technical sense as applying to waders only. It is used as a liberal collective term applying to all birds normally found along the shore, regardless of reason or scientific classification.

birds specifically adapted to significant roles in the completion of diverse patterns of life-chain correlations. The number and variety of birds found along the shore on any one occasion depend upon many physical and biological variables, especially during the seasons of migrations. The direction and intensity of the wind, for example, may account for large concentrations of shore birds, or for their complete absence. The significance of these variables has been taken into consideration in the preparation of the bird lists and text which follow.

Earth-shaping glaciers expended their awesome force at the edge of the sea some thousands of years ago. Stark, vertical cliffs, sculptured ledges, rounded boulders, and offshore islands stand as granite monuments to their passing, and to the land's gradual submergence into the sea. Now the sea is the dominant architectural force. With the unceasing wash of the waves, the rhythmic flow of the tides, and the surging violence of storms, it shapes its own boundaries.

Along the Rocky Coasts

The rocky coast is a picturesque area with a distinctive character of its own. It is moody, temperamental, and mysterious. Days can be clear and blue, bleak and gloomy, or wildly vicious. When an east wind blows the warm air from the Gulf Stream inward over the colder waters, an advection fog rolls in and shrouds the coast in an impenetrable blanket of gray. Fog horns moan their warnings, but boats and ships are harbor-bound. The "keouk—keouk" of a passing gull and the "wock" of a returning night heron come from somewhere within the depths of the thick, gray mist. Moisture drips from the coastal spruces festooned with the gray-green hangings of usnea; parula warblers build their basketlike nests within the entwining masses. The damp air aids the growth of algae and rock mosses, and they, too, become a part of life patterns along the shore. The engulfing shroud will persist until the breeze blows once again from the mainland.

Regardless of the weather, the sea rushes ashore with imperturbable consistency. It washes and splashes among the rocks and then recedes in curling designs of white foam. With it come countless numbers of marine life, some of which become entrapped in the washed-out basins, or tidal pools. There are microscopic forms, small sponges and worms, killifish, shrimp, jellyfish, limpets, periwinkles, and barnacles. Rockweed and Irish moss harbor matted colonies of minute bryozoan and shelter other aquatic creatures. Crabs crawl about the rocks, and beneath the shallow water there are starfish, sea urchins, mussels, clams, minnows, sea cucumbers, and a seemingly endless variety of wriggling life. The deeper waters teem with herring, cod, smelt, and other fish indigenous to the colder parts of the sea. Life is variable, and life is profuse. Otherwise, the great concentrations of birds along the rocky coast could not survive en masse. Enormous quantities of food must be available within the vicinity of an island that harbors thousands of birds in a single colony.

Yes, birds—thousands upon thousands of them—are irrevocably tied to the rock-bound coast and the adjoining sea. They must have their crustaceans, their mollusks, and their schools of herring, for the adaptations of time have so shaped their bodies and characterized their habits that they are akin only to the sea. Even man is captivated by the lore of these mysterious coastal waters; he must build his ships, follow the cod, trap the lobsters, and rake the clams.

Most of the great concentrations of birds supported by the bounteous waters of the rocky coast are to be found on the offshore islands—rocky promontories that were once a part of the mainland. To endeavor to list all the birds one might see on a trip along the coast and outer islands would be both precarious and presumptive, for this is an area of the unusual—the stragglers, the migratory wanderers, and storm-blown victims. With possibly two or three exceptions, the list on the next page includes those species which, in one way or another, are ecologically associated with the sea. No attempt has been made to include the woodland and grassland birds. Most of the following species nest during the early part of summer.

For bird watchers along our eastern coast, the gannets are surely the most entertaining and the most fascinating

Auks, Murres, and Puffins,
    Guillemot, Black
    Murre, Common
    Murre, Thick-billed
    Puffin, Common
    Razorbill
Cormorants,
    Double-crested
    Great
Gannets,
    Gannet

Gulls and Terns,
    Gull, Great Black-backed
    Gull, Herring
    Gull, Laughing
    Tern, Arctic
    Tern, Common
    Tern, Roseate
Herons,
    Great Blue
    Night Heron, Black-crowned

Ospreys,
    Osprey
Ravens,
    Common
Sandpipers,
    Spotted
Storm Petrels,
    Petrel, Leach's
Swallows,
    Cliff

of all the avian performers. Watching a large colony, such as the one on Donaventure Island off the tip of Gaspé Peninsula, will challenge the full gamut of one's emotions, from sheer joy to utter sorrow. For the gannets themselves embody these traits and transmute them to the observer in moments of joyous flight and inherent ceremonial displays, in the terror of fitful panic, and, seemingly, through their own tragic stupidity.

In the air, the gannet is the personification of graceful flight. The sleek, streamlined body is a perfect airfoil, and it glides through the air silently, effortlessly, and with incredible speed. At times, the gannet flies just for the solitary exhilaration of flight. It will ride the updrafts of cliff-deterred air currents, hover on the lift of passing winds, or power-dive to near the water's surface. But mostly, the gannet patrols the coastal waters in search of a passing school of smelt, herring, or other fish. When a school is sighted, gannets gather and attack it en masse. From a predetermined height, sometimes as high as 100 feet or more, the gannets dive upon the school in a spectacular display of grace and agility. The dives are continuous, simultaneous, and often side by side, but they are skillfully controlled, and interference does not seem to be a problem. The dive is a fast, streamlined, arrowlike plunge into the school. The momentum of the dive will carry the gannet to the proper depth and help plane it upward beneath the school. The gannet captures the fish from below the school, as it returns to the surface.

On land, the gannet is a different bird; gracefulness and agility cease upon landing. In a manner bordering on comedy, it waddles and stumbles about, often to the consternation of its wing-tip-to-wing-tip neighbors. Courting ceremonies are diverse performances of dancing, bill clacking, gift exchanging, preening, and similar displays of affection. Should one bird suddenly panic, which it will sometimes do at the slightest provocation, the entire ledge may erupt in frenzied fright, knocking eggs and young into the sea. The gannet's normal method of departure from the high ledges is to hurl itself into space and plummet downward until it gains flying speed. This is a precarious maneuver for the young, and occasionally broken remains on the lower ledges attest to their misjudgment. But despite the gannets' specialized habits, and their pathetic tragedies, their numbers are increasing.

No other bird is so symbolic of the sea as the gull. Wherever one goes along our continental shores, there are always the gulls—"sea gulls," the collective term given to all members of the family by the uninformed, are everywhere. They follow our ships, congregate about harbors, and scavenge our beaches. But they are not of one species; they differ as do the herons, the swallows, and the sparrows. I have visited islands off the coast of Maine that have been dominated by great black-backed gulls, others by herring gulls, and on one occasion, a single island that held a small colony of laughing gulls determined to extend their range into the cold waters of the Northeast. Of these three species, the great black-backed is the most easily recognized and remembered, for its name implies both size and coloration. It is our largest gull and has a black back and black wings. The herring gull is the most common and often is used as a comparative basis for identifying other gulls (see page 138).

Your first trip to the offshore bird islands will be a surprising and memorable experience, but first, one thought of caution: Don't try it alone or with an inexperienced boatman. The tides rush between the islands in treacherous currents, and the fog can roll in quickly—an opaque curtain of white that can close behind you suddenly. Also, landing amid the rocks from a surging sea takes the right kind of boat and an experienced handler. If you contemplate such a trip, hire the services of a native, someone who knows the waters and the weather and has the proper equipment. It is also advisable to have a knowledgeable birder with you, because there are certain precautions that should be taken to protect the birds as well as the observer.

Islands dominated by nesting gulls seem to be places of constant alarm and confusion. There are screaming gulls in the air, on the ground, and in the water. If you should go ashore, the confusion becomes chaotic. Individual nesting territories are quite small and close together, and must be guarded almost constantly. The male usually does this from a favored rock or mound. Vegetation may be sparse, but the nest, or a portion of the defended territory, will be protected by the broken shadows of a clump of grass or weeds. This helps hide the young from overly zealous neighbors. Protective parents will not hesitate to kill trespassing young from an adjacent territory. The reaction is instinctive, and probably adds a sense of discipline to the colony. Select your travel route carefully—one that will cause a minimum of excitement among the nesting birds. Any extensive observations should be made from a blind.

Birds select a nesting island by its physical features and the availability of food. Whereas gulls prefer an island, or a portion thereof, with some shadowy cover, cormorants seem more secure in the open on high, rocky areas. An open island with a covering of sandy topsoil may appeal to the burrow-nesting Leach's petrel. The puffin also nests in burrows, but it prefers the crevices in craggy rock promontories. Similar areas are selected by the black guillemot—anywhere it can seclude its two eggs under a rock or in a crevice. The terns along the rocky coast will nest on mainland or island exposures of sand, gravel, or rocks, often in close association with gulls.

The cormorant can hardly be considered a beautiful or graceful bird. Surely, these attributes are nowhere in evidence about a nesting island. I recall visiting Old Hump Ledge off the coast of Damariscota, Maine, with the na-

tionally famed ornithologist Allan Cruickshank. Allan had warned the landing group that it was not a place for anyone with a squeamish stomach. The guano-covered ledge reeked with the acrid pungency of ammonia. In addition to the penetrating odor of the excrement, there was an unpleasant odor of fish—fish no longer fresh—some of which came from the regurgitated deposits of disturbed young cormorants. This, after a bounding ride in a small motor launch!

We also visited Matinicus Rock and observed a large colony of Arctic terns, a number of black guillemots, and the southernmost colony of common puffins on the Atlantic Coast. Puffins are more abundant along the coasts of New Brunswick, Nova Scotia, Newfoundland, and Labrador. Nesting puffins on Machias Seal Island, New Brunswick, for example, were estimated at 1,000 pairs for the 1971 season.*

The puffin is a clown. It is a short-necked, stocky bird that reminds one of a penguin, but the brightly colored facial makeup and the solemn dignity of its actions impart a reminder of circus comedy.

Things to look for while observing puffins include:

• Their tameness and calm dignity as you approach. This unsuspicious nature has undoubtedly contributed to their scarcity near populated areas.

• The exceptionally large, brightly colored, triangular bill. Outer portions of the bill are shed after nesting. Winter birds have smaller bills.

• The orange-red feet and legs.

• Only one egg per nest and one nest per year.

• Flight under water. The puffin literally "flies" through the water. This can be observed with binoculars, especially when the birds start their dive.

• Note the difficulty of a water takeoff in the absence of a strong wind.

• The landing. Whether on land or water, it is not particularly graceful—more of a stalled-out drop.

• Adults arriving at the nest with fish (usually capelin, a form of smelt). Although the adult may have a half-dozen

* Davis W. Finch, "Regional Report," *American Birds*, Vol. 25, No. 5 (Oct. 1971), p. 835.

fish in its large bill, observe the arrangement—perfect alignment, with tails on one side and heads on the other.

• An answer to a riddle often posed by Roger Tory Peterson: "How can it hold onto the slippery fish while adding another to its collection?"

Most any trip along the rocky coast or amid the offshore islands will undoubtedly add birds, other than those already mentioned, to your daily list. Murres and razorbills may be spotted about the cliffs, and a raven may be seen scavenging along the water's edge. Cliff swallows sometimes find an overhanging ledge to their liking and will nest in large colonies. Spotted sandpipers rear their young along the gravelly beaches of open, grassy islands. And perhaps a Wilson's petrel, escaping the cold winter of its Antarctic breeding grounds, will wing its way across your bow. Also, you will find that each isolated area has an ecology of its own. An inquisitive approach to the differences and to the relationships will bring you rewards more exciting than mere bird recognition.

Grain by grain, the sand comes and goes along our beaches —millions of tons of it every year. The long, sandy shoreline is not a stable boundary; it is constantly in the process of changing—now building, now receding—at the whimsical mercy of the winds and the waves, by the dreaded force of storms, and by the incessant power of ocean currents. Through these forces, over the centuries, extensive barrier islands, or outer beaches, have built up along our eastern seaboard. The barriers protect the mainland from the full fury of these same awesome forces.

Along the Sandy Beaches in Summer

As the sand builds along the shore, much of it is carried beyond the normal tide line during periods of storms and exceptionally high tides. This process builds the inner, or middle, beaches. When the sand dries, it is carried farther inland by the wind until it is dropped or deterred by protruding vegetation. In some places, and over long periods of time, such action is sufficient to build high sand dunes. These dunes may be stabilized by pioneering beachgrass and succeeding vegetation, or they may creep inland, as sand is lifted off the windward side and dropped on the leeward, or inland, side. Bayberry, high-tide bush, poison ivy, and other coastal plants become established as sufficient humus is added to the sand by decay and wind. Birds play a pioneering role through seed distribution, excrement deposits, and nesting activities. Cottonwoods and pines may become established and prepare the soil for succeeding oaks. Eventually, the soil may become rich and moist enough for beeches and maples to become dominant. At each level, and at each stage, the bird life will change.

Along the water's edge, the moisture-soaked beach abounds with such life as sand hoppers (beach fleas), mole shrimps, and sand-collar snails. Sanderlings, sandpipers, plovers, and other shore birds pick and probe about the wet sand in search of these small marine creatures. At the highest reach of the tide, a drift line forms along the beach. Sea weeds, an occasional dead fish or bird, and assorted debris accumulate until disturbed by an even higher tide. Flies, beetles, and other insects swarm about the decaying debris and provide an additional source of food for birds that follow the shore. Life is relatively sparse on the dry inner beaches, but becomes abundant again in the line of coastal vegetation. Many spring and fall transients from other habitats can be found here, including swallows, warblers, hawks, thrushes, and flycatchers. The offshore waters teem with floating and swimming organisms. From the myriad of tiny, single-celled plant diatoms, microscopic protozoa and other minute crustacea, through swimming mollusks, minnows, and larger fish, a dynamic life chain energizes the sea and furnishes sustenance for the diving birds.

During the nesting season, one often is surprised by the small variety of birds to be found along the ocean beach. There are reasons for this. First, and perhaps the most decisive, is the lack of cover required by most nesting species. The offshore waters do not contain the abundance of larger plant and animal forms as found in the waters along the rocky coast, so the life chains are more specialized. Also, many of the shore birds, which are so numerous along the beaches during spring and fall migrations, nest

COMMON SUMMER BIRDS OF THE SANDY BEACHES

Gulls and Terns,
  Gull, Great Black-backed
  Gull, Herring
  Gull, Laughing
  Tern, Caspian
  Tern, Common

Tern, Least
Tern, Royal
Oystercatchers,
  American
Plovers,
  Piping

Wilson's
Sandpipers,
  Willet
Skimmers,
  Black

in northern interior regions. However, there are birds, such as gulls, terns, and black skimmers, that nest in great colonies on protected beaches.

At one time or another, a majority of our eastern birds can be found along the beaches, or in the vicinity of adjoining coastal waters and vegetation. An endeavor to list them all could hardly produce accurate results. The list at the top of this page contains only those species closely associated with the beaches during the nesting season. Migratory and wintering birds are covered elsewhere in this chapter, and the tropical species are included in the following chapter.

In addition to the nesting species, other birds often can be observed along the beaches during the summer months. Herons and egrets come to the water's edge to feed; grackles and crows forage along the drift line. You may see a hunting sparrow hawk, or get a glimpse of one of the coastal sparrows in the adjoining grasses. The shore holds the element of surprise at any season.

Terns are likely to be the first, and often the most common, birds you will see when visiting the beach during the summer. They are very active and excitable birds, mostly white with black caps, pointed wings, and forked swallow-like tails that have earned them the collective name of "sea swallow." You will see them hovering and then suddenly dive head first into the water after their favorite prey. The terns fit into the shore's ecological pattern by feeding mostly on a variety of small minnows.

With few exceptions, terns nest in sizable colonies. This

TERNS ASSOCIATED WITH EASTERN BEACHES

CASPIAN TERN

Identifying field marks: Nearly gull-sized, but has a black cap, a heavy blood-red bill, and a forked tail.

Range: Breeds in scattered colonies, both along the coast and inland, from Canada south to the Gulf Coast.

Nest: Coastal birds prefer the security of offshore islands. The nests are mere depressions in the sand and shell fragments. Seaweed and grass are sometimes used to line or shape the nest.

Food: Dives for fish like other terns, but often feeds from the surface in a gull-like manner. Also, it has some of the gulls' predacious habits, and has been known to rob nests of eggs and small birds.

Habits: The Caspian often is referred to as "the king of the terns," and rightly so. It is the largest and most aggressive of the terns; it is also less gregarious and more independent than other members of the family. Often associates with the ring-billed gull.

COMMON TERN

Identifying field marks: Orange-red bill with black tip.

Range: The most widely distributed tern. In the East, from Canada south to around Florida and the Gulf states. Also abundant along the larger inland lakes.

Nest: Prefers open sand or gravel beaches of offshore islands, or isolated sections of the main shoreline. The nest may be just a slight depression in the sand or pebbles, or it may have a skimpy lining of grass or seaweed.

Food: Mostly small fish such as the pipe fish, sand launce, and the fry of alewives, menhaden, and other coastal species. In some sections, small crustacea form a substantial part of their diet.

Habits: Dainty and graceful in flight. Often follows schools of feeding mackerel, bluefish, or striped bass to feed on the scraps and crippled minnows left in the wake of these voracious feeders.

LEAST TERN

Identifying field marks: Our smallest tern. White patch between the bill and black cap. Yellow bill.

Range: On the coast, from Massachusetts south to Texas. Also breeds along main inland river systems.

Nest: Favorite coastal sites are extensive sandy points that reach out into the sea. A small hollow in the sand and bits of broken shells; contains two or three buff-colored, brown-spotted eggs, which match their surroundings.

Food: Small fish, a few crustaceans, and aquatic insects obtained mostly by diving.

Habits: Excitable, noisy, but harmless to other species. Often nests in the same localities and in harmony with piping plovers and Wilson's plovers.

ROYAL TERN

Identifying field marks:	*A large tern. Long, slim, orange bill. Black cap ends in tufted crest. Deeply forked tail. Wings extend beyond tail when perched. Often confused with Caspian tern.*
Range:	*Breeds from Virginia along the coast to Texas. Wanders as far north as New Jersey in the summer.*
Nest:	*Nests in very compact colonies on sandy offshore islands. Two tan, brown-spotted eggs are laid in a slight depression in the sand.*
Food:	*Small fish caught by diving, or by following surface schools, and quickly dipping into the water for individual fish.*
Habits:	*Feeds mostly in offshore ocean waters. Nesting birds are so close together they almost touch. One wonders how they can find their own nests repeatedly.*

gives them the advantage of mutual protection, and concentrates the nesting period for all pairs into a minimum length of time. But this dense concentration of nesting sites is sometimes a disadvantage to the species as a whole. Their habit of nesting on comparatively low sand and gravel beaches makes the entire colony vulnerable to ocean storms and exceptionally high tides. If you approach a nesting colony, you will be subject to the diving attack of screaming, irate birds, the same reception given to any intruder. The smack of a wing, the scrape of a foot, or a peck from a sharp bill at one's head should be sufficient warning to deter further intrusion. Actually, colonies should not be disturbed. Exposed eggs will bake in the excessive heat of the sun and be subject to predation by gulls, crows, rats, and even ants.

The species of terns most closely associated with our eastern beaches are the Caspian, common, least, and royal. A brief account of each is given in the table opposite and above.

At times, the shore seems to belong to the gulls alone. They patrol the water's edge, feed from the surface, and are ever on the alert for a free handout from a passing boat or a surf fisherman. They are garrulous, noisy, and quarrelsome. The harsh, defiant screams of the great black-backed

and herring gulls are heard from the Arctic south to Long Island and northern New Jersey. The laughing gull maintains a slim and precarious hold along the New England coast, but it is basically a warm-water bird. Its hysterical laughter of "ha-ha-ha" is a common sound along the southern Atlantic and Gulf coasts. Coastal islands with grass and other low vegetation are favored as nesting sites. The small size, black head, solid dark mantle, and white trailing edge of the wings distinguish it from the two preceding species.

Special adaptations to the unique and varied ecological niches of the coastal waters are exemplified by the black skimmer and the American oystercatcher. In each case, the bill is adapted, and almost limited, to feeding in a specific manner. Such specialization limits competition for preferred foods.

The black skimmer is a comparatively large, slim, black and white bird with a wingspread of more than 3 feet. The bill is most diagnostic; it is long, bright red, and tipped with black. It appears to be quite heavy, but actually it is compressed flat and thin vertically. The lower mandible is nearly a third longer than the upper one. The skimmer has been known by many colloquial, but apt, names such as cutwater, scissorbill, sea crow, and sea dog. Cutwater is undoubtedly the most appropriate name of all, for it implies the manner in which the bird feeds. It does not skim, but flies low over the water, cutting the surface with its long, thin, lower mandible. When a fish or shrimp is touched, the upper mandible snaps shut like a trap, pulling the bird's head back beneath the body.

The skimmer feeds mostly in the early morning or late evening hours, when small school fish are nearest the surface. If you watch it feed, you will notice that it cuts the water in a long, straight line, reverses itself, and follows the same line in the opposite direction. There is considerable conjecture among ornithologists as to whether the repeated traversing of the same general line attracts feeding fish to the surface, thus making capture easier. From personal observations of skimmers feeding in the canal adjacent to my backyard, I believe this to be true. I have watched individual birds feeding continuously for 10 minutes, and as they traversed back and forth lengthwise of the canal, their feeding lines were no more than 6 inches apart, even though the canal is more than 60 feet wide.

The American oystercatcher is a large spectacular bird of the shore. The contrasting black and white plumage, long, red, chisel-shaped bill, and pinkish legs are the best identifying features. It feeds mainly on oysters, clams, mussels, snails, and other crustaceans. When exposed bivalves open their shells, the oystercatcher inserts its strong chisel-bill and severs the muscle that holds the shells together. The contents are then helpless and easily obtained.

Both the skimmer and the oystercatcher seek the security of offshore islands for nesting, their nests being mere "scrapes" in the sand. They are most abundant on selected islands from Virginia southward, and along the Gulf coast to Texas. Loud and garrulous, their presence adds an audible charm to the shoreline that is as characteristically significant as the defiant call of the gull or the excited cry of the tern. Peterson describes the black skimmer as "yelping like a small lost dog." The call of the oystercatcher is a sharp, piercing, and oft-repeated whistle of "wheep-wheep-wheep."

But not all birds of the shore are involved in the raucous melee of the nesting season. The piping plover, sand-colored and inconspicuous, goes about the business of rearing its family in a quiet, unhurried manner. As we watch this pale "ringed" bird feeding along the water's edge, it reminds us of a robin feeding on our lawn. It patters ahead, stops, cocks its head slightly to the side, and watches for some morsel of marine life. Insects, larvae, marine worms, small crustaceans, and tiny mollusks are the main items of food. The piping plover's soft, plaintive call of "peep-lo" does not emulate the hysteria of its neighbors.

Another "ringed" plover, the Wilson's, is found along our eastern beaches. Not as common as the piping, it can be recognized by its larger size and proportionately large, heavy, all-black bill. The call is also distinctive—an emphatically whistled "queep, queep." Both species nest amid the sparse grass of sandy offshore islands. The piping plover

breeds from the Gulf of St. Lawrence south to the Carolinas, but the heaviest concentrations of the Wilson's plover are between Virginia and Texas.

A number of these same coastal islands are also home to the willet, a medium-sized wader that reminds one of the greater yellowlegs. However, a sharply contrasting black and white wing pattern gives the willet an unmistakable identity in flight. Its normal call during the breeding season is a very distinct and somewhat melodious "pill-will-willet."

Undoubtedly, you will find other birds along the sandy beaches during the summer months, but for the species that nest there, you will find a few points in common: all are adjusted to survival in the bleak environment of nearly barren sand and excessive heat. And each species, through certain physical adaptations, is irrevocably bound to a specific ecological niche which forms part of the total shoreline community.

Migration along the Shore

Since the eastern coastline of our continent runs in a general north–south direction, it forms a natural flyway, or route of travel, for many migrating birds. In the fall, hundreds of thousands of shore and land birds funnel their way through river valleys and across mountain ridges until they come to the barrier of the Atlantic. Then the coast becomes an avenue that is followed south to Florida and the Gulf states. In the spring, this route of travel is reversed by many species. In addition to the values of orientation, the long, irregular shoreline provides an abundance of food and many ideal resting areas for the migrants. Places like the sandy spits of outer Cape Cod, the beaches and inlets of Long Island, and the numerous peninsulas and outer beaches of the New Jersey, Virginia, and Carolina coasts literally teem with thousands of resting and feeding birds.

Shore birding is best during late summer and fall. Inland, at this season, there is a strange quietness to the woodlands and meadows. Nesting has ceased. Birds are molting and difficult to find, but now the shore becomes

BIRDS ALONG OR NEAR THE SHORE IN WINTER

Auks, Murres, and Puffins,
  Dovekie
  Guillemot, Black
  Murre, Thick-billed
  Razorbill
Cormorants,
  Double-crested
Gannets,
  Gannet
Grebes,
  Horned
  Red-necked
Gulls,
  Bonaparte's

Glaucous
Great Black-backed
Herring
Iceland
Kittiwake, Black-legged
Jaegers,
  Pomarine
Loons,
  Common
  Red-throated
Ospreys,
  Osprey
Plovers,
  Black-bellied

Sandpipers,
  Dowitcher, Short-billed
  Dunlin
  Purple
  Sanderling
  Semipalmated
  Spotted

DUCKS OF THE SHORE IN WINTER

Bufflehead
Duck, Harlequin
Eider, Common
Eider, King
Goldeneye, Barrows

Goldeneye, Common
Merganser, Common
Merganser, Hooded
Merganser, Red-breasted
Old-squaw

Scaup, Greater
Scaup, Lesser
Scoter, Common
Scoter, Surf
Scoter, White-winged

"alive" with the long-distance travelers. This is the time to follow the edge of the sea—the time when you will see such birds as sandpipers, plovers, dowitchers, knots, sanderlings, turnstones, yellowlegs, scattered terns and gulls, and wandering egrets. You will see land birds, too—swallows skimming low and feeding as they travel, perhaps bobolinks weighting down the reeds and phragmites, or maybe a Savannah or Ipswich sparrow. Pigeon hawks and sparrow hawks work their way southward along the coast, and adjacent stands of shrubs and trees often harbor migrating vireos, warblers, and thrushes. A trip to the shore at this time of year is the way to build your bird list in a hurry.

Along the Shore in Winter

Birding along the shore in winter is more rewarding than one might suspect, often more so than during the nesting months. A number of nesting species merely extend their range southward along the coast; others, notably waterfowl, loons, grebes, and other species from inland lakes, winter in the open waters along the coast. Numerous species appear sporadically because they are affected directly by the winds of ocean storms, or they may follow bait fish seeking the security of coastal waters. The species you find on any one trip will depend upon these and other factors. Your chances of seeing the rarer pelagic birds will be best on extensions into the ocean such as Cape Cod and Long Island or on the offshore islands.

A "possibility" list of birds to be found along or near the coast in winter is given on the preceding page (see also the separate list of ducks, again on page 157).

One has but to check the regional reports in *American Birds* to realize that any list could not be considered complete. Invariably, someone is reporting such rarities as the marbled godwit, mew gull, or lapwing. But these are the finds that make winter birding along the coast such a challenging experience.

Perhaps the greatest single addition to the birds along the coast in winter is the tremendous influx of ducks. Some, like the mergansers, may appear singly; others such as old-squaws and buffleheads, may be in small flocks; and still others, like the scoters and scaups, will raft up by the hundreds. They are largely fish eaters and spend most of their time offshore. Depending on your location, you may find some or all of the ducks given in the following list.

Just as the unknown has lured man to follow the sea, so the unknown lures the bird watcher to follow the shore. For here one really finds the "unknown," the unexpected, and the spectacular inhabitants of the avian world. Here the watcher is challenged—in identification, by behavioral studies, and by the mystery of survival itself.

Southern Florida is the only semitropical area in the eastern half of our continent, so when we think of tropical birds, we naturally think of Florida.* Here is where we see flights of egrets, stark white against the black clouds of tropical storms, the magnificent frigatebird patrolling along the beaches, and the grotesque and primitive anhinga drying its wings in the sun. These, and similar vivid scenes, make Florida one of the most exciting birding areas of our entire continent.

Geologically speaking, southern Florida is still an infant, for it was just some 5,000 years ago that the ocean receded and the peninsula emerged from the eastern ridge of the ancient Florida Plateau. During this relatively brief span of time, the peninsula continued to build on a base of sand, pulverized shells, and skeletal marine life. Today, it encompasses a variety of ecological niches uniquely different from those found anywhere else in our country.

Florida visitors are frequently amazed at the size of the state, and by the diversification in terrain and vegetation. If islands, bays, coves, and other coastal indentations are included, Florida's shoreline is nearly 4,000 miles. It is difficult to believe, but nevertheless true, that when one is

* The word "tropical" as used in this chapter should be interpreted liberally, whether it applies to birds, vegetation, or climate. Mostly, I have used it as a collective term to include those birds indigenous to the state of Florida. However, this does not imply that all birds mentioned are found in Florida exclusively.

12 Watching Our Tropical Birds

in Pensacola, he is closer (by land) to Chicago than to Key West. Florida has its pinelands dotted with hundreds of lakes, scrublands, swamps, prairies, beaches, and salt marshes, as well as its renowned Everglades and Keys. Collectively, these habitats support a great variety of birds. The state list approximates 500 species.

With a few exceptions, the list on the facing page includes those species closely associated with our southernmost habitats and not covered in any detail elsewhere. It will be noted that many of the species are also found well beyond Florida's boundaries. In addition to the birds listed, others are included in the course of the text.

Typical Roadside Scenes

For economic reasons, many of Florida's highways are built of fill obtained from the adjacent roadside, leaving extensive drainage ditches or canals. While this bit of engineering folly sometimes claims the lives of unfortunate motorists, it does provide hundreds of miles of aquatic habitat for birds. Some typical roadside scenes often observed by motorists include:

• A lone, large, white bird, usually standing motionless amid the vegetation in shallow roadside ditches: Common Egret.

• Similar, but noticeably smaller, white bird hunting in the same manner: Snowy Egret or immature Little Blue Heron.

• Flocks of still smaller egrets following cattle or mowing machines: Cattle Egrets.

• A large, dark, long-necked bird sitting on a post or limb with its wings and tail spread open to dry: Anhinga.

• Flocks of long-legged, white birds with long, thin, decurved bills, feeding about puddles and wet areas in pastures: White Ibises.

• The largest of all roadside waders. Grayish blue in appearance. Stalks the shallows in a manner similar to the common egret: Great Blue Heron.

• A smaller and darker heron. Appears to be a solid slate-blue in color: Little Blue Heron.

• Large, long-tailed "blackbirds" about the cattails: Boat-tailed Grackles.

Anhingas,
    Anhinga
Blackbirds and Orioles,
    Grackle, Boat-tailed
    Oriole, Spotted-breasted
Bulbuls,
    Red-whiskered
Caracaras,
    Caracara
Cranes,
    Sandhill
Crows and Jays,
    Crow, Fish
    Jay, Scrub
Cuckoos and Anis,
    Ani, Smooth-billed
    Cuckoo, Mangrove
Ducks,
    Duck, Mottled
    Fulvous Tree
Flycatchers,
    Kingbird, Gray
    Scissor-tailed
Frigatebirds,
    Magnificent
Gallinules,
    Common
    Purple
Herons,
    Egret, Cattle
    Egret, Common

Egret, Reddish
Egret, Snowy
Heron, Great Blue
Heron, Great White
Heron, Green
Heron, Little Blue
Heron, Louisiana
Night Heron, Black-crowned
Night Heron, Yellow-crowned
Honeycreepers,
    Bahama
Ibises and Spoonbills,
    Ibis, Glossy
    Ibis, White
    Ibis, Wood
    Spoonbill, Roseate
Kites and Hawks,
    Hawk, Short-tailed
    Kite, Everglade
    Kite, Mississippi
    Kite, Swallow-tailed
Limpkins,
    Limpkin
Owls,
    Burrowing
Pelicans,
    Brown
    White
Pigeons and Doves,
    Dove, Ground
    Pigeon, White-crowned

Plovers,
    Snowy
Sparrows and Buntings,
    Bunting, Painted
    Sparrow, Cape Sable
    Sparrow, Dusky Seaside
    Sparrow, Java
Stilts,
    Black-necked
Tanagers,
    Blue-gray
Terns,
    Gull-billed
    Sandwich
Vireos,
    Black-whiskered

• Owl on fence post or mound of dirt during the day-time: Burrowing Owl.

• A small group (usually two to six or eight) of extremely large, all-gray birds flying low over open prairies or grass-lands: Sandhill Cranes.

• A rapidly swirling flock of hundreds of small, dark and white birds, usually over a damp, shrubby area: Tree Swallows.

New Birds for Your Life List

A trip to Florida affords most birders the opportunity for adding new birds to their life list. If a trip is your first one, or if you are a beginning student, you will be able to add a considerable number of birds to your list. However, there are certain species that may require some special effort to find—species of restricted areas, and in most cases, not found elsewhere. Some of these could be once-in-a-lifetime observations, so be sure to take binoculars, field guide, and notebook; positive identification will deter frustration. Any of the following species will be a memorable addition to your list:

Everglade kite: A rare species restricted to sections of the Everglades near Lake Okeechobee and in the Loxahatchee Wildlife Refuge. Your best chance of finding it is to employ the services of a local fishing guide who knows the area and the bird.

Short-tailed hawk: A rare, crow-sized buteo of swamps, hammocks, and coastal areas of south Florida and the Keys. Check your field guide for the two color phases—dark and white.

Caracara: A long-legged scavenger with a hawk-buzzard appearance. Usually spotted sitting on a post or on the ground feeding with vultures. Not a common bird, but can be found in the central prairie regions of Florida. Also in south Texas.

Great white heron: The largest of our herons, but the most restricted in range—the southern tip of Florida and the Keys. Its larger size and yellowish legs distinguish it from the common egret.

Roseate spoonbill: A large, pink wader with a broad spatulate bill. Found in the shallow salt-water flats of southern Florida. Also in Texas and Louisiana.

Limpkin: Look for the limpkin in wooded fresh-water swamps and marshes throughout Florida, where it feeds on a large snail of the genus *Pomacea.*

White-crowned pigeon: An all-dark pigeon with a distinctive white crown. Limited area in the Florida Keys.

Mangrove cuckoo: Similar to the yellow-billed, but with a black mask through the eye and buff-colored underparts. Found mostly in the mangrove swamps of southwest Florida and the Keys.

Smooth-billed ani: Looks like a grackle except for the short, heavy bill. Travels in small flocks. Ranges from Lake Okeechobee south through the Keys.

Gray kingbird: Distinguished from the more common eastern kingbird by its heavy bill, notched tail, and lack of white tail band. Becoming quite common all around coastal Florida and in the Keys.

Red-whiskered bulbul: Introduced in the Miami area in 1960. Its range now extends northward through Broward and Palm Beach counties. This is a striking, jay-shaped bird with a dark crest, red facial patches, and red undertail coverts. Often seen around fruit trees in residential areas.

Bahama honeycreeper: A house wren-sized bird with a decurved bill. Frequents flower gardens. Usually seen probing blossoms. A casual wanderer in southeast Florida.

Black-whiskered vireo: Similar to the red-eyed, but with black facial "whisker" marks extending from the base of the upper and lower mandibles. A bird of the mangroves and hammocks. Mostly coastal from Tampa south through the Keys. Rarer on the southeast coast.

Spotted-breasted oriole: An introduced species that is extending its range rapidly. From Miami, it now reaches northward through Palm Beach County. Mostly orange and black with a spotted breast. Larger than the Baltimore oriole. The song reminds one of a cardinal's, only it is slower and more continuous.

Blue-gray tanager: Another introduced species. As the name implies, it is a soft blue-gray in color with deeper shades of blue in wings and tail. Most abundant in the Hollywood area.

Dusky seaside sparrow: A rare sparrow found in the salt marshes of only two areas: Merritt Island, and on the east side of the St. Johns River, north and south of Route 50. About 95 percent of the total population is in the latter area.

Cape sable sparrow: Another rare sparrow found only in the brackish marshes of southwest Florida near Shark River.

Java sparrow: An introduced species, now considered to be an established breeder in the Miami area.

Florida Habitats

Although the ecological niches and microcosms indigenous to Florida could be listed as an endless number of variances, for the purpose of birding, the following eight habitats are generally accepted as being totally representative. These habitats are not necessarily self-contained units. In certain sections, there is considerable evidence of overlapping, intermingling, and relationships that, technically, could qualify these areas for a broader and more inclusive classification. However, each habitat does have a number of birds closely associated with it.

The Everglades

The Everglades are the most renowned topographical feature of Florida, yet they are the least understood. Ever since their discovery, they have been looked upon as a land of mystery and intrigue—a land that held many secrets beyond the findings and the comprehension of man. In a sense, this is still true, for even though their ecological significance is coming to light gradually, there are those who exploit the Glades without concern, or without a knowledgeable understanding of the potential results of their destruction.

In reality, the heart of the Everglades is a river of grass —a river approximately 100 miles long, more than 50 miles wide in places, with an average depth of less than one foot, and a current that flows less than one mile a day. The river is slowed by the luxuriant growth of saw grass, a tall sedge deeply rooted in the layer of muck overlying the limestone basin. Other plants associated with this watery environment attain varying degrees of dominance. In the open areas, there are spikerushes, pickerel weed, maidencain, false maidencain, sloughgrass, cattail, water hyacinth, water lettuce, white water lily, and other low-growing species. Submerged plants include the bladderworts, muskgrass, waterweed, and southern naiad.

Birding in the Everglades requires understanding. Contrary to popular belief, the area is not a biological haven where thousands of birds pass by the observer in endless profusion as they do on an edited television film. True, one can still find sizable concentrations of egrets, herons, ibises, ducks, and other species, but the birds here are subject to the same biological laws of survival as the birds of other areas. The flocks require a tremendous amount of food; consequently, they must feed over vast areas. The glorified picture of a blue sky filled with great white birds had considerable authenticity a couple of decades ago, but man is altering this lone world habitat with incredible rapidity. Its waters are being stored or drained under the guise of flood control, and they flow with excessive nutrients and poisons from agricultural runoffs. In addition, the borders of the Everglades are being narrowed as "developers" apply their technological know-how in an ever-tightening circle.

The Everglade kite, long symbolic of this wetland region, now numbers perhaps no more than 50 pairs; its demise seems inevitable. It feeds exclusively on large fresh-water snails of the genus *Ampullaria*. Drainage and poisons continue to narrow the snails' range. The limpkin is also a snail cater, but its fate is not so precarious because it does feed on other aquatic life and is not so tightly bound to a singular ecological niche. In addition to feeding in the shallow waters of the Glades, the limpkin ranges extensively through wooded swamps and marshes, and along sluggish rivers and canals.

The feeding methods of the two birds are quite different. The Everglade kite flies along slowly just above the saw grass, dipping, turning, and doing most of the maneuvering with its long, broad tail. It hunts mostly in the early morning or late evening when the snails are on the vegetation just above the water line. The kite seizes the snail with its claws, flies to a favorite feeding perch (usually a myrtle or willow bush), and extracts the snail from the shell with its sharply curved beak. Quantities of shells accumulate beneath such feeding perches. The limpkin has long legs and a long, decurved bill. It hunts by stalking the shallows and edges. The captured snail usually is carried to drier ground and eaten on the spot. The limpkin is active at night, and one often hears the humanlike "cry of the night bird."

If there is one scene about the Everglades (or the marshy borders of the Gulf states) that birders are not likely to forget, it is surely the exquisitely beautiful flight of the swallow-tailed kite. Imagine, if you will, a striking

black and white bird with a wingspan of 4 feet, and a correspondingly large, deeply forked, swallowlike tail. Add to this the mastery of aerodynamics, from power dives to graceful and effortless soaring, and you envision the swallow-tailed kite—a bird for which all superlatives seem inadequate.

This large bird will remind you of a swallow, not only in appearance but in many of its actions as well. It is somewhat gregarious and often hunts in small, loose flocks similar to those of swallows. Also, like swallows, it captures its food while on the wing and eats it in flight. It feeds on grasshoppers, cicadas, dragonflies, crickets, locusts, tree toads, lizards, frogs, small reptiles, and similar foods that can be taken while flying.

I have seen the swallow-tailed kite along the shores of Lake Okeechobee, along Route 29 on the eastern edge of the Glades, at several places on the Tamiami Trail, and while crossing Alligator Alley between Fort Lauderdale and Naples.

Actually, within the Everglades there is rarely a moment when birds cannot be seen or heard. This is especially true during the winter months, when feeding is done in more compact flocks, and when numerous migrants have returned from the North. One may see flocks of wood ibis, white ibis, and smaller gatherings of glossy ibis. Egrets and herons move constantly from one feeding ground to another. Ducks congregate in feeding flocks. Gallinules and coots are abundant in the acres of duckweed that float amid the cattails and sedges. Anhingas feed in the deeper waters, rails and snipe feed in the marshy areas, shore birds frequent the mud flats of lowered canals, and yellowthroats are common along the watery ditches. Overhead, a hawk hunts, an osprey fishes, and if you are lucky, you will see a bald eagle soaring on flattened wings.

The Keys   The Keys are a chain of narrow, limestone islands that arc south and westward from the Florida mainland for 120 miles. They are connected by bridges and U.S. Route 1. Even though they are geographically isolated—the Atlantic Ocean on one side and the Gulf of Mexico on the other— they cannot be considered representative of a singular type of habitat. For in reality, the natural community of the Keys is a composite of sandy beaches, coral reefs, shallow bays, mangrove swamps, hammocks, and even wooded drylands. It is a land where names like allamanda, marl-berry, coco-plum, mahogany, and gumbo-limbo roll from one's tongue with poetic intonations and the rhythms of an island bongo drum. It is a land of cerulean waters and giant sea turtles, of colorful tree snails and glamorous birds—a land controlled largely by the surrounding waters and the passing of tropical storms.

The stately and statuesque great white heron is the most symbolic bird of this tropical region. Although it is our largest heron and a strong flier, its range is limited to the Keys and the southern tip of the mainland. Unlike most herons and egrets, it is not a far-ranging wanderer during the fall, but seems ecologically bound to its restricted homeland. Rarely is the great white heron seen north of the Tamiami Trail. Physical factors such as light and temperature, and innate feeding and nesting habits, undoubtedly hold the secrets of its confinement. It is mostly a fish eater and nests in the mangroves during the winter months. The great white heron can be observed from the Overseas Highway (U.S. Route 1) and in Everglades National Park.

Birding along the Overseas Highway requires an extra degree of alertness in both driving and bird recognition. For the most part, the route can be considered a two-lane highway, and it is heavily traveled. There are numerous places (except on the bridges) where one can pull off the road and observe the bays, shorelines, and islands. Some of the bridges have walkways, designed for fishing, which provide safe, unobstructed observation points. Occasional short side roads will lead you inland and to other water locations.

Bird observations should not be made hastily. The pigeons you see flying across the highway may not be the common domestic variety, or rock dove, but the rarer white-crowned. The kingbird you see sitting on the utility wires is likely to be the gray kingbird rather than the more common eastern one. A cuckoo in the mangroves or hammocks may not be the expected yellow-billed, but the mangrove cuckoo. Look for the dark eye mask. And if the song of a vireo doesn't sound quite right, you may be hearing the black-whiskered virtuoso.

Be alert for the magnificent frigatebird (man-o'-war bird), for it is more common around the Keys than elsewhere along our southern coasts. You will see it soaring effortlessly over the open water not far from shore. Recognition will be instantaneous because of its large size and distinctive shape. It has long, narrow wings and a deeply forked tail. With a wingspan of 7½ feet, and a body weight of only 3½ pounds, it is a soaring specialist. This and other unusual characteristics make the frigatebird extremely interesting to watch. As you watch it soar, or hover motionless against the wind, it may suddenly peel off, skim low over the water, and deftly lift a fish from the surface with its long hook-tipped bill. Schools of feeding bonita, albacore, jacks, or other predacious fish are followed; the scraps and wounded bait fish are easy fare. Often the jumping mullet or other small school fish are captured in midair. Tropical flying fish are caught in the same manner. Gulls, boobies, and pelicans are frequently robbed of their catch, hence the name "man-o'-war bird." Although this magnificent bird feeds exclusively from the sea, it does not enter the water. Its feathers are not waterproof, and it is doubtful whether the bird could become airborne from the surface. Even on shore, it roosts and nests in an elevated location in order to launch itself directly into the wind and have immediate lift and flying speed. The comparatively small feet and legs are of little value in takeoff procedures.

In addition to the birds which are considered as being generally native to the Keys, many other species are to be observed throughout these picturesque islands. Great flocks of gulls follow the shrimp boats; brown pelicans sit on pilings or dive into the harbor waters. There are herons, egrets, ibises, and other long-legged waders. And terns, black skimmers, cormorants, and scores of migrants. This far-reaching chain of islands is a natural flyway for both shore birds and land birds. Occasional wanderers include the sooty and noddy terns, which nest in great numbers in the Dry Tortugas some 60 miles beyond Key West. Also, the brown booby—and, less frequently, the blue-faced booby—are tropical visitors. Always, the Keys have a captivating enchantment—especially for the bird watcher.

If we adhere to our previous definition of a swamp as being a low, wet, wooded area, we confine ourselves to a habitat which, for the most part, is ecologically different *Swamps* from the Everglades and marshes. Swamps may be inland or coastal, and they are usually characterized by the dominant plant growth, such as mangrove swamps and cypress swamps.

Unlike many life species emanating from the sea, the mangrove trees did not adapt and extend their range across interior lands. Instead, their development was confined to the shallow margins of the sea, and now they fulfill one of the most important ecological niches of tropical Florida. Perhaps no other single species of tree is so ecologically significant as the red mangrove. For approximately 700 square miles, mangrove habitat surrounds the mainland and coastal islands of southern Florida. This area bears the brunt of tropical storms, and protects the interior from extensive intrusion by salt water. In fact, the red mangrove is a soil builder; its arched roots, and roots that drop vertically into the sea, trap and hold quantities of detritus—the mudlike bottom matter consisting mostly of decomposed vegetation. This detritus is the basis of numerous life chains that support the majority of marine species in the surrounding waters. And the detritus itself is composed largely of rotted leaves from the red mangrove.

This muddy, brackish world is not one of a single plant species, but of many. The red mangrove is the most seaward of the trees and the most adaptable to environmental conditions. It will survive as a shrub or, when conditions are favorable, grow as a tall, straight tree to a height of 70 feet or more. Moving inland, it is backed by the white mangrove, black mangrove, tropical buttonwood, and other trees, shrubs, vines, ferns, and flowering plants. In most areas, the growth habits and mixing of these plants form a nearly impenetrable jungle. Observing these tangled vegetative designs, one becomes conscious of a feeling of

movement; the forest seems to be creeping forward. The roots of the red mangrove arch in giant steps of 20 or 30 feet; the black mangrove sends up canelike quills from its roots to gather needed oxygen. The buttonwood moves forward like a measuring stick. When the tall straight tree is toppled by the wind, new straight shoots spring up from the top. Over years of time, this process is repeated again and again as the buttonwood "measures" its way through the forest. The mahoe moves with an almost deliberate walk; it grows to a height of 10 feet or more and arches over; then new plants sprout from the soil-encased tips. An abundance of wildlife lives within these creeping, massive tangles.

Fiddler crabs seem to be everywhere; their myriad holes aerate the methane-laden soil. There are blue crabs and hermit crabs. Land crabs scurry away noisily, and the horseshoe crab, the oldest of earth's creatures, comes ashore like a miniature armored tank. Thousands of dragonflies hover on gauzy wings, and zebra butterflies drift by on the constant winds. Tree frogs croak from their shaded recesses, and brightly colored tree snails feed on the fungi from the trees' bark. To these littoral margins of mangroves comes a variety of birds, each adapted to a particular niche within the tropical community.

The structure and remoteness of these mangrove stands provide security for the rookeries of the larger water birds. Herons, egrets, ibises, and roseate spoonbills nest in colonies that are but remnants of the great rookeries of years gone by. Dredging and filling continue to alter the environment, and the tenure of these spectacular water birds becomes increasingly questionable.

Surely the most glamorous among them, especially for the beginning student, is the roseate spoonbill. To see these large, pink birds gliding in to roost against a contrasting evening sky is an unforgettable sight. Also, to see them feed on the small aquatic life of the muddy shallows is a unique experience. Food is obtained by the continuous working of the long, spatulate bill, as it is swung back and forth, stirring up the muddy bottom.

The wood ibis (the only American stork) is similarly adapted to feeding in the muddy shallows of ponds and

NESTING SPECIES OF FLORIDA SWAMPS

Anhingas,
   Anhinga
Bitterns,
   American
   Least
Blackbirds,
   Grackle, Boat-tailed
   Red-winged
Cormorants,
   Double-crested

Ducks,
   Duck, Mottled
   Duck, Wood
Flycatchers,
   Acadian
Gallinules,
   Common
   Purple
Grosbeaks,
   Cardinal

Hawks,
   Short-tailed
Limpkins,
   Limpkin
Warblers,
   Parula
   Yellowthroat
Woodpeckers,
   Pileated

bays. If we examine the bird somewhat critically, we notice that the long legs and the long bill seem exceptionally heavy and rugged. Both are used in the feeding process. The wood ibis muddies the water by scratching, thereby forcing small fish and aquatic animals to the surface, where they can be captured with the strong bill.

Of course, when in the mangroves, one should always be alert for the black-whiskered vireo and the mangrove cuckoo. The prairie warbler is there, also. Its song of "zee, zee, zee" ascends the scale, and at times it seems as though this beautiful little warbler were the only bird enjoying the hot days of summer.

Northward from this tropical region, the swamps of Florida change in character. Some are dominated by cypresses, and others by a mixture of hardwoods. These variations are exemplified best by the Big Cypress Swamp in the southwestern part of the state, and by the Wakulla River area in the northern section. Both swamps are accessible and rich in bird life.

Although most of the vast swampy areas of Florida have been subjected to lumbering, fire, fill, drainage, and other encroachments, the remaining second-growth areas still support a large number and variety of birds. In addition to many of the species already mentioned, there are many nesting species, including those given in the list at the top of the page.

Hammocks

Florida's expansive wetlands of grass are punctuated by hundreds of wooded islands known as hammocks. These hammocks may be large or small—measured in square yards or in square miles. They are densely covered with tropical or semitropical hardwoods and a thick, tangled undergrowth of shrubs, vines, ferns, mosses, air plants, and wild orchids. The vegetation on some hammocks is so thick that Florida's brilliant sunshine reaches the lower strata only in the form of refracted light. The thick, jungle-like growth, the subdued light with its green refractions, and the unfamiliar sounds give one an eerie feeling—a feeling that the hammock is a strange island world apart from its surroundings.

The distinctive character of the hammocks makes them especially attractive to a number of birds. Here, as well as in the cypress swamps, one may be lucky enough to find the rare short-tailed hawk. Red-shouldered hawks and barred owls find nesting sites in the larger trees; the red-bellied woodpecker is common; and towhees and cardinals frequent the open margins. Some hammocks also attract a variety of the long-legged waders.

Beaches and Salt Marshes

The Gulf Coast still retains more salt marshes, open beaches, and undeveloped offshore islands than most other areas in the United States. Here one may find the snowy plover, Sandwich terns mingling with royal terns, and a variety of smaller shore birds. In addition to the more common marsh species, there are clapper rails, long-billed marsh wrens, and seaside sparrows.

Prairies and Fresh-Water Marshes

Most of Florida's vast prairies lie to the north and west of Lake Okeechobee. Hundreds of square miles of this flat cattle country are covered with grass, saw palmetto, and fresh-water marshes. The landscape is broken by lakes, scattered stands of pines, and hammocks of cypress, oak, and cabbage palm. It is in this type of habitat that we find the sandhill crane, caracara, burrowing owl, and grass-hopper sparrow. Other species likely to be seen would include herons, egrets, ibises, anhingas, limpkins, red-tailed and red-shouldered hawks, loggerhead shrikes, plus many smaller land and water birds.

Florida is not all sand and water. The central and northern highlands are characterized by open pine and hardwood forests. But this, too, like every other land type in the state, is prime real estate for someone. The great citrus desert spreads its sterility across the land. *Pinelands*

Birds of the pinelands that would be of special interest to visitors include the red-cockaded woodpecker, brown-headed nuthatch, yellow-throated warbler, and Bachman's sparrow. And I would include the rufous-sided towhee because it is likely to be the white-eyed variety.

Localized sections of Florida have a soil base of white sand. Lacking any appreciable amount of nutriments, they support a stunted, scrubby growth of vegetation. Dominant plants include sand pine, saw palmetto, myrtle, rosemary, gallberry, and various oaks of a shrubby nature. The most interesting bird of such areas is the scrub jay. Look for it on utility wires and the tops of scrub oaks along the roadside. The beginner will recognize it as a jay without a crest. Also, its white throat has a collar of blue rather than of black as does the more common blue jay. Like most jays, it is garrulous and noisy. It is shy and is apt to disappear in the undergrowth before a good sighting can be had, but it is quite a curious bird and a little patience is soon rewarded. *Scrublands*

• Avoid excessive exposure to the sun; the tropical sun can burn you severely before you realize it. If you plan to be afield for an extended period of time, cover up. Above all, do not wear shorts, especially on boat trips. Your lily-white knees can blister in less than an hour.

• Do not rent a boat and head off into the Everglades without an experienced guide. The waterways are a criss-crossed maze, and it is easy to become lost. Remember: the Glades are big. There are places where you can see nothing but saw grass from horizon to horizon. **Field Trip Precautions**

• Tropical storms develop quickly and often are accompanied by strong winds. If you get caught while boating, seek land shelter until the storm passes. Carry rain gear, even on the sunniest of days.

• Carry insect repellent. The presence of mosquitoes and sand fleas is unpredictable, depending upon such factors as wind direction and intensity, rainfall, and temperature.

• Florida has a variety of wildlife, including snakes, alligators, wild boars, black bears, and panthers. Alligators will not bother you unless cornered and deliberately molested. A glimpse of a bear, wild boar, or panther would be a real find. Rattlesnakes sometimes are seen in dry areas, and water moccasins along the water's edge. They are just as scared of you as you are of them. Avoid deliberate encounters, and you will not have any difficulties. However, a snakebite kit is a good precautionary item.

• Don't be a sampler; avoid unknown wild fruits. Plants poisonous to the skin include poison ivy, poison sumac (thunderwood), machineel, and Florida poisontree (poisonwood).

Despite the increasing pressures on the natural environment, Florida is still one of the most exciting birding areas to be found anywhere. Just how long it will remain this way is a matter of conjecture. Thousands of people flock into the state each month, and the demands for living space, farms, water, oil, and other needs associated with growth increase accordingly. One thing is certain: when the graceful flight of the elegant water birds can no longer be seen against the tropical sky, much of what people come to Florida for will be gone also.

The word "garden" is relative; it may refer to a tiny plot in the center of a city or to several acres in the suburbs or country. In either case, the birds attracted will be determined by the available needs of survival—protective cover, nesting sites, food, and water. For most of us, the garden is a compromise between these two extremes. Of course, larger areas are likely to have a greater diversification of vegetation, and thus attract more birds.

Although the garden can be managed in a manner that will attract a great variety of birds, there are other established factors that influence bird distribution. Each species survives within a certain temperature range. We do not expect to find the purple finch nesting in the pines of Georgia, nor the painted bunting in the hedgerows of New England. Also, the vegetation upon which each species depends is limited with somewhat parallel temperature extremes. The hours of daylight influence birds' arrival and departure dates. Even conditions hundreds of miles beyond your garden may determine the presence of certain species. Far-reaching storms may bring in wind-blown victims, or the scarcity of food in distant areas may account for a sporadic influx of nonresident birds. These and other indeterminate factors, along with the results of management, help make the garden an exciting place to watch birds. The rarities or the "finds of the year" may be observed sometimes in our own gardens; we have but to be alert to find them.

13 Bird Watching in the Garden

Common Birds of the Garden

Seasonally, we think of birds being divided into four groups: the permanent residents, those that are with us the year round; the summer residents; the winter residents; and the spring and fall migrants. To these groups we could add the casual visitors which may appear at any time of the year. Obviously, to list and consider all the birds one might find in his garden during a year is beyond the scope of this book. Mostly, in this chapter, we are concerned with the nesting species—permanent and summer residents.* Even such a list will vary according to geographical location and other factors. The species listed opposite have adjusted to living adjacent to mankind and are generally conceded to be our most common garden birds.

Niches within the Garden

As you watch the birds about your garden, it will soon become obvious that each species is associated more closely with one particular niche, or section, than with the others. Some will feed in open areas; others will stick to the security of dense hedges and borders; and others will be at home in the taller shrubs and trees. The common variations in garden habitats and the birds associated with them are discussed in the following sections.

Open Lawns

A number of garden birds do much of their foraging around open grassy lawns but, for obvious reasons, do not nest there. The robin, for example, is our most familiar lawn feeder, but it nests in tall shrubs or small trees. The first nest of the season is usually in a spruce, red cedar, or other dense evergreen that affords early protection. Subsequent nests (two or three broods), when the deciduous plants are in full leaf, will be found in such favorites as lilacs, dogwood, and maples.

The starling, common grackle, and brown-headed cowbird do much of their feeding on the ground. The starling, despite its rather ribald reputation, is a voracious ground feeder. It walks around the lawn, head down, and probes constantly. The starling always seems to be in a hurry, but

* For winter birds about the garden, see Chapter 14, "Watching Songbirds in Winter."

THE MOST COMMON GARDEN BIRDS

Blackbirds and Orioles,
    Cowbird, Brown-headed
    Grackle, Common
    Oriole, Baltimore
Chickadees and Titmice,
    Chickadee, Black-capped
    Chickadee, Carolina
    Titmouse, Tufted
Doves,
    Mourning
Flycatchers,
    Kingbird, Eastern
    Phoebe, Eastern
Goatsuckers,
    Nighthawk, Common
Grosbeaks, Finches, Sparrows,
and Buntings,
    Cardinal
    Finch, Purple
    Goldfinch
    Grosbeak, Rose-breasted

Sparrow, Chipping
Sparrow, Song
Towhee, Rufous-sided
Jays,
    Blue
Nuthatches,
    White-breasted
Owls,
    Screech
Starlings,
    Starling
Swallows,
    Martin, Purple
    Tree
Swifts and Hummingbirds,
    Hummingbird, Ruby-throated
    Swift, Chimney
Thrashers and Mockingbirds,
    Catbird
    Mockingbird
    Thrasher, Brown

Thrushes,
    Bluebird, Eastern
    Robin
    Thrush, Wood
Vireos,
    Red-eyed
Warblers,
    Yellow
Waxwings,
    Cedar
Weaver Finches,
    Sparrow, House
Woodpeckers,
    Downy,
    Flicker, Yellow-shafted
    Red-bellied
Wrens,
    Carolina
    House

it always seems to find an abundance of food. It helps free our lawns of grubs, cutworms, armyworms, and other insects, and is one of the few birds that will eat the destructive Japanese beetle. The common grackle walks more deliberately as it probes for the same foods. The brown-headed cowbird has a waddling gait; it feeds on insects and weed seeds. Often, both the grackle and the cowbird will interrupt their foraging with a vocal and visual display. Their somewhat harsh and squeaky songs are accompanied by the fanning of the tail and wings, and by ruffing the feathers on the neck and upper back.

The mourning dove patters around the lawn in search of grass seeds and weed seeds; however, it is seen more often in driveways and along bare edges, picking up bits of gravel, an essential part of its digestive system. The flicker spends a lot of time on the ground looking for ants, its chief source of food. Sparrows, cardinals, and blue jays may find a certain amount of their food in the grassy areas of the garden.

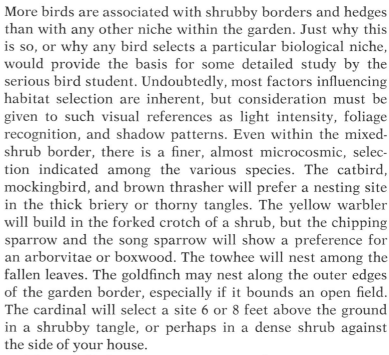

More birds are associated with shrubby borders and hedges than with any other niche within the garden. Just why this is so, or why any bird selects a particular biological niche, would provide the basis for some detailed study by the serious bird student. Undoubtedly, most factors influencing habitat selection are inherent, but consideration must be given to such visual references as light intensity, foliage recognition, and shadow patterns. Even within the mixed-shrub border, there is a finer, almost microcosmic, selection indicated among the various species. The catbird, mockingbird, and brown thrasher will prefer a nesting site in the thick briery or thorny tangles. The yellow warbler will build in the forked crotch of a shrub, but the chipping sparrow and the song sparrow will show a preference for an arborvitae or boxwood. The towhee will nest among the fallen leaves. The goldfinch may nest along the outer edges of the garden border, especially if it bounds an open field. The cardinal will select a site 6 or 8 feet above the ground in a shrubby tangle, or perhaps in a dense shrub against the side of your house.

There is little competition among the various species attracted to the garden border. Some food preferences may be similar, but there are differences in where and how they are obtained. The towhee will scratch in the leaves for grubs and worms in an area close to its nest, but the goldfinch will range farther afield for its seeds and insects.

As you study the birds about the hedges and borders of your garden, you will find them to be mostly common species. There are reasons for this: shrubby borders are also common and widely distributed throughout the East, and they provide a profusion of food, nesting sites, and cover.

You will discover, also, that your own garden is a good place to conduct detailed studies. The birds are relatively tame, and repeated observations can be made without the need of travel. Even though the birds may be considered as common, they do, nonetheless, include some of the most

fascinating species. The cardinal, for example, is a familiar bird in many gardens, yet surely it is one of the most beautiful and most admired of all birds. The male's cheerful whistle starts with the first hint of dawn, and his bright red brilliance about the garden never fails to stir a spontaneous flash of admiration. Mated cardinals are extremely devoted to each other. During the nesting season, the male frequently brings favorite morsels of food to the female, feeding her as though she were a fledgling just out of the nest. They stay close together when feeding and resting, and when the young have left the nest, they in turn become intensely devoted parents. Both parents will bring food to the young, but the male's main role seems to be one of protection. He does most of his hunting within a few feet of the fledglings.

No matter what your special interests of study may be, your own garden is the ideal place to start.

Trees do more for birds and the garden community than fulfill the obvious needs for food, cover, and nesting. By the very nature of their size, they receive the full impact of the sun, wind, and precipitation. As a deterrent to these factors, and through the process of transpiration, they alter the garden climate. The garden becomes a more pleasant place to be, not only for us, but for the birds as well.

Garden Trees

From one point of view, a single tree in your garden can be looked upon as a microcosmic neighborhood within the garden community, and as such, it affects the lives of birds in many ways. Each tree, depending upon the species, size, and nature of growth, supports an abundance of life from microscopic forms to the dominant birds. Rain-filled knotholes may harbor mosquito larvae, sow bugs, and the rat-tailed maggots of the beelike syrphid fly. Ladybird beetles fly and crawl about the trees, feeding on plant lice; birds eat the beetles. There are bark beetles and wood borers, and myriad insects that swarm about the foliage providing provender for the warblers, vireos, and flycatchers. Finches and grosbeaks feed on the tender spring buds. Spiders, lizards, and tree frogs may find a home about the tree and become prey for still another species. Egg cases

*Garden
Flowers*

and cocoons provide food and nesting materials; humming-birds, gnatcatchers, and wood pewees gather tree lichens to camouflage their nests. Blue jays, cardinals, and mourning doves gather the small twigs. Chipmunks burrow beneath the trunk, and squirrels inhabit the hollow limbs.

As you watch the tree-nesting birds, you will soon note that each species has decided preferences for locating its nest. There will be differences in the kinds of trees and in the nesting levels selected. Evergreens appeal to several species because they provide thick cover in early spring. Robins show a preference for the larger red cedars; pines appeal to the grackles; and spruces are favored by purple finches, blue jays, song sparrows, and chipping sparrows. Look for the swinging, cradlelike nest of the Baltimore oriole in larger trees in the open: elms, sycamores, and willows are favorites. If your garden is deeply shaded and borders on a woodland, wood thrushes and red-eyed vireos may nest in the dogwoods, hornbeams, witch hazels, and other understory trees.

A colorful array of flowers about our gardens does more to attract birds than we may realize. Our first thoughts turn to the ruby-throated hummingbird, because it is dependent upon flowers for its chief source of food, nectar and tiny insects. But flowers attract a great variety of insects, and these in turn are a source of food for many birds. It is not unusual to see sparrows, warblers, flycatchers, and other birds feeding around the flower beds. When flowers go to seed, certain varieties provide foods for sparrows, finches, buntings, and other seed eaters.

The ruby-throat is the only nesting hummingbird in the eastern half of our continent. Fortunately, it is quite common and widely distributed; it is likely to be found in gardens from southeastern Canada southward to the Gulf states and Florida. It is our smallest bird; it is tame, pugnacious, and beautiful. These features make it one of our favorite garden birds.

The habits and behavioral patterns of the ruby-throat make it a fascinating bird to watch. It is easily recognized by its rapid, insectlike wing beat, and by its ability to hover and to fly backwards as it flits from one flower to another.

Both sexes are burnished green above and white underneath, but the male sports an iridescent ruby gorget that may appear black in subdued light. This tiny hummer can be confused only with the hawk moths which sometimes feed about the flowers in a similar manner.

The male ruby-throat arrives in our gardens about the time the first wild columbines bloom. In addition to feeding amid the early spring flowers, he spends much of his time on an exposed perch watching for the arrival of a female. When she arrives, usually several days later, the male goes into his courtship antics. In long, pendulous arcs, he swings back and forth in front of the female. Once he has been accepted and mating is completed, his role in rearing a new family is mostly finished. He may spend time defending the territory against all intruders, but the female assumes the duties of nest building and caring for the young.

The ruby-throat's nest is so small and so well camouflaged that it is difficult to locate. The completed nest is about the size of a golf ball and sits like a saddle on a small horizontal or downward-sloping limb. It is built of plant down and bound together with spider and caterpillar webs. The exterior is covered with lichens and bits of moss, and the nest appears to be just another knot or natural protrusion on the limb. Hornbeams, beeches, maples, and birches seem to be favored trees.

One can attract hummingbirds to gardens by growing their favorite plants, which include the following: dwarf buckeye, mimosa, Japanese flowering quince, azaleas, bee balm, columbine, gladiolus, honeysuckles, larkspur, lupine, sage, and trumpet vine.

Some birds have become so adapted to the presence and ways of man that they will accept his shelter as their own. Today, more phoebes nest on porches and under bridges than in their original habitat of sheltered ledges. Robins, too, will build their nests in the shelter of a porch or other outbuildings. Chimney swifts are probably chimney dwellers exclusively; the use of hollow tree stubs seems to be a thing of the past. House wrens and Carolina wrens do not hesitate to build in our garages or carports; they will tuck

Around Buildings

their sticks behind a box, a paint can, an old shoe, or anything else that will hide and support them. House sparrows and starlings will occupy any holes along the eaves of buildings.

If you have a barn on your property, barn swallows may nest on the exposed beams; cliff swallows may plaster their gourd-shaped nests beneath the eaves; and perhaps a barn owl will find a high ventilator or silo top to its liking.

Garden Ponds and Streams

A garden pond or stream adds a whole new dimension to the bird life within a garden. The presence of water alone may add a dozen or more species to your garden list.

The larger the pond, and the more diversified its borders, the greater the variety of birds it will attract. But even a small pond is a definite asset to the garden. Herons and egrets will come to the pond to feed on minnows, frogs, tadpoles, and aquatic insects. A kingfisher may find the fishing easy, and a pair of mallards or black ducks may find enough seclusion to nest along its borders. The beautiful wood duck is likely to accept your man-made nesting box.

Along the garden stream we may hear the waterthrush and the yellowthroat, or the "peet-weet" of the spotted sandpiper. The yellowthroat may stay to nest. And at one time or another, most of the garden birds will drink from the stream and bathe in its sandy shallows.

Watching Birds Drink and Bathe

As you watch your garden bath, you will notice differences in the way various species approach it, and in the way they drink and bathe. Any drinking usually precedes bathing, and most species drink in a manner similar to that of a chicken, i.e., they must raise their heads in order to swallow the water. Doves are an exception to this procedure; they can drink their fill without removing their beaks from the water. In the standard procedure of bathing, the bird hops into the water, flattens itself against the bottom, and splashes water over its body by a vigorous flapping of the wings. This is done rather quickly and may be repeated several times, but invariably, the bird will shake off all excess water and take a quick look around between each dip. Birds seem innately concerned for their own safety when the quickness of flight can be hampered by water-soaked and disarrayed feathers. When the bath is finished, birds will shake off the water, fly to a nearby perch, and quickly preen their feathers into place.

As in most households, there is a definite priority in the use of the bath. The order of dominance at a birdbath depends upon the variety of birds in the garden. If blue jays are present, they will hold the key and usurp the bath whenever they want it. Next come the grackles and starlings. Starlings are communal bathers, and at times they will arrive in such numbers that even the jay's boldness cannot deter them. The remaining order of priority is determined mostly by size: robins, thrashers, mockingbirds, catbirds, orioles, sparrows, and finally, the warblers.

Blue jays approach the bath in bold direct flight from a distance. They come flashing in, often screaming like a hawk, and any other bathers are quick to relinquish the bath. Blue jays are vigorous bathers, throwing water in all directions, often nearly emptying the bath by the time they are finished. Usually, they will repeat this procedure several times before they are satisfied, but will shake off the excess water between flurries; they will not stay water-soaked for a prolonged period of time. Robins also use a direct approach to the bath, but they usually have just one good dip and are finished. They shake off the water, fly to a nearby perch, and rearrange their feathers.

When a flock of starlings descends upon the bath, there is a squabbling melee as they all try to bathe at once. When they are finished, you can be sure the bath will need a good cleaning and fresh water. Most of the water will be gone, and the little that remains will be saturated with seeds, droppings, and lost feathers.

Thrashers and catbirds are more cautious in their approach to the bath. They work their way through the low shrubbery, gradually getting as close as possible before flying to the edge. A drink and one quick bath is their usual routine. Warblers are perhaps the most cautious of all the garden bathers. I have banded hundreds of them by using water traps. Their approach to the water was nearly always the same. They would land high in a nearby tree and gradu-

ally work their way downward. They were constantly alert and always seemed nervous, but they could not resist the temptation of dripping water.

In the absence of a birdbath, garden birds must resort to other means of obtaining water for drinking and bathing. Some will travel quite far to enjoy the shallow edges of some pond or stream. Rain puddles, no matter how muddy they may be, are used by many species. I have seen mockingbirds, cardinals, catbirds, flycatchers, and other garden birds bathe by taking rain showers, by flying through the spray of lawn sprinklers, and by pushing their bodies through rain-soaked foliage or dew-covered grass. Certain species, such as the downy woodpecker, black-capped chickadee, and slate-colored junco, will sometimes bathe in the snow.

For the bird watcher, the greatest advantage of a garden birdbath is that it attracts birds into place for close observation—birds that otherwise would go unnoticed. Many "firsts" have been recorded by watching a birdbath.

Watching Bird Activities in Your Garden

Anting

At least 150 species of birds have been observed anointing their feathers with ants. This is done in one of two ways: the bird will pick up the ant, crush it, and quickly rub the feathers (usually the underside of the wing tips and the undertail coverts) with its bill, or it may spread its body over the ants and allow them to crawl through the feathers. In the latter, or more passive, type of anting, it is believed that the type of ants selected exude a repugnant mist. The most plausible explanation of this seemingly strange behavior is that the body juices of ants contain formic acid which helps rid the bird of mites. However, this is but one of many theories, and the positive reason for anting is unknown.

Watch the mockingbird while it is on the ground. It has the very common habit of "flashing" its wings, i.e., it will raise its wings repeatedly to an angle of about 45 degrees. Often this is done in a series of successive steps rather than by one continuous movement. When the wings are raised in this manner, the white underneath wing patches are displayed, or exposed. The reason for this wing flashing by mockingbirds is still one of the unsolved mysteries of bird behavior. Several theories have been advanced, suggesting that wing flashing is a courtship display, a means of flushing insects from the grass, or an outlet for emotional frustrations. But if you watch the procedure, and note when and under what circumstances it is performed, not one of these theories seems to have much basis. Additional detailed studies are needed to reach a positive conclusion on the reason for wing flashing.

Wing Flashing

The edges of flower beds and driveways are favorite places for garden birds to sun themselves. Usually, the bird turns one side toward the sun, fluffs up its feathers, and spreads the tail and one or both wings. Practically all birds engage in this activity, but about the garden, I have noticed it most frequently among mourning doves, blue jays, mockingbirds, cardinals, and robins. The significance of sun bathing remains obscure, but it is likely that birds obtain some physical benefit from the practice, and that it is not done merely for the enjoyment of the extra warmth.

Sun Bathing

Some birds bathe by dusting. They scratch a depression in the dry dirt surface and force the powdery soil through their plumage. This method of bathing is the one used by pheasants, grouse, bobwhites, whip-poor-wills, and chuck-will's-widows. Within the garden, it is most likely to be noticed among members of the sparrow family. Dust bathing undoubtedly helps birds get rid of external parasites.

Dust Bathing

This is the birds' method of caring for their plumage. Frequently, it is engaged in after bathing or some disturbance that disarranges the feathers. As you watch a bird preen, you will observe that it takes the feather in its bill and gradually works toward the tip. By working the mandibles, or by drawing the feather through the bill in one continuous action, the bird cleans the feather and interlocks any separated barbs. When oiling the feathers, the bird will touch the oil gland with its bill. This oil may be applied directly by the bill, or it may be transferred to the foot and

Preening and Oiling

then applied. Preening is needed not only for comfort and appearance; more importantly, it is essential to maintaining maximum aerodynamic efficiency.

Fighting Reflections

Most of us have seen a robin, cardinal, mockingbird, or some other species wage a relentless battle with its own reflection in a hub cap, bumper, window, or similar reflective surface. This is an act of territorial defense. The bird (usually a male) looks upon the reflection as an intruder and is doing his best to chase it away. The battle may persist for days, and the only way to stop it is by covering the reflective surface.

Attracting More Birds to Your Garden

To me, the most exciting aspect of garden bird watching is managing the garden so that it will continue to attract an increasing number and variety of birds. This can be done without interfering with the aesthetic values of any landscaping plans. Remember this main point: birds are attracted to an area that provides them with the means of survival. There are obvious differences in the needs of birds, and the garden that provides a variety of food, cover, and nesting sites will attract the greatest numbers.*

Keeping Records of the Birds in Your Garden

Whether you keep any other bird records or not, you will find much pleasure in keeping a few simple records of the birds about your garden. Over a period of years you will be interested in knowing the total number of species you have seen in your garden, the total for each year, and the arrival and departure dates for certain species. If you do not start keeping these records now, there will be many times in the future when you will wish you had done so.

More complete information on record keeping will be found in Chapter 17, "Techniques Afield."

* At this point I can do no better than to recommend my own book, *The New Handbook of Attracting Birds,* 2nd ed. (New York: Alfred A. Knopf, 1960). It contains detailed information on numerous projects that will attract birds to your garden.

During the cold days of winter, all life must yield to the demanding laws of nature. The falling snow, the biting winds, and, above all else, the bitter cold rule the land with a violence and a tenacity unknown to other seasons. For birds, and all other creatures of the wild, there is but one law: survival. And survival is not easy, for a single life endures only as long as it can find sufficient food and escape its natural enemies. The constant search, the incessant hunt, the capture or the escape—life and death—these are the judicial decrees in the applied law of survival.

The white world of winter belies its serenity; it is not kind. Its grip upon the land is unrelenting and without mercy. Deep snows cover food and shelter, but it is now that winter wildlife demands an abundance of food to maintain body temperatures, and adequate shelter to protect it from the intense cold and ever-searching predators. It is not a season of reproduction, and all plant life lies dormant in the cold grasp of winter. All life must subsist on the harvest that remains from the previous growing season.

Despite the demands and cruelties of winter, the outdoor community survives. The number of inhabitants it can support is limited in many ways. Some hibernate and live off their accumulated fat; others stay secluded within protective shelters and feed from their granaries of stored seeds and nuts. Most species of birds have migrated to a warmer climate and a more abundant food supply. Those

14 Watching Songbirds in Winter

that replace them from farther north are fewer in number and variety; like the permanent residents, they are specially adapted to survive in a winter environment.

Winter Bird Populations

The preparation for the onslaught of winter begins as the lush growth of summer slows and the cooler days of autumn become noticeable. Leaves build a corklike separation layer of cells at the base of their stems; the leaves are sealed, and chlorophyll is no longer produced. Without the dominant greens, other pigments present in the leaves now appear. The yellow carotene in the leaf cells of the aspens, birches, and shaded sugar maples gives them a golden hue. The sugar-rich cells in the leaves of maples, oaks, and sumacs bring out the varying shades of red and purple, their brilliance depending upon the amount of exposure to the sun. Bright sunny days and cool nights produce autumn's most colorful displays. Frost crystals penetrate the cells of the separation layers and loosen the leaves, which flutter to the ground and are gradually returned to the soil.

Preparation for winter continues. Woodchucks fatten on the last growth of clover; white-footed mice build their caches of acorns, beechnuts, and seeds from maples, pines, wild cherries, tulip trees, dogwoods, knotweed, and other local plants. The squirrels have stored or buried a supply of acorns, hickory nuts, and walnuts. The furred animals have acquired a heavy winter coat, and the birds—most of the birds have departed for warmer climates.

Food, either directly or indirectly, is associated with all the climatic and geographical factors that influence bird migration. It is known that shortening or lengthening of of the periods of daylight brings about certain biological changes in birds that are directly allied with migratory movements. But it is equally true, and perhaps just as influential, that days with fewer hours of daylight provide less feeding time during the season when it is needed most.

Robins, bluebirds, house wrens, catbirds, chipping sparrows, hermit thrushes, and palm warblers may be considered common winter residents in the more southern states, but with the exception of a few stragglers, they will be absent from the northern regions. States in the northern half of the country will experience an influx of slate-colored juncos, evening grosbeaks, and a number of other species. The terns and plovers that were common along the New England coastline during the summer have gone, but from the beach we can see flocks of mergansers, scoters, old-squaws, and other sea ducks.

And so it is in every habitat. There is a constant fluctuation in populations that makes winter bird watching an ever changing and challenging experience.

From the viewpoint of bird watching, there are some rather obvious advantages in maintaining winter feeding stations around your home or garden.* First of all, birds attract birds. A flock of birds at a feeder (even if they are mostly house sparrows) will attract additional species, often ones you didn't know were in the area. Second, winter feeding affords the opportunity for exceptionally close observation. This fact should be kept in mind when locating your feeders. Place your feeders where they can be watched from a convenient window. A number of well-placed feeders will bring you daily companionship and opportunities for intimate studies of your favorite species.

"In regard to food preference, the species attracted by an artificial food supply can be divided into two general classes: insect-eating birds such as woodpeckers, brown creepers, and warblers, and seed-eating birds like the sparrows and juncos. A definite grouping cannot be made, as some species, including the blue jays, chickadees, and nuthatches, eat both types."†

Feeding Birds in Winter

Feed and Feeders

* The information included here is covered in much greater detail in my *The New Handbook of Attracting Birds*, 2nd ed. (New York: Alfred A. Knopf, 1960). It includes complete information on preferred foods, species attracted, feeders and how to build them, plantings, etc. The subject is presented here only as an aid to bird watching.

† *Ibid.*, p. 27.

What to feed: Insect-eating birds are exceptionally fond of beef suet. It is a particular favorite of woodpeckers, chickadees, brown creepers, nuthatches, and blue jays. In addition, most seed-eating species welcome bits of this body-warming fat on exceptionally cold days. Peanut butter (the chunky type is best) is another cold-weather favorite. It is eaten by most of the species that enjoy suet.

Commercial birdseed mixtures are available now in most grocery stores. These mixtures are satisfactory if you have just a few birds around, and you feed modestly or only sporadically. They are usually loaded with inexpensive kaffir corn—a second-choice food at best. For an extensive feeding program, you will find it advantageous (and less expensive) to buy your seeds separately and compound your own mixture. With a little experimentation, you can soon develop a formula that will be most satisfactory for the numbers and varieties of birds in your area. Any mix should contain an abundance of sunflower seeds, because they are eaten avidly by so many species—chickadees, nuthatches, tufted titmice, cardinals, purple finches, evening grosbeaks, and others. In fact, you will probably find it more satisfactory to provide the sunflower seeds separately. With certain types of feeders, you can make the seeds available to chickadees and other small birds without having them devoured quickly by the ravenous blue jays or squirrels.

In experimenting with any mixture, you will find that hemp seed is favored as much as sunflower seeds. It has an oily texture and is most popular on the coldest days. For juncos, white-throats, tree sparrows, redpolls, and other small-seed eaters, any of the millets are excellent. A small amount of cracked corn can be used, but it will be eaten mostly by house sparrows and blue jays.

Cautions: An intensive feeding program is likely to attract more birds to a given area than the area can support by natural foods alone. For this reason, once the program is started, it should be continued unabated throughout the winter. Also, remember that birds need a certain amount of grit to help digest their food. During extended periods of heavy snow, some sand, fine gravel, or crushed shells (available from most food stores) should be mixed with the grain or made available separately. Birds have been known to "starve" amid an abundance of food because they couldn't digest it.

Feeders: There are many and varied bird feeders on the market; some are more aesthetic than practical. If you are handy with tools, you may want to build your own. You can be as ingenious as your skills permit.

For the purpose of watching birds, the glass-topped window feeder is ideal. Chances are, you won't be able to purchase one that suits you (or fits your window) exactly as you might wish. You may have to build it yourself, or have a carpenter build it for you from your design. The glass top not only protects the food from the weather, but it helps light the entire interior of the feeder. This is important for observation purposes, particularly if any windowsill photography is planned. There is no need to put a back in the feeder, so it can be filled quite easily from within the house. The glass top should extend at least 2 inches beyond the feeder's base. This will carry any water runoff beyond the food.

The window feeder will attract a greater variety of birds if containers for suet and peanut butter are placed on the interior ends. Thus, with a mixture of seeds, plus suet and peanut butter, your feeder will contain at least one favorite food for any species that may be in your area.

Birds are individualists. Some are docile and tame; others are wild and unapproachable. Some are considerate and sociable; others are scrappy and belligerent. Some will become pets, and others enemies. As you watch your feeders throughout the winter, your emotions will run the gamut from love to hate. But this is the excitement of winter bird watching—the excitement that will have you looking out the window at every opportunity.

One of the first things you will discover is the manner in which various species approach the feeders. (A little food scattered on the ground beneath a new feeder will help the birds discover the source quickly.) The chickadee is bold and inquisitive, and probably will be your first customer. It is quick of flight, and at first it will dart in, grab a sunflower seed, and fly to a nearby tree to extract the

Watching Birds Feed

kernel. Later, and when the feeder is not occupied by other birds, it will be content to sit on the edge of the feeder and hammer open several seeds in succession. The nuthatch approaches the feeder with an undulating flight, landing on the upcurve. It, too, prefers to open its prize in a nearby tree. House sparrows flock in quickly, eat greedily, and flash away at the slightest provocation. Redpolls or evening grosbeaks may settle on the feeder in flocks. Blue jays flash in with a lot of color and noise, and will command the feeder until they have their fill. The juncos and white-throated sparrows are somewhat docile; they gather gradually and will feed contentedly until disturbed by a more dominant species.

In addition to your grain feeders, you undoubtedly will want at least one suet feeder on the trunk of a tree where it can be easily observed. Here again, it is interesting to watch the methods of approach. The quick little chickadee and the domineering blue jay will fly directly to the suet. The nuthatch will land above the suet and approach it head first in a squirrellike manner. The downy woodpecker comes in with an undulating flight and lands somewhere near the suet, usually above it. The downy seems to have a nonchalant attitude about the whole procedure, pecking about the tree as though it were unconcerned with anything else. After occasionally jerking its head in a quick side-to-side fashion, it will hitch down the tree to the suet. By contrast, the brown creeper will land below the suet and spiral its way upward. It is a bit reluctant to leave a tree to feed, but on occasion it will accompany the chickadees to a window feeder. A bit of peanut butter will make the creeper a steady customer.

You will soon become aware that the "table manners" of various species (and individuals) vary considerably. The task of opening a sunflower seed, for example, is done in several ways. The chickadee holds the seed with its feet and hammers it open with a number of blows from its sharply pointed bill. The nuthatch, being more resourceful, wedges the seed in a crevice and then proceeds to open it. The nuthatch is also quite provident; it will carry seeds from your feeder and store them in small cracks or behind pieces of bark in a favorite tree. These are often discovered and stolen by other nuthatches, chickadees, or blue jays—an act of thievery that is the cause of many a backyard scrap.

Cardinals and purple finches turn the sunflower seed in their bills as they apply pressure from their strong, sharp mandibles. They retain the kernel and let the split hulls roll out either side of their mouths. Evening grosbeaks simply pressure the seeds open with their powerful beaks, and can open them just about as rapidly as they can pick them up. The grosbeaks (also redpolls and pine siskins) are rather sporadic in their winter movements. One winter you may be overwhelmed with them, and then not see a single one the following winter. This fluctuation in numbers is generally attributed to severe climatic conditions and the availability of food in their northern range.

Sunflower seeds are not a problem for blue jays. The jays may be content to sit on the edge of the feeder and open a few seeds, but when nervous or in a hurry, they will gobble them down whole in rapid succession.

A certain pecking order—which species dominates which other species—will be noticeable among the birds at your feeders. This order of dominance can be seen also in a flock of a single species; members of the flock will be subordinate to an individual bird. The order of social preeminence about any feeder will depend upon the numbers and varieies of species attracted.

Two or three blue jays at a feeder are seldom challenged by other species. A flock of evening grosbeaks will take complete possession of feeders filled with sunflower seeds, but invariably scrap among themselves. However, they will yield to the more belligerent jays. The downy woodpecker has little trouble in protecting its favorite suet feeder. The white-breasted nuthatch will not hesitate to exert its dominance over the chickadees and titmice. The finches are great scrappers, and the little pine siskin will defend its feeding spot with all the flurry and pugnacity of a Haitian fighting cock.

One final point about watching your feeders: examine feeding flocks closely, and do not assume they are all one species. This is where you may find the unusual or the rare winter visitor.

The two lists of birds on the opposite page include those species you may see around a winter feeding station in the cold and snowy regions of our eastern states. The first list includes those species that are usually considered normal or common feeders; the second list includes the uncommon species, the stragglers, and the rarities. Both lists are general and, of course, cannot be considered complete for any one given place. A bird that is considered relatively common in one area may be a rarity in another. Also, early and late migrants affect winter populations. Nevertheless, these lists will give you an idea of the fascination and excitement that winter feeding can bring to the bird watcher.

Winter Birdbaths

A supply of water for drinking and bathing* is often just as attractive to wintering birds as a well-stocked feeder. The trick, of course, is to keep the water from freezing. There are two simple ways of doing this: one, for pedestal-type baths, place a light bulb in the top of the pedestal just under the basin; two, for any type of bath, place an electrical aquarium heater (the kind used for tropical fish) directly in the birdbath. All extension cords should be waterproof.

A Winter Walk through Field and Forest

A cold front has passed. The snow stopped falling in the early evening, and the night cleared. The morning is cold with a slight breeze from the north. A light blanket of new snow covers the ground, and the sky seems bluer than ever. It's an invigorating morning to be afield.

We start across the meadow toward the woods. The snow squeaks beneath our feet, but the rising sun promises warmth. The snow has drifted only slightly and clings like powder puffs on the dried thistle heads. Grass and weed stems are weighted down, but they will soon be relieved of their burden by the wind and the sun. The meadow is a barren sea of white, seemingly void of all life.

* Information about the bathing habits of birds can be found in Chapter 13 of this book. For details on the purchasing, building, placing, and maintenance of birdbaths, see McElroy, *The New Handbook of Attracting Birds,* pp. 44–53.

COMMON WINTER FEEDERS

Blackbirds,
    Cowbird, Brown-headed
    Red-winged
Chickadees and Titmice,
    Chickadee, Black-capped
    Chickadee, Carolina
    Titmouse, Tufted
Doves,
    Mourning
Grosbeaks, Finches, Sparrows,
and Buntings,
    Cardinal
    Finch, Purple
    Goldfinch
    Grosbeak, Evening

Junco, Slate-colored
Redpoll, Common
Siskin, Pine
Sparrow, Fox
Sparrow, Song
Sparrow, Tree
Sparrow, White-crowned
Sparrow, White-throated
Jays,
    Blue
Mockingbirds,
    Mockingbird
Nuthatches,
    Red-breasted
    White-breasted

Starlings,
    Starling
Weaver Finches,
    Sparrow, House
Woodpeckers,
    Downy
    Hairy
    Red-bellied

LESS-COMMON WINTER VISITORS

Chickadees,
    Boreal
Grosbeaks, Finches, Sparrows,
and Buntings,
    Crossbill, Red
    Dickcissel
    Finch, House
    Junco, Oregon
    Longspur, Lapland
    Sparrow, Chipping
    Sparrow, Grasshopper
    Sparrow, Harris's
    Sparrow, Lark
    Sparrow, Lincoln

Sparrow, Vesper
Towhee, Rufous-sided
Jays,
    Gray
Orioles,
    Baltimore
Thrashers and Mockingbirds,
    Catbird
    Thrasher, Brown
Thrushes,
    Hermit
    Robin
Warblers,
    Myrtle

Orange-crowned
Palm
Wrens,
    Bewick's
    Carolina
    House

Life? We wonder about the grasshoppers, crickets, and countless tiny insects that were so abundant here just a few months ago. Most of them have succumbed to the first freeze of winter; their grasp on life is now in the dormancy of eggs, larvae, and pupae that must survive the cold and

the endless search of the winter foragers. To some, the cold is a necessity; the eggs of the short-horned grasshopper would not mature without an extended period of low temperatures. They lie dormant in the soil beneath the snow.

Our first bird is a surprise: a wintering meadowlark. It flushes from a clump of ragweed and flies to a fence post across the meadow. We watch it fly. Its wing beat is a rapid flutter. It soars on downcurved wings. Another flutter, a soar, and it lands on the post. We lift our binoculars for a closer look, but the lenses are frosted over. (We should have put them outdoors to adjust to the temperature change while we were having breakfast.)

Our course takes us along the frozen spring ditch that meanders through the meadow. The alder catkins have been a favorite source of food for visiting redpolls, but this morning not one can be found. We settle for a pair of goldfinches, and note their dull olive coloring as they bound away in a pronounced undulating flight. At the far end of the ditch, a sparrow hops and flits about amid the tangle of briers, sedges, and weeds. It has a dark back and a rusty cap. Its throat is nearly white, and its breast a dull gray; it has to be a swamp sparrow. We consider it a lucky find. A number of slate-colored juncos are here, too, feeding on the seeds of ragweed and bristlegrass.

Now we follow the multiflora rose hedge that will lead us to the wood's edge. A fox has preceded us. Its tracks are doglike, but in a straight line. The hind feet step almost exactly into the tracks made by the front feet. The fox has been hunting during the night. Hunger and cold are harsh companions.

The multiflora hedge towers above us, and it must be at least 10 feet wide. The interior is a massive tangle of heavy briers; the outer edges hang red with clusters of tiny rose hips. The hedge provides cover and food for a number of wintering species. If there is a mockingbird in the area, this is where we will find it. (The northward expansion of the mocker's range has coincided with the extended use of the multiflora rose in conservation projects.) This morning we find four—a pair at each end of the hedge. They flit along ahead of us, eventually circling and landing at their starting point. We decide the pairs have definite feeding boundaries, and that they respect each other's territory. A male ring-necked pheasant is sighted momentarily as he runs along the ground beneath the overhanging briers. We wonder how he can travel so fast through this barbed maze. He doesn't flush, and we do not see him again. A flock of about a dozen robins and a lone wintering brown thrasher complete our list for the multiflora rose hedge.

Turning south along the eastern edge of the woods, we welcome the partial protection from the wind and the growing warmth from the sun. An old stone wall divides the forest from the original field boundaries. But now the vegetation extends into the field 30 feet or more; it is a mixture of grasses, weeds, briers, shrubs, vines, and young encroachment trees from the forest—an ideal habitat for birds. The wall, undoubtedly built by the farmers who first cleared the land, is mostly granite that has been rounded and smoothed by glacial travel.

In a large, impenetrable patch of greenbriers, we notice a cluster of birds. Some are obviously juncos, and the others are sparrows of some kind. The pronounced white bib beneath the dark bill, and the narrow-striped crown, tell us they are white-throats. We notice a larger bird deep in the tangle. The first squeak on the back of a hand confirms our suspicion; the inquisitive catbird comes close to investigate. Its survival depends largely on the blue fruit of the greenbrier. Chances are good, for there is an abundance of fruit, which will cling tightly to the briers throughout the winter.

Our first chickadee is not among the trees and shrubs, where we expected it. It is some distance out in the field on the top of a giant mullen stem. As we watch it pick at the seeds, some of which fall and drift across the snow, we get our first lesson of the day in seed dispersal.

Slowly trudging along the wood's edge, we sight a male downy woodpecker (the red head patch is plainly visible) feeding on the white berries of the poison ivy that abounds along the stone wall. Evidently, his search for wood-boring larvae was not rewarding enough for such a cold morning; the berries will sustain him while he resumes his drilling in the freeze-hardened wood. The fruit of the red-osier dogwood hangs in white clusters, and the small prunelike fruits of the black haw still cling to this large viburnum. A branch of a black cherry tree extends across our path. We examine it closely and discover the varnished ringlets of tent caterpillar eggs.

A flock of small birds settles in a red cedar tree far ahead of us. Through binoculars, we note they are sleek and brown, crested, and have a yellow band across the ends of their tails; we add cedar waxwings to our list. There is considerable activity in a large patch of bayberry that extends into the field. Using binoculars from a distance, we see at least two cardinals, another meadowlark, and a number of small birds showing yellow rumps flitting about. This is the field mark of the myrtle warbler. The gray, waxy fruits of the bayberry will be their chief sustenance for the winter. A single call note of "twee" comes from another patch of greenbriers. A male towhee hops on a brier in the open, giving us an excellent view. It is easy to see why the authorities have finally settled on the name of rufous-sided towhee. We wonder why he didn't migrate with the others. He, too, will depend mostly on the fruits of the greenbrier for his winter diet.

A flock of about 50 evening grosbeaks settles in a box elder tree. They are beautiful in the bright sun—a burnished yellow with contrasting black-and-white wings. We watch them feed. They bite the winged seeds off the twigs and extract the kernel in virtually the same motion; the seedless wings spiral down onto the snow. They are quite tame and continue feeding as we pass them by and turn into the woods on an old lumber road.

The cold, tall trees creak and crack from the warming sun and the increasing breeze. Snow falls from the higher crotches and limbs—some in clumps, but mostly filtering down through the branches in a white mist. Compared to the forest's edge, there is little evidence of winter foods.

The tapping of a woodpecker—loud and slow, not the rhythmic drumming of springtime—is our first sign of life. We search the area with our binoculars and discover a male (again, the red head patch) drilling a cavity on the underside of a dead oak limb. Is it a hairy or a downy? He seems large, but could it be just the magnification of our binoculars? We move closer. He *is* large—the size of a robin, and his bill is long and heavy. It is a hairy, without a doubt. He continues drilling his new roosting shelter; this one will be completely protected from future snows of the winter.

Our next find—a lucky one—is also a woodpecker. A shower of snow from a large limb overhanging the trail ahead of us attracts our attention. Through our glasses, we watch a downy woodpecker taking a bath on the snow-covered limb.* It bathes just as though it were in a bath filled with water. The downy pushes through the snow on its chest, and splashes snow over its body with a rapid flutter of wings. We watch two performances, and then it shakes itself dry and wings away to a distant tree.

Continuing along the old woodland road, we add the brown creeper, the white-breasted nuthatch, and several more chickadees to our list. Someone hears a high-pitched "see, see" in the treetops. Two tiny birds flit about nervously and are gone before anyone can make positive identification. We *think* they are kinglets, golden-crowned or ruby-crowned, but they are not added to the list. A pair of blue jays flush from beneath a lone white pine just off the trail. Their startling cry of "thief, thief" causes us to investigate. We expect to find an owl. The owl has gone, but the telltale signs of its having been there are obvious; the fur and skeletal remains of a cottontail rabbit are scattered in the snow. We conclude that the owl—probably a great horned—dropped the remains after gorging itself on the night's lucky kill. Now the jays scavenge among what is left. Tiny tracks and tunnels in the snow tell us that the shrews have been there, too. They will be back if crows do not carry the remains away.

A small brown bird in a pile of brush is obviously a wren, but which one? It doesn't have an eye stripe, and we aren't near a marsh. This eliminates all but the winter wren, or possibly a stray house wren. The tail is just a stub, and its belly is barred crosswise. Our field guide tells us it has to be a winter wren. And there are tracks—large bird tracks—leading away from the brush pile. They are broad

* During all my years of bird watching, I have observed this procedure only twice, both times in Connecticut.

and shallow, and we learn of the ruffed grouse's "snow-shoes"—the spiny feathers that grow on its feet each winter. Did the grouse spend the night in the brush? Not likely; it probably flew into a deep drift (leaving no tracks) and slept beneath the snow.

The old lumber trail leads us to a big, open field, our direct route home. But our attention is once again attracted to the wood's edge; we hear the unmistakable tinkling of tree sparrows—like wind chimes on the back porch. We consult our Peterson guide and verify the "rusty cap" and the "black stickpin." A flock of them was feeding in a large patch of panicgrass. Some would land and feed on the seed heads of the most sturdy stalks; others would glean the seeds that were knocked into the snow. Some would walk out the inclined stems until their weight forced the seed heads down, then they would stand upon the heads and eat.

As we cross the open field toward home, a small flock of snow buntings wheels overhead, skims low over the snow, and lands in a mixed stand of ragweed and bristlegrass. We watch from a distance with our binoculars, and note that their feeding habits are somewhat different from those of the tree sparrows. The snow buntings fly up against the seed heads and knock the seeds loose with their beaks and wings, and then pick the seeds from the snow.

We check the sumacs along the roadside, hoping to add a wintering bluebird to our list. But this morning they must be feeding on something else—perhaps rose hips or bayberries. A lone hawk soars above the field—broad-winged and broad-tailed—one of the buteos. It banks away from us, and the rufous tail can be seen quite clearly. It's a red-tailed hawk for sure, and we wonder about his chances for hunting success on such a cold morning. But this we know: just across the road there is a pot of hot coffee awaiting us; the remainder of our birding will be done from the kitchen window.

As the final song of the wood thrush is hushed by the gentle flow of darkness, a mysterious quietness stills the wild land. The daytime foragers have sought the quiescence of sleep and the protection of the night's enveloping shroud. But for the nocturnal creatures, it is the time of awakening, and the brief moments of silence vanish amid the rising sounds of a newborn chorus. For in darkness, as in light, the pulse of life within the natural community continues unabated.

The incessant buzzing and droning of insects fill the night air. Fireflies have turned the dampened meadow into a twinkling fairyland; the enzymes within their bodies have turned on the cold luciferin lights. Beneath the lone mulberry tree in the garden, we pause and listen to the mellow orchestrations of the snowy tree crickets. They are not soloists, but play in unison—the only insects which do so. Their rhythm depends upon the temperature. We count the wing-against-wing sounds for exactly one minute: 128. We divide this number by 4, add 40, and determine the night's temperature to be 72 degrees. Other insects compete with this novelty orchestra; they buzz, scrape, whir, or drone their songs in an ear-piercing cacophony of vibrations.

But the night does not belong to the insects alone. Nature's more timid creatures find security in the darkness. The mice, voles, and shrews now venture forth in greater numbers. The cooler night air protects certain reptiles and

15 Birds in the Night

amphibians from excessive body evaporation. The cotton-tail rabbit leaves his hide to mate and to feed on the fresh clover and plantain, but the night is damp and still; his scent is followed more easily by the hunting fox. The raccoon, opossum, and skunk are astir, and the muskrat and the mink forage along the water's edge. The deer browses throughout the night.

Birds, too, have a particular role to play in this night-time drama. The black-crowned night herons have left the seclusion of their daytime roosts. Their familiar "quock" can be heard as they fly overhead en route to favorite hunting areas. Nighthawks and whip-poor-wills have replaced the swifts and swallows; the relentless pursuit of flying insects continues. The most feared of all nighttime creatures, the owls, have relieved the day-flying hawks of their predacious task. They glide over field and forest as silently as a passing shadow.

The high-pitched insect orchestra is joined by other stars on the nighttime circuit. From the low wetlands come the more profound chords of the batrachian choir. The gray tree frog trills a musical obbligato, and the great basso profundo, the bullfrog, provides a rhythmic accompaniment of "more rum, more rum, more rum." A discordant note is sounded as an owl screeches defiance at a territorial intruder. But the exhilaration of the night is unrestrained. The solo of the field sparrow descends the scale; the chat whistles; the mockingbird mimics the performers. And from across the pond comes the hysterical laughter of the gallinule, as if the whole performance were a joke.

The night is dark, but the night *lives*.

Owls: The Night Hunters

Owls are the silent marauders of the night. They hunt, and they kill. But this is an essential part of maintaining a functional equilibrium in the outdoor community. They are chiefly rodent eaters, and without this night and day predation by the raptors, the natural environment could suffer from drastic ecological changes. Rodents are prolific breeders, and lacking natural controls, their numbers could soon multiply to devastating proportions. Considering man's interests, owls are among the most beneficial of all bird species, yet they are still persecuted through ignorance and superstition. In addition to rodents, owls do capture a number of other small mammals, reptiles, amphibians, insects, and birds. But we must remember: predators are present in numbers proportionate to the available food supply.

There are eight species of owls that can be considered residents of the eastern United States; four are "eared" (feather tufts), and four are round-headed. They are listed in the table on pages 206–7, together with aids to their identification. All have large heads and big eyes, and appear to be neckless. The best chance for visual observation is at dusk.

Owls are most active at night, secretive, silent-winged, and often quiet except during the nesting season. This combination of factors makes them more difficult to observe than most other birds. If you want to find owls, other than just accidentally flushing an occasional one, you must know something about their preferred habitats and the telltale signs of their presence.

Finding Owls

Always investigate a flock of noisy crows. They seem to delight in tormenting a sleeping owl—especially the great horned. And with just cause, I am sure, because the great horned owl can cause quite a ruckus amid roosting crows. Many a great horned has eaten crow.

Many times, the screech owl will rest in whatever dense cover is nearby when it finishes foraging for the night. Its presence in a decorative evergreen, thick vines, or other heavily shaded spots about our gardens and orchards is frequently revealed by mockingbirds. Once the resting owl is discovered, it is subject to the continuous scoldings and attacks of the wrathful mockers. Yet this little owl is reluctant to leave its daytime perch, not because it cannot see to do so, for owls can see exceedingly well during daylight hours, but because it would be subject to vicious attacks while in flight and at its next resting spot. For this reason, it is often possible to observe the screech owl quite closely during the daytime.

Evergreens, singly or in a cluster in a predominantly

hardwood forest, provide an island of refuge for the woodland owls. Here you may find the great horned, the barred, or a number of long-eared owls. Look for their white splashings, and search the ground for pellets, fur, and feathers. If the evergreens are isolated stands, and you do not find any of these telltale signs beneath them, you can be reasonably sure there are no owls in the area.

Check any large tree (dead or live) that has one or more natural cavities; it may be a nesting tree or a roosting tree. Again, look around the base of the tree and beneath any logical perch for droppings and pellets. If there are indications that owls are present, watch the tree at dusk. It may be an ideal spot for some intensive study. Also, be sure to investigate the area beneath any large nest. Although most owls prefer to nest in cavities, lacking these, they often will appropriate old nests previously inhabited by hawks, crows, or squirrels.

The resting habits of woodland owls vary somewhat. In addition to the screech owl, the great horned and the barred owls may change their resting sites from day to day. But the tiny saw-whet will return to the same bush or limb on succeeding days until it is no longer satisfied with the feeding area. Saw-whets are quite tame, and often can be picked up by hand.

Look for the short-eared owl over marshes, pastures, and sand dune country. It hunts day or night, but is seen most often during the evening and early morning hours. When hunting, it flies just a few feet above the grass and sedges. The more slowly the owl flies, the better its chances are of spotting and capturing an unsuspecting mouse. To maintain a minimum flying speed, it dips and turns, gaining some lift with each erratic maneuver. It will also sit on a post or other low perch and watch a mouse runway in a catlike manner. You can sometimes flush the short-eared from tall grass by making a sharp loud noise, such as clapping your hands or closing your field guide with a sharp "bang." This owl nests and roosts on the ground. Occasionally, resting short-ears will seek the protective cover of available evergreens.

Barn owls are strictly nocturnal, and they are seldom discovered during the daytime. They shun the bright daylight and seek protection in the darkness of old buildings, barns, silos, church steeples, mine shafts, caves, tunnels, and tree cavities. These places are also favored for nesting. Barn owls hunt over open country and are quite tolerant of human habitation. They are chiefly rodent eaters—beneficial friends of the farmers.

Usually, barn owls are found accidentally. Someone discovers a nesting site, and the word soon gets around. If the owls are not disturbed unduly, the site will be used year after year. There are records of the same site being used for a century or longer.

Keeping a nighttime vigil with a family of barn owls is a most interesting experience. It becomes a bit eerie at times as the night's quietness is broken by rasping screams, discordant clackings, the stuttering "ick-ick-ick" of approaching adults, and the contentious hissing of the young. A strong flashlight aids in observation, but it should be used sparingly.

Your best chance of seeing burrowing owls in the eastern part of our country is in central and southern Florida. Look for them around the perimeter of airports, or in the open flatlands of cattle ranches. They can be seen sitting next to their burrows, or on a post, nearly any time of the day, but they are most active during early morning and evening hours. They feed mostly on night-flying beetles and small rodents. Burrowing owls have the peculiar habit of bobbing or bowing when they become concerned about the intentions of the observer.

Owls will respond to the calling methods described elsewhere in this chapter, especially during the nesting season, when they are concerned with the protection of established territories. The calls of owls are distinct and not very difficult to imitate.

Calling Owls

First, study the calls and learn to imitate them with a reasonable degree of accuracy. This can be done by listening to the actual calls at night or to recordings. Then select an area where you have heard owls call, or have seen signs of their presence. Seclude yourself in some cover, or stand against the trunk of a large tree. You are now ready to call *Otus* and *Bubo,* or other members of this night-roaming

IDENTIFYING OUR RESIDENT OWLS

BARN OWL

Description: Best field mark is the white, heart-shaped face. Comparatively small brown eyes. Long legs. Soft rufous and gray-colored back—very light underneath.

Voice: A screaming hiss "kschhh."

Range: In the East—southern New England and the Great Lakes south to the Gulf.

BARRED OWL

Description: Round-headed—no tufts. Barred horizontally on neck and chest, vertically below. Brown woodland owl with brown eyes.

Voice: "hoohoo-hoohooo—hoohoo-hoohooaw," verbally translated as: "Who cooks for you—who cooks for you all?"

Range: Southern Canada south through all of the eastern and central United States.

BURROWING OWL

Description: Screech owl size, but not tufted. Long legs. Often seen in the daytime at the entrance to a burrow or on a fence post. Found around airports and open prairie-type land.

Voice: A soft cuckoolike call of "coo-hoo."

Range: In the East—central and southern Florida. Occasionally in Louisiana.

GREAT HORNED OWL

Description: "Horned" or tufted. Our largest owl—twice the size of a crow. Tufts far apart. White throat.

Voice: A low guttural hoot, "hoo-hooho-hoo-o."

Range: Hudson Bay south through the United States.

LONG-EARED OWL

Description: Tufts closer together and more vertical than on the great horned. Crow-sized. When perched, seems thin and tall. In flight, long wings and tail.

Voice: A soft hoot, "hooo, hooo, hooo."

Range: Central Canada south to Virginia and Texas.

SAW-WHET OWL

Description: A tiny, tuftless, brown owl. Quite tame. Seen most often in winter. Not abundant.

Voice: A rapid and continuous whistling of "too, too, too."

Range: In the East—central Canada, New England, just south of the Great Lakes; in the mountains—south to West Virginia.

SCREECH OWL

Description: Our smallest "eared" owl. Two color phases—red and gray. Common around gardens, orchards, and woodlots.

Voice: A mournful, descending cry of "wheeoo-ooo-ooo-ooo."

Range: Southern Canada south through all of the United States.

SHORT-EARED OWL

Description: *"Ears" are barely noticeable. Round face. Hunts mostly over sloughs and marshes, often in the daytime. Flies low with irregular dipping flight similar to the marsh hawk.*

Voice: *Almost a bark, "kee-yi" or "kee-wow."*

Range: *In the East—the Arctic south to the Illinois and New Jersey line.*

clan. If you keep still, don't be surprised if the investigating owl comes quite close—perhaps closer than you would like. This ruse will work as well during the day, particularly in the nesting territory of the great horned owl.

Owls have an exceptionally keen sense of hearing, and can be lured quite close with high, squeaking sounds that resemble the distress call of a rodent or some other creature.

Owls are an exemplary illustration of adaptation. Every detail of their physical structure contributes to their success as nighttime hunters. Their bodies are light in weight, softly feathered, and aerodynamically designed for swift and silent flight. The eyes are large, with exceptional light-gathering capacity. The eyeballs are elongated and elastic, permitting instantaneous focusing on close or distant objects; pupils can be opened or closed for proper adjustment to light intensity, much like the lens of a camera. The eyes are fixed in a straight-ahead position (which undoubtedly provides good binocular vision and exceptional depth perception), but this is compensated for by extra neck vertebrae which enable owls to turn their heads in an arc of more than 180 degrees.

Special Adaptations of Owls

The hearing of owls is so keen that they can capture by sound alone a mouse hidden beneath the leaves of the forest floor. (This has been proven with captive owls.) The ears (not to be confused with the feathered tufts) lie beneath the facial disk, and face forward. A funnellike feather covering of the ears in many species helps in gathering sounds.

Being largely carnivorous, owls have long, sharp, strong claws for grasping and holding their prey. Their beaks are heavy and hooked for the purpose of tearing. Beetles and small mammals are swallowed whole by adult birds, usually head first. Large mammals are torn or pulled into bite-size pieces. This, of course, is necessary when feeding the very young.

The eggs of owls are white. There is no need for protective coloration, because incubation begins as soon as the first egg is laid. The number of eggs varies from two or three for the great horned and barred owls, to as many as five to eleven for the barn owl. Since incubation begins immediately, there is often a difference in the size of the fledglings. This becomes more noticeable as the young grow larger. If there is ample food available, all may survive. If the food supply becomes relatively scarce for some reason, the older and stronger fledglings will dominate the feeding, and the weaker ones may not survive. This is one of nature's ways of ensuring the survival of the strongest, and of adjusting the surviving numbers to the carrying capacity of the land.

Other Night Hunters

As the owls maintain their constant vigil over forests, fields, and meadows, other segments of the outdoor community are exposed to the forays of additional avian hunters in the night. Whip-poor-wills, chuck-will's-widows, and nighthawks resume their aerial patrols; night herons stalk along the edges of ponds and streams; the woodcock and the snipe probe for earthworms in the mud flats and bottomlands.

Nighthawks make their appearance with the setting of the sun. They feed strictly on airborne insects, and their erratic flight gyrations can be observed over both city and country. Originally, they nested on barren ground and pebbly beaches. (The last ground nest that I observed was in the middle of a cow path in an abandoned pasture.) With the advent of flat gravel roofs on many of our town and city buildings, nighthawks accepted these new man-made "beaches" as ideal nesting sites. They are disturbed less often there, probably, than on the ground. Two eggs, mottled to blend with the background, are laid directly on the gravel, without any supporting nesting materials.

Whip-poor-wills and chuck-will's-widow are more nocturnal, and they, too, feed on the wing, but not exclusively. Their exceptionally large mouths (opening to 2 inches) are used as scoops when flying through swarms of mosquitoes or other insects. Stiff bristles on both sides of their mouths help funnel the insects into the wide openings. Both species prefer to lay their two eggs on the shadowy, dappled forest floor.

With the diminishing light of the day's ending, there is a "changing of the guard" among the herons. As the common egrets and the little blue herons return to their communal roosts in scattered flocks, the night herons can be seen heading toward the fresh-water swamps and tidal marshes, either singly or in small, loose flocks. There is an abundance of food to be harvested—minnows, frogs, toads, aquatic insects, crayfish, and other crustaceans. Night hunting is easy along the water's edge during the season of proliferation.

Even in the darkness of night, every facet of the outdoor community is involved in the continuous struggle for the energy of life. This struggle cannot stop, for the survival of all species depends upon the continued functioning of a dynamic pattern, developed over millenniums.

A number of birds sing at night, but surely the mockingbird is the lead chorister of all the nighttime singers. He is a mimic and a clown. His exultations bubble forth in endless profusion both day and night. His ecstasy reaches its zenith on moonlit nights during the mating season. It is then that he sings incessantly from your TV antenna or the utility wires outside your bedroom window. He denies you sleep, for his song does not have the soothing qualities of a lullaby. It is loud, ebullient, and so intriguingly melodious that it demands your constant attention. His amorous antics are displayed with equal exuberance. Often while singing, he will spring into the air, do a complete somer-

Voices and Sounds in the Night

sault, and return to his perch without missing a single note. At times, the fervor of his courtship seems to reach an exhausting pinnacle, and he will flutter to the ground on stiffened wings.

Perhaps it is the constant rejoicing of the mockingbird that challenges other songsters to emulate his nightly performance. The yellow-breasted chat is a versatile night singer, and often is credited with being quite a mimic. Actually, I think its seemingly endless conglomerate of vocal noises unavoidably includes some notes or calls identifiable with other species. I believe this to be true of the catbird, also—an occasional night singer. The field sparrow joins the night chorus with a single hurried trill as though it had been awakened suddenly and wanted to announce its presence. The grasshopper sparrow is another night singer, but its high-pitched buzz can be mistaken for an insect by the untrained ear. In heavily grassed areas, the quick "flee-sic" of the Henslow's sparrow can be heard sometimes at night. And down in the marsh, we can hear the chatterings of the marsh wrens.

The whip-poor-will and the chuck-will's-widow enunciate their names so clearly and vigorously that they are immediately recognizable. The whip-poor-will's call consists of three distinct syllables, with the accent on the first and last syllables ("whip'-poor-weel'"). The chuck-will's-widow's call is four-syllabled with the accent on the "wid" (chuck-will's-wid'-ow"). The "chuck" is often inaudible when the bird is not close to the observer. While there is considerable variation in the frequency and rapidity of their calls, both species have a habit of embarking on a series of consecutive calls, as though they were competing for the endurance record of their respective species. Alexander Sprunt, Jr., noted ornithologist from Charleston, South Carolina, once counted a sequence of 834 continuous calls by the chuck-will's-widow. It is not uncommon for the whip-poor-will to repeat its name 100 times or more in rapid succession.

The most fascinating ritual of all the night performers is the aerial courtship flight of the woodcock. Every spring, hundreds of birders go afield with the hope of witnessing this exciting show; some are successful, but many are disappointed. If you lack an experienced birding friend who can tell you when and where to go, the following points will increase your chances of success.

• The aerial performances take place during the periods of mating and incubation. This can be as early as mid-winter in northern Florida and Alabama, and as late as early May in Maine. March and April are the most likely months for most of the East. Through friends or literature, determine the time for your area.

• During the day, locate what you believe to be the best possible habitats—alder bogs, brushy meadows, or bottom-lands with low stands of red maples, willows, buttonbush, and similar wetland plants.

• Performances begin shortly after sunset, but will continue into the night when the moon is bright. Select an observation spot where you have a good view of the sky above the bog or meadow. (It is usually impossible to see the preliminary strutting on the ground.)

• Listen! Listen for the giveaway "peent." It will remind you of the "peent" call of the flying nighthawk. Once you hear this, you have reasonable assurance the performance is about to begin.

This is what you will see and hear (based on personal observations in an alder bog along the Machias River in Maine).

The "peent" was repeated several times, and twice I heard a low, guttural, froglike call. (I've no doubt the male was strutting in his most pompous manner for the benefit of his mate, but I could not see this owing to the dim light and thick undercover.) Then a batlike silhouette rose from the alders and began circling higher and higher. All the while, I could hear a whistling sound that seemed to vibrate in the still night air. As the bird gained altitude, the rapidity of the whistling (made by the wings' outer primary feathers) continued to increase until it ended in a blurred twitter at the climax of the bird's ascent, a height of 200 feet or more. The woodcock circled the area twice and then began to spiral downward, but now his song was a sweet, warbling exclamation of his devotion. It continued intermittently until he was a few feet above the alders. He

landed at his point of departure, and immediately resumed his "peent" call. Within two or three minutes, the display was repeated. As I retired to my tent on a high bank along the river, I could hear the courtship performance of the woodcock continue on into the night.

For those of you who would venture afield at night, there awaits a new world of mysterious and enchanting sounds that add the elements of surprise and intrigue to bird watching. The eerie hoot of an owl permeates the darkness with a haunting mysteriousness that will set the mood for the night. A strange winnowing high in the air above the meadow tells you the snipe has returned. A "wak-wak-wak" sound from the marsh causes you to wonder, and the "squawk" of a surprised heron startles you. In the South, the "kuk-kuk-kuk" of cackling coots, the frenzied laughter of gallinules, and the wailing cry of the night bird, the limpkin, remind you of faraway jungles. But there is one night call you never will forget. It is a call from the wild north country—the resonant cry of the loon echoing across a spruce-bordered lake. This is a call that embodies the spirit of wildness and freedom—a call that lures you northward again and again.

Moon Watching

During the height of spring and fall migrations, there is a constant movement of birds both day and night. Hawks, falcons, herons, swifts, and hummingbirds are daytime travelers. The migratory flights of geese, ducks, loons, gulls, terns, and shore birds can be observed day or night. But the great majority of our songbirds do their most extensive traveling in the protective hours of darkness. In the daytime they rest, feed, and renew their energy for the continuing journey.

On nights when migrations are at their fullest, there are many more birds in the air than we realize—hundreds of thousands of them at the same time. Many of these night migrants can be observed through a spotting scope as they pass the face of the moon. The first systematic approach to obtaining practical figures that would indicate the density of night migrants on a nationwide basis was conducted by

Louisiana State Universtiy in the 1950's. In October, 1952, more than 1,500 "moon watchers" manned nearly 700 observation stations throughout the country. The numbers and directions of flight silhouettes against the moon were recorded and reported on special forms. Then through a series of complicated formulas, involving time, location, angles, a constantly moving moon, etc., it was possible to express the results in a theoretical total indicating the number of passing birds per mile of front per hour. The following examples will give you the number of birds (to the nearest hundred) passing a mile front during the hour between 9 and 10 o'clock on the night of October 3, 1952, for the stations indicated: South Hadley, Massachusetts, 2,400; Brooklyn, New York, 1,600; Moorestown, New Jersey, 4,600; Charlotte, North Carolina, 8,600; Robins A.F.B., Georgia, 4,100; Pensacola, Florida (October 2), 28,200.*

This concerted effort, under the supervision of Louisiana State University, gave us not only the first mathematical deduction of our migration traffic rate and density, but it did much to promote the interest of moon watching among amateur birders.

Moon watching is easiest and most enjoyable when the moon is full, or nearly so. During this period you have the largest area to observe, and the complete circular shape of the moon simplifies the recording of flight directions on a clock-face basis. Past observations indicate that the largest number of birds is on the move during the middle of the night.

Selecting a Time and Place to Watch

The place of observation should be an open area where you can follow the course of the moon without the interference of trees, buildings, or other obstructions. Avoid areas where street lights or automobile headlights interfere. The quieter the area, the better will be your chances of hearing and identifying flight calls. Within city limits, flat-roofed buildings are usually the best locations for observation stations. Of course, moon watching will be most exciting if your point of observation happens to be on a

* Robert J. Newman and George H. Lowrey, Jr., *Selected Quantitative Data on Night Migration in Autumn* (Baton Rouge, La.: Museum of Zoology, Louisiana State University, 1964).

EQUIPMENT NEEDED FOR MOON WATCHING

Spotting scope with 20x eyepiece
Sturdy tripod with telescope mount
Lens tissues (for mist or condensation)
Adjustable lawn chair (comfort is essential)
Pillow (for that final adjustment)
Warm clothing
Watch
Flashlight
Notebook and pencils
Insect repellent (a precautionary item)

major flyway; but this is not essential. For just the fun of it, your own backyard may provide all the excitement you wish. Certainly the results will be of greater personal interest.

Procedures The first requisite of moon watching is the comfort of the observer. It is impossible to maintain continuous or accurate observations if you have to keep twisting your head or body to see through the scope. You can't operate from a standing position except for momentary sightings. These are the reasons for using a lawn chair and a pillow. An adjustable, aluminum-framed, webbed lawn chair is ideal; it is light in weight and folds for easy transportation.

Moon watching is much more fun if the station is manned by two or more people. In fact, if accurate records are to be kept, this is almost essential. One person acts as observer while another does the recording. The following steps will help you get set up in an efficient manner.

• Face your chair toward the moon. If the moon is kept slightly to the left of the chair, you can watch it for a longer period of time without having to readjust the chair's position.

• Mount the scope securely on the tripod. For best results, make sure the eyepiece does not exceed 20x. Greater power will not permit you to view the entire moon at one time, and the light collected is too brilliant for continuous viewing.

• Position the tripod over the chair so that the ocular is somewhere near the desired viewing position. Depending on the leg spread of your tripod, you may have to invert the center post to get the scope low enough.

• The observer (now in position) makes the final adjustments to bring the ocular to the viewing eye. A pillow beneath the observer's head adds comfort and a certain degree of stability, and it can be used to raise or lower the head slightly for this final adjustment.

• Focus on the moon. Start with the moon at the left edge of your field of view. You can make continuous observations until the moon begins to move off the right edge of the field.

• Readjust the chair's position until the moon is again at the left edge of the field of view.

Passing birds will appear as small, fast-moving silhouettes against the bright background of the moon. Some will be recognizable as to families, but most will not. Some birds will be in sharp focus, and others will seem hazy. Most crossings are made in a fraction of a second, the speed depending largely on the bird's distance from the scope—the nearer the scope, the smaller the viewing plane.

Recording Results

Record keeping is a matter of choice. You may want to moon-watch for the pure fun of it, or you may be interested in accumulating some comparative records for your area. Picture the moon as an imaginary clock face, 6 o'clock being at the bottom nearest the horizon. The observer will call out the passing of birds—for example, "Bird 9 to 3." This means a bird is passing the face of the moon in a direction from 9 o'clock to 3 o'clock. The recorder makes this notation. Sightings are usually blocked into time periods of 30 or 60 minutes. Field notes can be transferred to circular diagrams with arrows indicating directions and numbers.

With experience, you will be able to recognize certain passing silhouettes and identify some of the chips and pipes of the flight calls. Moon watching adds a new dimension to birding by providing a visual conception of the magnitude of migration.

16 Using Binoculars and Scopes

With so many makes and models of binoculars on the market today, the beginning birder is bound to experience a sense of frustration when making a selection. Good binoculars are comparatively expensive—so much so that few of us can afford a hit-or-miss method of buying until a satisfactory instrument is found. The purpose of this chapter is to help you develop an understanding of binoculars so you can make the right purchase the first time, and to help you acquire a knowledge of their use for the utmost in enjoyment. In birding, as in any other activity we might pursue, the most satisfactory results are obtained through the intelligent use of good equipment which fulfills the needs of the individual participant. Binoculars are designed for various purposes, and many of them are not practical for birding.

Generally speaking, there are three types of instruments to choose from: the nonprismatic "field glass," the prism binocular with individual eyepiece focusing, and the prism binocular with center focusing. The nonprismatic "field glass" is basically two simplified telescopes—tubes with a concave eye lens in one end and a convex objective lens in the other. They are not powerful enough to be practical because, as the magnification increases, the size of the area that can be viewed diminishes rapidly. These glasses are of little value for bird watching and are a sheer waste of money, no matter how cheap.

Prism binoculars with individual eyepiece focusing are good for distant viewing only. Once each eyepiece is accurately set, everything from the horizon to as close as 40 or 50 feet will be in focus. For birding, they are satisfactory for offshore viewing of water birds and for watching migrating hawks. They are of no help in observing a warbler flitting about in a nearby tree; the individual focusing of each eyepiece is just too time-consuming to be of any use in such situations.

The most practical binocular for birding is the prism type with a central focusing mechanism. By the slight movement of finger or thumb, one can observe at a distance or close-up. Remember: a good binocular is a lifetime investment, and the center-focusing type automatically compensates for any changes in the condition of your eyes. This is definitely the type of binocular the beginning student should buy—the type that will be considered in the remainder of this chapter.

Choosing Binoculars for Birding

Select the Right Type

The main purpose in using binoculars for birding is to produce an enlarged image of birds at various distances so that their colors and physical features are recognizable. The degree of clarity and brightness of this enlarged image is, therefore, one of the most important features to be considered when selecting a binocular. Second, you want a binocular that will not cause unnecessary eyestrain when used for prolonged periods of time. Eyestrain can be associated with clarity, alignment, and magnification. These features (and how to check them for quality) will be discussed in more detail in the section that follows.

Consider These Features

Of course, one expects durability in any product. Quality binoculars should last a lifetime if they are not dropped, immersed in water, or otherwise abused. Quality is determined by such things as the type of glass used, the manner of mounting prisms and lenses, and the precision of moving parts; it must be built in by the manufacturer. Unfortunately, quality (or the lack of it) is difficult to detect in the store. Even the cheapest models have a "quality look" on the outside, but it's what's on the inside that counts. For this reason, the prospective buyer should have some knowledge of how to test for quality (see following discussion of numbers and terms).

Buy from a Reputable Dealer

Today, it is possible to buy binoculars in drugstores, souvenir shops, tourist centers, discount houses, and similar purveyors of "quick-buck" items. Binoculars carried by this type of merchandiser are likely to be of inferior quality, overpriced, and without recourse in the event of dissatisfaction. Buy from a reputable dealer and choose from proven brand names. Check such items as the length of the guarantee, return or exchange privileges if not satisfied, and procedures for repairs in case of damage. You are making a sizable investment, so protect yourself with all the surety possible. Also, remember that the man behind the counter is primarily a salesman; he probably knows little about binoculars other than price. The final responsibility is yours.

Understanding Numbers and Terms

We hear people speak of "seven by thirty-five" binoculars, or we see it written as "7x35." What do these numbers mean? Basically, they are a simple numerical designation that will help you select the right binocular for a specific purpose. The 7x indicates the power of magnification; the object being viewed will appear to be seven times closer or seven times larger than it appears to the naked eye. The number 35 is the diameter in millimeters of the front (objective) lens. Thus, a 7x35 binocular is one that magnifies an object 7 times and has an objective lens with a diameter of 35 millimeters.

Power or Magnification

What power binocular is best for birding? Actually, this is a matter of personal choice. What you want is a binocular that is best for *you*. Factors such as the condition of your eyes, whether you wear glasses or not, and the steadiness of your hands should be considered. Your choice will undoubtedly be one of the following: 6x30, 7x35, 8x40, or 9x50. Remember: the greater the power, the more difficult it is to hold the glass steady. When using binoculars of 9 power and above, such movements as breathing and heartbeat can cause your image to "jump." This is hard on the eyes. Anything above a 9 power should be supported by a tripod or rest.

The most popular binocular among birders is the 7x35. This seems to be the most practical compromise of power and the size of the area being viewed. Personally, the 7x35 is my favorite; the 8x40 is my second choice.

How to check: The proclaimed power of a binocular can be checked by a simple method of viewing. With the binocular on a rest or tripod, focus on a distant single object such as a shrub or post. Now, view the object with one eye looking through one side of the binocular and the other eye looking along the *outside.* You will see two images—a large one through the binocular and a smaller one with the naked eye. Next, move the binocular slightly until the smaller image is superimposed over the larger one. If you are using a 7 power binocular, the larger image should be 7 times the size of the smaller one.

A binocular's field of view is simply the width of the viewed scene at a designated distance (1,000 yards is the accepted standard for comparative distance). It is often expressed as a single number, such as 420 feet. This means you see an area 420 feet wide at a distance of 1,000 yards. Within reason, a wide field of view (as opposed to a narrow one) is a desirable feature for birding binoculars; it enables you to locate a bird more easily and to follow it for greater distances without moving the binoculars. The field of view depends partly on power and partly on design. In standard field binoculars of similar design, a simple law of physics applies: the greater the magnification, the smaller the field of view. This is partially compensated for by manufacturers of "wide-angle" or "wide-field" designs. (Field of view is sometimes expressed as the angle between two lines extending from the binocular to the outer edges of the viewed area.) I find the standard field of view of the 7x to be quite satisfactory. When using wide-angle glasses, I have a tendency to become distracted or to lose a small bird in the multiplicity of scenery. The design of wide-angle binoculars requires the use of extra lenses, and they are, therefore, usually more expensive.

Field of View

Caution: Many people believe a wide-objective (front) lens indicates a wide field of view. This is not necessarily so, for the field of view is determined largely by the size of an interior field lens. A large objective lens simply collects more light than a smaller one.

How to check: To compare the field of view of two or more equally powered binoculars, focus each binocular in turn on a distant object or scene that is obviously wider than the area the binoculars could possibly include. Such objects as a long row of buildings, a wide stand of trees, or a distant power line are ideal. The binocular that includes the greatest span on either side of a given center point will have the widest field of view.

Exit Pupil and Light Transmission

If you hold your binocular at arm's length and point it toward the bright sky, you will see a bright disk of light emanating from each eyepiece. This disk of light is known as the exit pupil. It concerns us only in that its area is a measure of the light transmitted (relative brightness) through a particular binocular. Its numerical designation is found by dividing the diameter of the objective lens by the power (exit pupil) and then squaring this quotient (relative brightness). For example, the exit pupil of a 7x35 binocular is 5 millimeters (35 divided by 7), and the relative brightness is 25 (5 squared). Effective light transmission is necessary for brightness and clarity.

Note: If the exit pupil is surrounded by a square shaded area, it is an indication of poor materials or faulty workmanship.

Alignment

Both barrels of a binocular should be optically parallel. When the binocular is adjusted for proper eye width, the image from both barrels should appear as one perfect circle. An instrument that cannot be adjusted to eliminate a double image is obviously not aligned properly. However, slight errors in alignment (and this is often the case with low-cost binoculars) are very difficult to detect because your eyes can automatically compensate for a certain amount of error. This often results in eyestrain, fatigue, or a headache.

How to check: There is no way of being certain your binocular is perfectly aligned without the use of a collimator, an instrument designed especially for this purpose. Most camera shops and repair centers that offer to "clean and check" your binoculars are not equipped to align them. If you have an indication of eyestrain each time you use your binocular, you should have it checked.*

Lens coating: Not all the light that enters the objective lenses gets through to form the image. Part of it is absorbed, but a larger part of it is lost through reflection. This loss can be greatly reduced by coating the glass surfaces with a thin metallic salt. Today, most binoculars have a certain amount of antireflection coating. (It is usually noticeable as a bluish cast when you look into the objective lens.) A quality binocular, with *all* surfaces coated, will reduce reflections as much as 90 percent and increase light transmission at least 50 percent.

Additional Items You Can Check When Selecting a Binocular

Bausch and Lomb, Inc., of Rochester, New York, suggests the following test for determining the amount of antireflection coating: "Hold the binocular so that you look into the large, or objective, end in such position that you can see the reflection of an overhead light bulb. If you hold it right you will see in the objective lens a series of reflections, one for each optical surface of the lens and prism system. Each reflection for a coated surface will be dull and blue or purple. If any internal surfaces are not coated, they will show as a bright reflection in the natural yellowish color of the light."

Distortion: If magnification is not equal throughout the field, straight lines in the viewed object will tend to bulge. Focus on a wall or building; straight lines should appear from edge to edge.

Curvature of field: Again, focus on a wall or building. The image should appear in a flat plane—not curved or bowl-shaped.

Color fringes: Avoid purchasing any binocular that tends

* The best place I know to have this done is the Mirakel Optical Co., Inc., 14 West First Street, Mount Vernon, N.Y. 10550. They will check binoculars free of charge and send you a cost estimate for any necessary repairs. This is a most cooperative and reliable company that has been serving birders for nearly 50 years.

to cast a colored fringe around objects silhouetted against a bright background. This is an indication that the lens system is inferior and cannot focus light waves of different length.

Hinge action: The center hinge (between the two barrels) should have a firm, smooth action. Any looseness will impair proper alignment. Avoid binoculars that show signs of grease at the hinge joints. It is sometimes used as a filler to smooth out nonprecision workmanship.

Weight: Many people are quite concerned about weight when selecting a binocular. This is understandable when you realize that a 7x35 binocular, for example, can weigh anywhere from slightly more than 18 ounces to as much as 40 ounces in the wide-angle models. With standard models, I believe a few ounces of difference one way or the other are of little concern if the remaining features and results are top quality. However, this is a matter for personal consideration. Birding sometimes requires the carrying of binoculars for a matter of hours; then a lightweight one is less tiring—or at least less annoying—than a heavier one.

How to Use Binoculars

It may be difficult to believe, but I have known people—including some birders—who have owned good binoculars for a number of years without understanding all their features, or without knowing how to use them well enough to enjoy their maximum capabilities. The five points that follow (plus the section on care and maintenance) will help you enjoy all the efficiency and quality built into your binocular by the manufacturer.

How to Adjust and Focus

For proper eye width: Not everyone's eyes are the same distance apart. This means there must be some adjustment capable of exactly aligning the eyes and the exit pupils of the binocular. Hold the binocular to your eyes in normal viewing position. Now, with a slight wrist action, swing the barrels around the center post until a single round image is seen when viewing with both eyes. Next, check the setting on the "interpupillary distance scale"—the small calibrations on the end of the center post. (The scale usually represents a possible eye separation of 56 to 76 millimeters.) If you remember this setting, you can automatically adjust your binocular to the proper eye width each time you use it. The only thing to learn here (and this will come automatically with a little practice) is to place the binocular to your eyes with the same amount of pressure each time. In other words, place it in the same position each time. A few millimeters' variation in distance from the eye pupil will tend to distort the field of view, and you will begin to question your original setting.

If you are buying binoculars for children, make sure they can be set for the normally shorter interpupillary distances.

For difference in eye strength: Binoculars have an adjustment to compensate for eyes of unequal strength or vision. You will notice only one eyepiece is independently adjustable (we are still talking about center-focusing models only), and that it has a scale marked off in diopters, the optical measuring unit for spherical power. To adjust your binocular for any difference in the strength of your eyes, first, using the lens cover or your hand, cover the objective lens which is on the same side as the adjustable eyepiece. (Some are on the right, others on the left, depending on the manufacturer.) With both eyes open to avoid distortion by squinting, look through the binocular and, using the central focusing mechanism, focus on a distant object until it is sharp and clear. Now, transfer the cover to the other objective lens. Again, with both eyes open, but this time using the adjustable eyepiece, focus on the same object until it is again clear. Your binocular is now properly focused for your use. Now, all you have to do is use the central focusing mechanism to focus for various distances. *Note:* The individual eyepiece setting can be considered permanent. The scale reading should be noted and checked occasionally, as it may be accidentally moved by handling or in moments of excitement.

There is no special grip (as with golf clubs) for holding binoculars. The main objective is to hold them *as steadily as possible*. This is accomplished best through *practice* and *concentration*. You will be surprised at how a "jumping" image will settle down if you *think about holding the*

How to Hold

glasses still. It is quite difficult to maintain a steady image of a bird and try to tell someone else what it is at the same time. Of course, it helps if you can rest your elbows on some rigid object such as a car top or fence. Otherwise, the best you can do is tuck your arms in against your body for a little extra support, and concentrate.

I find that I can gain a little extra steadiness, when needed, by making sure the eyepieces are firm against the bone below the eyebrows and then extending my thumbs against the cheekbones. This, of course, will not work if you wear glasses.

If You Wear Glasses

Binoculars with single-depth eyecups are designed to be worn without eyeglasses. They are constructed so the exit pupil (the smallest diameter of the emerging light rays) is on the same plane as the pupil of eye—9 to 11 millimeters in front of the ocular lens. If you wear eyeglasses and use this type of binocular, the fixed-depth eyepieces and the normal protrusion of your glasses keep the exit pupils and your eye pupils some distance apart. This results in a restricted field of view. Fortunately, most manufacturers now recognize this problem, and you can buy binoculars with adjustable eyecups or with eyecups especially designed for use with eyeglasses. If you must wear glasses, avoid buying binoculars with fixed-depth eyecups.

Adjustable eyecups are usually made of rubber that can be turned back, or of plastic that screws inward, permitting the ocular lens to be brought closer to the eyeglasses. For use without glasses, the eyecups are left extended and help shade the eyes from extraneous light.

Positioning and holding binoculars against eyeglasses requires a bit more caution than placing them against the naked eye. Here's the way to do it: grip both barrels of the binocular with three fingers, leaving the thumb and index finger extended somewhat inward toward you. As you raise the binocular into viewing position, the extended thumbs will make the initial contact against your cheekbones; the index fingers should be extended and braced against your brow just above the eyes. The binocular can now be eased into position against your eyeglasses. This gives you a firm hold for steady viewing.

If there is any problem associated with the use of binoculars, it is most likely to be the difficulty experienced by many beginners: spotting a bird with the naked eye and then trying to locate it quickly through binoculars. On most any field trip, there are usually at least two or three people who consistently fail to locate a bird before it is gone. If you watch them, they can be seen weaving their heads in all directions trying to find a reference point; some even have difficulty in finding the right tree. There is a reason for this, and I shall try to analyze it here so you can avoid this rather embarrassing situation.

Invariably, the problem develops when the observer takes his eyes off the bird or reference point and looks down to find his binocular. It is compounded when the observer puts the binocular to his eyes as he raises his head. He is now blinded to the original reference point, and he must search the landscape until he finds it. The following points will help you avoid this problem.

First, when you spot the bird, notice some reference point next to it, such as the tip of a branch, a forked limb, some colored leaves, or a knothole. In other words, you are making a quick mental note of where the bird is. At the same time you are reaching for your binocular, if it is not already in your hand. (You know where it is, and there's no need to look for it.) Lift the binocular into position (you are still watching the bird, or the spot where it was last seen), holding it as nearly as possible at the same angle as your line of sight. With a little practice, all this will be done simultaneously in a fraction of a second. Practice on a stationary object; you will soon find you can center it in your field of view every time.

There is a slight variation of this procedure that is equally effective. As you continue to watch the bird or the reference point, lift the binocular to a point in front of your eyes so that you are sighting the bird across the top of the barrels. Now, bring the binocular to regular viewing position. You should not lose the bird with this slight transition.

There are three things that should influence the way you carry your binocular when going into the field. First of all, you want it ready for instant use. This means it must

How to Sight
Birds
through Binoculars

be out of the case and have all lens covers removed. Also, it should be adjusted to the predetermined settings for interpupillary distance and any difference in eye strength. Second, you will be carrying a sizable investment, so you want to avoid the possibility of damage. Finally, you will want to carry it with the least amount of annoyance and discomfort.

How to Carry Binoculars

Most birders carry their binoculars by simply placing the carrying strap around the neck. (I know of a few who prefer to carry them over one shoulder. This may be more comfortable, but surely less safe.) Carrying straps are often too long for maximum comfort. The binocular should rest high on your chest and not on your tummy. Also, long straps permit the binocular to dangle and swing dangerously, especially when you have to stoop to go under an obstruction. Straps can be shortened by tying a knot in the center, but this is a temporary measure at best. If you have qualms about cutting off one end of the strap and replacing the fastener, have your local shoe repairman do it.

L. L. Bean, Inc., of Freeport, Maine, sells an over-the-shoulder and around-the-waist type of harness designed to keep binoculars or cameras snug against the chest, but ready for quick use. It is called a Kuban-Hitch. The price: about $6.00 postpaid.

In order to enjoy the clearest and sharpest image your binocular can produce, it will be necessary to keep it absolutely clean—just as you would your camera lens. You are concerned with cleaning the exterior surfaces only.

How to Care for and Maintain Binoculars

Steps in Cleaning Binoculars

• First, blow on the exterior lenses to remove any grit or loose dirt.
• Second, brush the lenses with a soft camel's hair brush (available in any camera store).
• Third, if a haze or film remains, breathe on the lenses and wipe carefully with a *clean*, soft cloth. Make sure the cloth does not contain any grit or dust from previous use or storage. Keep your cleansing cloth in a plastic envelope.

226   THE HABITAT GUIDE TO BIRDING

- Fourth, if fingerprints or stains still persist, add one or two drops of alcohol to the cleansing cloth.
- Fifth, wipe dust and dirt from all metal surfaces, especially the moving parts—ocular tubes and adjustable eyepiece.

- Handle with care. Don't bump or jar binoculars, as this may ruin the alignment.
- Never take binoculars apart for any reason. This is one sure way of ruining the alignment and nullifying any warranty you may have.
- Do not oil. Oil collects grit and also thins the original lubricant, causing looseness and poor alignment.
- Keep clean. Fingerprints or stains can eventually cause permanent damage. Check the interior for dust or dirt particles by looking through the objective lens at various angles. Have the interior cleaned by a qualified optical concern only.
- Store your binocular in a dry place. If you use it only occasionally, and live in a hot or humid climate, remove it from the case and leave both the case and the binocular exposed to the light. This will help prevent the growth of fungus—usually first noticeable on the interior of the lenses.
- Always place your binocular in the case in the same position it was when you first unpacked it.

Maintaining Binoculars

I have been field-testing a variety of binoculars for a period of several months. The condensed results of these tests printed here (representing only four makes) are intended solely as a guide and as a comparative basis upon which you can base your own selection. There are a number of binoculars available, other than those included here, which will undoubtedly produce equally satisfying results. For obvious reasons, not all makes and models could be tested, nor the total results printed, short of doing a complete book on the subject. The binoculars represented here were selected on the following basis:
- All were established, proven, quality products.

Some Results of Field Testing

• For fairness in comparative results, only one model, the 7x35, was tested.

• They represent a fair range in price.

• They include innovations in features and design.

• They represent the three countries manufacturing quality binoculars—the United States, Germany, and Japan.

I would hasten to mention here that these findings represent my personal analysis based on in-the-field use for the purpose of birding only. I am sure not all birders, manufacturers, and retailers will agree with me. (Some have disagreed already.) But results of field tests are not changed by personal opinion.

Four binoculars and their specifications are listed in the table opposite, as well as being discussed below.

• Bausch & Lomb binoculars have always enjoyed the honor of being among the world's finest. Much of this reputation, I am sure, is based upon their ruggedness and durability, for they are truly a lifetime investment. I know a number of birders who have used their same B & L binoculars for more than forty years.

When field-testing the Bausch & Lomb—7x35, I found such things as clarity, image definition, and brightness to be all that company laboratory reports claimed. However, I did find that most beginning students had more difficulty in locating a given object with this binocular than with several competitive brands. I believe this was due mostly to the smaller field of view, but partially to the comparatively smaller eyepiece and ocular lens. This smaller eyepiece seems to fit "into" the eye (for non-eyeglass wearers) rather than the eye fit into the eyepiece. Students had a tendency to rest the smaller eyepiece against the eyeball, thus restricting its ease of movement.

These findings are somewhat minor and should be weighed against the other qualities of this glass.

Although Bausch & Lomb no longer manufacture a binocular line in Rochester, New York, I have included this binocular in this listing because their models, including the 7x35, are so popular and no doubt will be available in stores for some time. Since June, 1973, they have been importing a 7x35 model made to their specifications, which

BAUSCH & LOMB—*7x35*

Magnification:	*7x*
Objective diameter:	*35mm*
Field of view:	*382**
Exit pupil diameter:	*5mm*
Relative brightness:	*25*
Weight:	*22 ounces*
Retail price:	*$269.00†*

LEITZ—*Trinovid 7x35B*

Magnification:	*7x*
Objective diameter:	*35mm*
Field of view:	*450**
Exit pupil diameter:	*5mm*
Relative brightness:	*25*
Weight:	*18.3 ounces*
Retail price:	*$411.00†*

BUSHNELL—*Custom Insta-focus 7x35*

Magnification:	*7x*
Objective diameter:	*35mm*
Field of view:	*420**
Exit pupil diameter:	*5mm*
Relative brightness:	*25*
Weight:	*23 ounces*
Retail price:	*$137.50†*

MIRAKEL OPTICAL CO.—*Miroptico 7x35*

Magnification:	*7x*
Objective diameter:	*35mm*
Field of view:	*367**
Exit pupil diameter:	*5mm*
Relative brightness:	*25*
Weight:	*20 ounces*
Retail price:	*$39.50†*

* Feet at 1,000 yards. † All prices given in this book were accurate at the time of publication. The reader may use them as a guide in comparing one binocular with another—but should be aware that prices change constantly.

are similar to those of the Rochester-made glass. Retail price: $175.00.

• The Leitz—Trinovid 7x35B, a little binocular, amazed me each time I used it. First of all, I was impressed by the light weight and compactness made possible through a new concept in binocular design. Second, no matter how it was tested, the results were outstanding. The field of view was considerably wider than that found in most standard 7x35 models. The image was bright, clear, and crisp from one edge to the other.

The only external moving parts on the Trinovid are the two wheels on the center hinge—one for eyepiece adjustment and the other for focusing. With true internal focusing, the binocular is sealed against dust and moisture.

The Trinovid's light weight makes it a favorite of the

ladies, but there's a lot more to the instrument than that; it's truly one of the finest binoculars made. If you need a new binocular, and the price is not prohibitive, you should at least give this one a fair test before making any purchase.

• The Bushnell—Custom Insta-focus 7x35 proved to be the most satisfactory of all the medium-priced glasses tested. In fact, it compared quite favorably with some costing twice as much. This Custom 7x35 comes with or without the Insta-focus feature. Personally, I like it and think it's worth the extra ten dollars in price. Insta-focus refers to the central focusing mechanism that operates with the slight movement of the right thumb rather than with the turning of the conventional center wheel. This feature enables you to focus rapidly without changing your grip or without moving the binocular; the focusing device is positioned naturally under your thumb. I found this to be a distinct advantage when viewing something like a fast-moving flock of shore birds.

The wide adjustable eyepieces with the comparatively wider ocular lenses are designed to fit over and around the eyes—not against them. This feature, along with a wide field of view, makes scanning an easy, unrestricted process.

When this binocular is removed from its case for field use, the case makes an ideal carrier for at least two of your favorite field guides; it is exactly the right size and shape.

• For a really cheap binocular, the Miroptico 7x35 is probably the best. As with all binoculars sold by Mirakel, each instrument is checked for alignment and clarity before being shipped. I know numerous birders who use the Miroptico exclusively and are completely satisfied.

Telescopes for Birding

Telescopes are practical for birding when the distance between the observer and the bird being viewed is too great for a definitive image through hand-held binoculars, or when there are special reasons for exceptional close-up observations. The telescopes most useful for these purposes are the prismatic spotting scopes.

Spotting scopes are reasonably compact and portable,

TELESCOPES AND THEIR SPECIFICATIONS

BAUSCH & LOMB—*Balscope Zoom 60*

Zoom lens:	*15x to 60x*
Objective lens:	*60mm*
Field of view:	*150 to 37.5**
Length:	*16-11/16 inches*
Weight:	*48 ounces*
Price:	*$169.95†*

Accessories:

Car window mount:	*$24.95*
Camera adapter:	*$34.95‡*
Carrying case:	*$24.95*

BAUSCH & LOMB—*Balscope Sr.*

Fixed power eyepieces:	*15x, 20x, 30x, or 60x*
Objective lens:	*60mm*
Field of view:	*140 to 28.6**
Length:	*16-7/16 inches*
Weight:	*48 ounces*
Price:	*$139.95† with choice of eyepiece*

Accessories:

Car window mount:	*$24.95*
Camera adapter:	*$34.95‡*
Extra eyepieces:	*$29.95*
Carrying case:	*$24.95*

BUSHNELL—*Spacemaster II*

Zoom lens:	*20x to 45x*
Objective lens:	*60mm*
Field of view:	*120 to 72**
Length:	*11⅝ inches*
Weight:	*36 ounces*
Price:	*$98.50† without eyepiece*

Accessories:

Car window mount:	*$22.50*
Camera body adapters:	*$3.75 or $6.25§*
Camera mount:	*$16.50‖*
Fixed power eyepieces:	*$29.00 and $34.00*
Carrying case:	*$16.95*

BUSHNELL—*Sentry II*

Fixed power eyepieces:	*20x, 32x, and 48x*
Objective lens:	*50mm*
Field of view:	*120 to 45**
Length:	*12⅝ inches*
Weight:	*25.4 ounces*
Price:	*$74.50† with choices of lens*

Accessories:

Car window mount:	*$22.50*
Camera body adapter:	*$3.75 or $6.25§*
Camera mount:	*$16.50‖*
Extra eyepieces:	*$26.00*
Carrying case:	*$16.95*

---

* Feet at 1,000 yards.

† All prices given in this book were accurate at the time of publication. The reader may use them as a guide in comparing one telescope with another—but should be aware that prices change constantly.

‡ Any SLR camera.

§ Depending on type of SLR camera.

‖ Camera mount and body adapter required for telephotography.

but even so, they are awkward to carry (along with a tripod), and they lack the versatility of binoculars. They are ideal for observing offshore birds along lakes, bays, and oceans. The scopes can be set up (which takes considerable time) and observations made over a large area from one location. They are also very practical for observing shore birds on distant sand bars, islands, and beaches. Birders often use scopes to watch rookeries, roosting areas, migration flocks, and for observations across open prairies and marshlands. They are also used quite extensively for moon watching (see page 212).

How to Use a Scope for Birding

Owing to the intensive power of spotting scopes (15x to 60x), satisfactory results cannot be obtained by hand-holding; a sturdy tripod or car window mount is essential. When selecting a tripod, emphasis should be placed on the word *sturdy*. A flimsy tripod may hold the scope safely, but it will be subject to vibrations from the slightest touch and from the wind. In addition to being rigid, the tripod should have an adjustable center post so that the scope can be positioned at a comfortable height. Telescoping legs should have positive locks, and the head must be operable both vertically and horizontally by a single handhold.

Car window mounts are practical where observations are possible from within an automobile, such as along a shore road or lake front. They fasten securely to the window glass and can be adjusted to the proper height by raising or lowering the window. A swivel head makes other adjustments quite easy. Their use is limited pretty much to one or two people; it becomes a bit awkward, to say the least, to shift a group of birders of all sizes and shapes into and out of the front seat of an automobile. If you do not have a car window mount for your scope, carry a soft pillow with you. With the glass turned down, a pillow placed on the bottom edge of the window will make a reasonably steady cradle for your scope or for a camera with a telephoto lens.

At first, you may experience some difficulty in being able to locate the desired bird through your scope. There are natural reasons for this. First of all, scopes are not as easily maneuvered as binoculars, and second, the field of view is much smaller. For example, the average field of view at 1,000 yards for a 7x binocular is about 400 feet; for a 60x scope, it is less than 40 feet. The following procedures, and some practice, will help you overcome this difficulty.

First: Adjust the center post of your tripod so that the scope is at a comfortable viewing height. Tighten securely.

Second: Keep the horizontal and vertical adjustments loose enough to permit you to turn or tilt the scope freely.

Third: Sight across the top of your scope, and aim it as you would a gun. This will put your point of aim somewhere near the object being sighted.

Fourth: Now, using your lowest power lens setting, focus on the area—waves, trees, or whatever happens to be near the object.

Fifth: Still looking through the eyepiece, swing or tilt the scope until you pick up the object.

Sixth: Adjust your focus. You can now switch to whatever power magnification you prefer. If the object is stationary, tighten all adjustments.

How to Select a Scope

During the preparation of this chapter, I conducted a survey among individual birders and Audubon groups to determine which scopes were preferred for birding purposes. Invariably, the answers showed a preference for either one of two brands: Bausch & Lomb (Balscope Zoom 60 or Balscope Sr.) and Bushnell (Spacemaster II or Sentry II). Many birders liked the versatility of a zoom lens, but others were satisfied with a fixed power lens, the 20x being the most popular.

Both brands are quality instruments, and the results are comparable. I use a Spacemaster II and find it completely satisfactory. It is compact, light in weight, and has a blue "Squint-pruf" filter built into the objective lens which helps eliminate the glare from water, snow, sand, and haze.

With special camera attachments, both the Bausch & Lomb and the Bushnell scopes can be used for telephotography. I

*For
Telephotography*

am not a professional in this field, but I have used my Spacemaster II (with a fixed 15x lens) with my Nikkormat camera and have been amazed at the results an amateur can get. At 15x, the effective focal length is comparable to a 750-millimeter lens. A sturdy tripod and a cable release are essential items for telephotography. (Sources of additional information on this subject are included in the Bibliography.)

If there is one disturbing factor about bird watching, it's people—particularly bunches of people. However, a gathering of humans with a mutual interest is just as characteristic of bird watching as it is of any other sport. And there is much to be said for birding in a group (as I have already stated), for it is here that the inexperienced learn from the experienced. But there comes a time when even the most fledgling of birders want to go it alone—away from the cavorting of kids and without listening to a running report on the "fantastic bargains at Jordan Marsh's."

Alone, or in a group, the first matter of concern is what to carry with you.

17 Techniques Afield

Binoculars: A must, as we have concluded previously.

Field guide: It is best to carry your own. Personal confirmation is the most rewarding, and it prevents having to interrupt the leader repeatedly. I try to limit myself to one guide, as books are rather awkward items to carry. Most trouser and jacket pockets are the wrong size or shape. Practical field-guide carriers can be obtained from O B Enterprises, Box A-21, Celina, Ohio 45622. These carriers have a separate pocket for lists and pencils. Price: $4.50* postpaid.

* All prices given in this book were accurate at the time of publication. The reader may use them as a guide in comparing one item with another—but should be aware that prices change constantly.

**What to Take
with You**

Note pad, check list, and pens: If you are interested only in the number and varieties of birds seen on a particular trip, a check list is sufficient. A pocket-size notebook is ideal for jotting down notes about behavior, habitats, plants, etc., and for making sketches for future reference or identification. Always carry a notebook; you will find it useful on almost every trip—perhaps just to record the address of a new birding friend. Include more than one writing instrument.
Insect repellent: This is a "just in case" item. There are places at certain times of the year where mosquitoes, black flies, or "sand fleas" can make life absolutely miserable. A Minnesota fishing guide introduced me to Cutter's insect repellent. I find this to be as effective as any on the market. Also, it is concentrated and packaged small. A one-ounce bottle fits into any pocket.
Snakebite kit: Carrying a snakebite kit is a precautionary measure that should be adhered to when hiking in areas likely to be attractive to snakes. There should be one kit in each group, or preferably, carry your own. The Cutter Compak Suction Kit weighs but one ounce. Cost $2.98.

How to Dress

Dressing for field trips is largely a matter of personal judgment. Your main concern is to be comfortable so you can enjoy the trip. Factors such as weather, time of year, and where you are going need to be considered. Don't wear anything you are afraid of getting wet or dirty. Subdued colors are preferred except during hunting seasons; at other times don't arrive looking like a psychedelic scarecrow. Remember: you are going to watch birds—not each other.
Jackets and trousers: Almost any old jacket will do for birding as long as it is comfortable. But eventually, most birders end up with a favorite jacket for field use. I prefer the lightweight tan "field jacket." (They are available from most sporting goods stores.) These jackets are wind-resistant, tough, and have large patch pockets ideal for carrying field guides, note pads, insect repellent, and other personal items. Matching trousers are often available, but these, of course, are not necessary. Any good khaki, cordu-

roy, or work-type trousers will do nicely for both men and women.

Footwear: This is one item of dress that should be given serious consideration. Comfort is of primary importance, but this doesn't mean wearing certain shoes because they are comfortable around the house. Some thought must be given to the weather and the type of terrain you expect to cover. Tennis shoes or sneakers are a favorite of many birders during the warmer months. They are comfortable enough for a couple of hours' walking, and if you get them wet, they are easily washed and dried for future use. (They will shrink noticeably after repeated soakings.) On early morning walks, especially in the spring, you are likely to find the grass drenched with a heavy dew. If you have an aversion to getting your feet wet, waterproof footwear is the only answer.

Oil-tanned leather hiking shoes with rubber or composition soles are ideal for most field work. They are comfortable, durable, and protect your feet and ankles. Even if they wet through, they will dry soft and supple if you keep them treated. Avoid leather-soled shoes, especially when hiking in the forest. They will eventually become polished and slippery, making your footing dangerously insecure.

Headgear: I wear an old baseball-type cap when I go bird watching, hiking, fishing, or indulge in similar outdoor activities. I find it serves a number of useful purposes: it keeps my hair out of my eyes on windy days; it protects my head from the sun; it provides protection from insects; it is literally "starched" with insect repellent and the visor serves as an eyeshade. Ladies seem to find enough protection from a simple scarf that can be tied around the head when needed.

Raingear: This is strictly a matter of judgment. The thin plastic raincoats (with attached hoods) that fold into a pocket-size package are easily carried and usually provide adequate protection from quick showers.

With some people, the exuberance of being afield seems to preclude good manners and common sense. There is nothing quite so distracting to a trip leader as having to talk, or listen to a distant bird call, in competition with a discussion on last week's bridge game or yesterday's golf score. Strangely enough, most of the "people chatter" emanates from the experienced birders—those who can't be bothered to look at "another catbird." If you must overflow with the excitement of the past week's events, keep your voice low, or better yet, save it until a rest period. Excessive jabbering is distracting to the leader and not fair to the beginning student. That catbird may be his first.

Field Trip Etiquette

Undisciplined children can disrupt a bird walk quicker than anything I know. If you take your children birding with others, have them understand the rules of being a part of a very special group.

Don't be a straggler. Stay with the group so the leader doesn't have to waste valuable time waiting for you to catch up. Also, if you lag behind, you are apt to miss the best finds of the day.

And finally, don't be too eager to display your newly found knowledge. Respect your leader; if he needs your help, he will undoubtedly ask for it.

How to Lead a Field Trip

The day will come when you will be asked to lead your first field trip. This is often a moment of panic, and you are likely to respond with, "I can't. I just don't know enough." This is probably not true. First of all someone thinks you are sufficiently competent, or you wouldn't have been asked. And second, you don't have to be *the* authority in the group in order to be a good leader.

If you plan the trip according to the six points that follow, you can proceed with confidence knowing that everyone will have the opportunity to get the most of everything this particular walk has to offer. Your reputation as a good field-trip leader will be established.

First: Make a preliminary survey of the area. If possible, explore the area the day before your scheduled field trip. This will help you discover the most interesting and productive places; you can then plan your route accordingly. You will also know what birds you are most likely to see the following day. This is a great boost to one's confidence.

Don't limit your survey to birds alone; study the total area. Tomorrow's trip will be a lot more interesting and meaningful if you can tell the group the surrounding hills are of glacial design, or that the ground on which they are walking was part of the ocean floor so many millions of years ago. Perhaps you can prove your point by moraine deposits, glacial striations, or fossilized shells. Know something about the plants, especially the dominant ones. What are their relationships with the birds attracted to that particular habitat? Is it food, cover, nesting, or what? Note the changes in succession from field to forest, or shore to swamp—and the accompanying changes in bird species and populations. What about mammals and predators? What keeps this particular area in "balance"? Some timely comments on items such as these will help make the field trip a more complete experience for everyone. A little time spent in the local library can provide you with most of the answers.

Second: Organize your group. Before you start, assemble your group and talk to them briefly. Tell them a little about the area, where you are going, and what you hope to see. This also provides a good opportunity to ask for their help and cooperation. This brief preliminary talk will help pique their interest in the trip, and get their minds off extraneous matters. As a result, your trip promises success from the very beginning.

Third: Use the talent in your group. Don't be afraid to ask for help. You may have a biologist, a botanist, or an ecologist among those in attendance. If so, ask them to help with their specialty, or at least call on them when you are in doubt. If there is an exceptionally good birder in the group, ask him to be your assistant or to help you when the occasion warrants. No one will criticize you for asking for help or admitting you do not know, but don't try to bluff your way; there is always someone ready to hang you with the nearest grapevine.

Fourth: Be alert constantly, and interpret what you see. At this point you should read (or reread) the section in this chapter entitled "Interpreting What You See and Hear (page 243).

Fifth: Use a check list. It is your duty as leader to keep a record of the birds observed on the trip. A number of participants may want to compare their lists with yours, or obtain a complete copy of the "official" list. Include all birds that were positively identified regardless of whether they were seen or heard by every member of the group. You should also note on your list such information as date, time, numbers, and specific locations. These notes will be a valuable reference the next time you are asked to lead a trip in that particular area. Also, over a period of time, they will give you an indication of the changes in that specific habitat.

Sixth: Summarize for the group. When your walk is completed, and you have returned to your original starting point, call the group together (they will have strung out somewhat by this time) and summarize the results for them. In addition to the total number of species observed, you can emphasize such points as the scarcity or abundance of a particular species, the best finds of the day, and the effects of ecological changes. Also, it will give you a chance to answer questions and to express your appreciation for everyone's cooperation and participation. Most important of all, everyone will leave with the feeling the trip was a real success.

Going It Alone

Once you have learned the fundamentals of bird recognition, you will find much satisfaction in birding alone. Many of our more common birds are so used to human habitation they can be observed easily. We have little difficulty in watching the robin, the mockingbird, or the house wren; however, the majority of our birds are quite wild and elusive. In order to observe them clearly, we must approach them in their natural habitat, or put ourselves in such a position that they will approach us. In either case, there are certain techniques we can use that will enhance our chances of success considerably.

Approaching birds: Here, the color of clothing is of paramount importance. Consider your background and wear outer garments that will blend with it. Camouflaged jackets or suits such as bow hunters wear are ideal. Dull tans, browns, and greens are also quite satisfactory. Avoid white (except on snow) and brilliant colors. Remember: the vision of most birds is far superior to ours. Colors that contrast sharply with the background are noticed more readily.

There are two things that disturb birds in the wild: movement and noise. Of course, it is impossible to approach birds without a certain amount of movement. This is your chance to "play Indian." Move slowly and take advantage of your background and available cover. Avoid stepping on dead twigs and limbs that are likely to break and make noise. If you can approach the bird (or call) from a downwind position, any sounds you make will be less noticeable. As you near the bird, give consideration to the available light. Try to make the final approach with the sun at your back. This is most important if you are planning to take any pictures. Colors are difficult to distinguish when you are looking toward the sun or into light reflected from water.

Birds of open areas, such as fields, meadows, and beaches, are usually the most difficult to approach. Lacking any substantial amount of cover, one is sometimes obliged to crawl through low grasses and shrubbery. Except for the most avid (not to mention athletic) of bird watchers, this becomes tiresome in a hurry. I have been quite successful in approaching birds in the open by moving slowly and by seemingly not paying any attention to their activities. A meandering approach is better than a direct one. I once walked to within 50 feet of a meadowlark and watched her build a nest without alarming her. I have also used this approach quite successfully with feeding herons and resting shore birds.

I have enjoyed good birding along stream and lake shores by using a canoe. A canoe, gliding slowly and quietly along the water's edge, makes it possible to observe herons, bitterns, rails, snipe, and other marsh birds in areas that otherwise would be inaccessible.

Calling birds: It is not necessary to indulge in an athletic sojourn across hill and dale to enjoy good birding. In fact, I have experienced some of my most rewarding birding while sitting beneath the shade of a forest tree and just watching what went on about me.

If things are slow and few birds appear, try calling them to you. This can be done by sucking on the back of your

hand so a squeaking or "kissing" sound results. Some birders have equal success by making a *psssh* sound through their teeth. Commercial bird calls are effective, also. They consist of a pewter key that turns in a small block of hard wood. A touch of powdered rosin helps produce a variety of high-pitched sounds. It is believed that birds respond to these various calls because they sound like a bird in distress.

Certain species can be enticed to come within close range by imitating their calls. This is especially true of owls, crows, and certain species of game birds. It works best in the early spring when males are protecting nesting territories.

Using decoys and blinds: We are familiar with the manner in which hunters use decoys to attract waterfowl within shooting range. The same technique can be used for observation or photographic purposes. The decoys should be placed along the lee edge of a lake or pond adjacent to some protective cover for the observer. If cover is sparse, it may be necessary to use a blind.

Blinds are almost a necessity for continuing nesting observations and for extensive photographic purposes. They can sometimes be built of native materials—brush, limbs, cattails, weeds, grass, etc. They can also be built of burlap, canvas, or any other durable cloth that will blend with the background. They should be secured well so the material doesn't flap and snap in the wind. Small, lightweight pop-up blinds are available commercially. They save a lot of muss and fuss if you have repeated use for a portable blind.

Also, birds can be attracted close to you by feeding. This is covered rather extensively in Chapter 14, "Watching Songbirds in Winter."

Your wanderings afield will be decidedly more interesting if you are continuously aware of what is happening about you. For everything you see and hear, from the cloud formations in the sky above you to the insect burrowings beneath your feet, contributes to the functioning of life within the outdoor community. Without this relationship among all things wild, the birds you seek would not be there. With nearly every step you take, you can find something new and revealing about the world in which you walk. Even the birds themselves often act as field assistants by revealing the excitement of the moment.

Although predation is a natural process within nature's cycle of life, this fact is not necessarily inherent in the pursued. Even the meek and the weak struggle to survive. Birds are the first to reveal that something is "wrong" within their seemingly serene community. Blue jays spread the alarm, calling "thief, thief." Other species gather and flit about excitedly, repeating their alarm notes. Some, more brave than others, will dart at the intruder. The excitement may be caused by a prowling cat or perhaps a snake that found an easy meal in a nearby nest. A marauding crow may be stealing eggs, or a hawk could be watching for mice from the dead limb of a tree. A sleeping owl, accidentally discovered on his secluded perch, may be the cause of all the ruckus.

A gathering of raucous crows, circling and diving over a small area, usually indicates the presence of an owl or fox.

A chattering red squirrel, flipping its tail and leaping from limb to limb, is a good indication that something is amiss. It may be nothing more than your presence, but more often than not, the snake, the owl, or the fox is the victim of its ridicule.

Telltale signs along your route will reveal the presence of unseen life. A scattering of droppings beneath a tree will often disclose the favorite roosting place of an owl, a grouse, or a wild turkey. If the tree is an evergreen, look for owl pellets. The ground beneath isolated stands of evergreens is an excellent place to look for these pellets.

An accumulation of seed hulls on the ground may divulge a favorite feeding area of siskins or finches. If you find a pile of drillings and chips at the base of a dead tree, look for the home of a woodpecker. If the chips are abundant and large, they may be the workings of a pileated. A dead elm will undoubtedly display the etchings of the engraver beetles, and the flakes of dried bark will tell the story of the woodpeckers that put an end to their artwork.

Interpreting What You See and Hear

Observing and interpreting such findings may not add a new bird to your list, but the outdoors will have greater enchantment for you and you will understand more about the birds' particular niche in the dynamics of a wild community.

Weather and Bird Watching

I am asked often whether it is worthwhile to go afield in search of birds on rainy or on stormy days. A number of factors could influence the answer to this question, but basically, I think it depends upon individual judgment and personal enthusiasm for the sport. Birds are with us regardless of the weather, so it is chiefly a matter of deciding if we want to brave the elements to find them.

I wouldn't go afield looking for spring warblers on a day when a passing cold front brought strong winds howling from the north. Even if there were warblers around, the movement of blowing limbs and leaves would make it virtually impossible to see or hear them. On the other hand, if there has been a high-pressure area off our southeast coast for a couple of days, with consistent winds from the south or southeast, northbound warblers may appear in waves as they take advantage of the helping winds. In the fall, when a strong northwest wind blows, birds will "stack up" sometimes along our eastern coastline while they wait for the wind to abate, thus preventing them from being blown out to sea on their southern migration.

Birds enjoy days of light, warm showers. During and after such showers, they can be seen bathing frequently in the newly formed puddles or in the rain-drenched grass. If the rain is sufficiently heavy to flood low-lying areas, swallows and martins will skim the grass tops, feasting on the disturbed insects. Around the edges, grackles, meadowlarks, egrets, an occasional heron, and other species will feed on escaping insects and rodents. Even the hawk perches nearby, watching for fleeing rodents, reptiles, or amphibians. But the days of really vicious storms are another matter; it is then that we wonder if there is a bird to be found anywhere.

When a northeaster howls across the land, or when a

hurricane comes roaring in from the Atlantic or the Gulf, birds seek the safest shelter they can find. It is then we see them huddled under the eaves of porches and outbuildings. Others seek shelter in abandoned tree cavities, while many seek what protection they can find by snuggling against the leeward side of a sturdy tree. Gulls and certain shore birds sense a greater degree of safety in open areas such as golf courses, airports, and fields. As far as birding is concerned, these storms can be exciting, tragic, or beneficial; it depends upon your point of view. We know that early tropical storms or hurricanes can do extensive damage to concentrations of colony-nesting species such as herons, egrets, gulls, and terns. Fortunately, most of these great storms are spawned in August, September, and October when most nesting has been completed. The majority have their beginning in the South Atlantic east of the Caribbean. Swirling their way westward and northward in cyclonic fashion, they follow the low-pressure troughs of least resistance. Many expend their energies far out at sea, but others may unleash their fury upon the land, anywhere along our eastern coast from Mexico to Canada. As a storm follows its erratic course across sea and land, birds are often sucked into its vortex and carried hundreds of miles beyond their normal range. When a hurricane strikes, the avid birder invariably faces a quandary: Should he seek safety, or should he wander afield in search of rare oceanic birds?

As hurricanes move inland and divest their energies upon the landscape, great environmental changes are often wrought. Drying marsh areas are filled suddenly with an abundance of water, making them attractive to ducks and other water birds; forests are partially leveled, and individual trees are broken and tumbled. Life cycles begin anew; where one species suffers, another thrives. The wood thrush may lose his shaded home, but the yellow-breasted chat, the towhee, or the white-throated sparrow may find the tangled undergrowth much to its liking. Storms—even violent hurricanes—are a part of nature's long-range ecological balance. No matter what changes the phenomena of weather may bring, population pressures will fill each "new" habitat with species adapted to survival therein.

Note Taking and Record Keeping

"If you're going to be a good birder, you must keep accurate records," a friend of mine once told me. (On that particular occasion, I doubt if my friend had actually seen half the birds he was so busy writing down. Nevertheless, I suspect there *is* an element of truth in his statement. Records become more meaningful as they accumulate over a period of years.)

One of the best and most avid field men I know has yet to keep his first record. He has watched birds throughout the United States, but he hasn't the slightest idea how many species he has seen during his lifetime. In a recent interview, I asked him about this. "It's not because I'm too lazy," he said. "I watch birds to escape from a world of statistics. The details of keeping records would detract from the complete simplicity and relaxation that birding has to offer." I am sure there are many of us who would agree with this philosophy. Yet, by contrast, I know birders who gain much of their enthusiasm from voluminous records. The totals become an insatiable challenge to their keepers, and provide the incentive for more additions or findings that will, in turn, renew this challenge.

If you are a beginning student, you should keep records of your observations. They will serve as a measurement of your progress and provide you with a feeling of satisfaction as you watch them grow. Also, at this initial stage, you are not completely familiar with all the facets bird watching has to offer. As you progress, you may want to concentrate on some special phase in which your preliminary records would be most valuable. Once you become proficient in identification, and are familiar with all the opportunities of bird watching, you can decide what records, if any, you want to continue keeping.

What Records Should Be Kept?

Field notebooks: When selecting a notebook for use in the field, there are several points to consider. Since the notebook is another item to be carried in conjunction with field guides and binoculars, a pocket-size one is most convenient. If you plan to file your actual field notes as part of your permanent records, select the loose-leaf type in a size that conforms to your filing system, such as 3-by-5 inches or 5-by-8 inches. Spiral-bound notebooks are quite popular for keeping permanent records. They open flat for easy use, and spoiled pages can be torn without damage to others. If you are artistic and plan to use numerous sketches, you may want to select a notebook (or paper) designed for this purpose.

Make your notebook a personalized record of all sorts of things that interest you in the field. You will certainly want to list the species of birds observed, and perhaps some notations as to their numbers. You should include the date, time, location, weather, and names of persons accompanying you. Make notes and sketches of newly identified species; they will be of help the next time you go afield. And, of course, do the same for doubtful species so you can look them up at home.

If your interest carries beyond birds alone (and to encourage your interest is certainly one of the objectives of this book), I would recommend the permanent type of notebook. In it you can make notations and sketches of wild flowers, tracks, animals, insects, and countless other things that may interest you. You may even want to include a bit of suddenly inspired philosophy, or a few lines of impassioned poetry. Such a notebook can become a veritable treasury of outdoor lore.

Check lists: The National Audubon Society and a number of state Audubon societies print pocket-size check lists that are very convenient for recording daily observations and for use on special trips. Birds are listed in the order established by the American Ornithologists' Union—the same order as your field guide. All the observer has to do is make a check mark next to the name of each species observed on a particular day or trip. The lists also provide spaces for recording observers, date, weather, and location.

I like to use a check list when birding with a group (there seems to be little time for taking detailed notes), and for keeping a total list of birds seen in a particular area. I keep just one card for each area, and indicate the birds seen by entering the date. When I bird alone, I favor my notebook, for I can record all kinds of observations and details. Any information I might want to keep in a permanent file is easily transferred from my notes.

Life lists: A life list is a permanent record of all the birds one has seen during one's lifetime. There are a number of ways this record can be kept. Some birders use the check list in their favorite field guide; others enter the date and location of their first observation in their guide next to the description of the species. In either case, a duplicate list (one that is more secure and permanent) should be kept. A field guide is easily lost, and records extending over a number of years would be difficult to replace with any accuracy. Other birders incorporate their life list in an all-inclusive permanent record file.

Permanent records: I realize that keeping permanent records is not a part of in-the-field techniques. However, since all records are based on the results of field work, and because we have included the keeping of other records here, I feel this is a logical place to make a few suggestions concerning their use.

The type of information you keep, and the manner in which you keep it, should be based on your personal interests or objectives. For general records, the most popular practice is to use 4-by-6 or 5-by-8 portable card files. The name of the bird is typed or printed in the upper left corner of the card, and then filed alphabetically. A new card is added (with the date) each time a new species is observed. Either size card is sufficiently large to hold entries of subsequent sightings (within reason), and any other information you want to include. This is a good method for beginners who have not yet developed any specialized interest. Pertinent information can be transferred later to cards designed to fill a specific need. This type of file, when kept up to date, automatically becomes a life list.

Many birders prefer to use commercially printed cards with ruled spaces for each type of entry. This does give a better sense of uniformity and makes the compilation of statistics much easier. Since specialized interests vary considerably, I do not know of any standardized form that is universally acceptable to all birders. Regardless of your interest, I think it is best to use hand-ruled cards until you are certain your format is completely satisfactory. You will probably change it several times before you arrive at this conclusion. You can then design your own card and have it printed quite inexpensively by your local offset printer.

To watch birds—a time, a place—it matters neither where nor when, for all the wild land is shrouded in a mysterious enchantment awaiting our personal discovery. We have but to go afield and open our minds and our senses to all that is around us. Yes, to go afield, to be outdoors, that is the most important thing.

The birds, the list—it matters not how many or what kind we see, for we have learned that watching birds is only an interim step to greater innovations. We find our rewards in new clouds racing across the sky, in the design of a wave that crashes upon the shore—a design of momentary beauty never to be seen again—in the ephemeral life of a lone primrose, and in the ethereal song of a thrush that transmutes its joy into our own sense of well-being. We find a new alertness and a new keenness of mind, and in moments of solitude, our contemplations reach deeper and become more meaningful than ever before. Surely, these are rewards enough to lure us afield in the pursuit of birds.

Bird watching is perhaps the most cosmopolitan of all outdoor activities; it is not limited by political or geographical boundaries; and it attracts a host of followers the world over. Undoubtedly, this universal appeal is bound to the fact that it provides an avenue of personal interest for everyone who would dare to accept its challenge. Whether by choice or by chance, for most of us who follow the lives of birds, there is one niche in the outdoor

18 Come Walk with Me

world that appeals to us especially. It may be the edge of the sea, where your senses are the keenest, where you can smell its pungent odors, hear the thunder of the surf, see the wheeling flocks of shore birds, and feel the freshness of wind-blown spray on your cheeks. Or you may find your contentment in the solitude of a distant evergreen forest, where the silence is broken only by the warblers singing from sunlit spires of spruce, or by the melancholy cry of a loon from some hidden lake. Or you may be one of many who seek new discoveries within their own gardens. But despite such personal affinities, there are those who must follow the birds wherever they go. The choice of habitat matters little, for each has birds to be seen, and each abounds in wonders that will carry us far beyond the mere act of watching. It is here, when birds lure us afield, that we both remember and forget—where we awaken but still dream.

I cannot recall how many times I was late for school because of birds, nor can I possibly count the hours, since those initial days of interest, that I have spent wandering across some abandoned field, or roaming the sandy beaches, or sitting on a log in the shaded depths of some forest. But this I remember: it was during those times, during those hours, that the sturdy stuff of profound decisions came to the fore. And I remember lessons learned more than two decades ago. I remember a cute little eighth-grade girl proving to me that the bird I heard singing was not a catbird, but a red-eyed vireo. Today, I could take you to the very hornbeam tree from which the vireo sang, but the hornbeam is an understory tree, and it has undoubtedly returned to the soil beneath the canopy of dominant oaks. I remember, too, my first waterthrush along Rock Run, and the chimney swifts funneling into the old hollow tree stub in Lytle's meadow. I remember the great V's of wild geese etched against the evening sky; their clamoring foretold the imminence of spring, and on their return trip they warned me that the cold of winter was soon to follow. And I remember, many years later, flying a glider wing tip to wing tip with the eagle, and for one brief moment sharing the exhilaration and freedom of effortless flight.

As you follow the ways of birds, you will remember, and at the same time build memories to be recalled in the future. You will feel the sudden surge of emotion and not be ashamed; you will find a shield from the grasping tentacles of concrete and steel; and you will know a world that cannot be measured by the yardsticks of technology and finance. You will rejoice in the elation of the moment and then ponder the significance of your discovery.

The realization that birds endured on this planet for uncountable centuries before the advent of man, and that they continue to succeed without the need of his technological bravado, comes as a rebuff to our domineering ego. Their ease and grace of flight humble our mechanical attempts at duplication; their innate response to the changing seasons stirs the pangs of envy. But in the humility of discovery, we sense a new perspective on life. For life's tenuous hold upon the land is manifest in a fragile chain of the living.

Come walk with me. Come; let us go down to the edge of the sea and walk the sandy beaches at the ebb of the tide. Come; let us wander across lush green meadows and along flower-strewn pathways of gardens.

Come. Walk with me. Let us watch birds.

Bibliography

Cruickshank, Allan D. *Birds Around New York City*. New York: American Museum of National History, 1942.

Pettingill, Olin Sewall, Jr. *A Guide to Bird Finding East of the Mississippi*. New York: Oxford University Press, 1951.

————, ed. *The Bird Watcher's America*. New York: McGraw-Hill Book Co., 1965.

Books Related to Bird Watching

Where to Find Birds

Blachly, Lew, and Jenks, Randolph. *Naming the Birds at a Glance*. New York: Alfred A. Knopf, 1969.

Peterson, Roger Tory. *A Field Guide to the Birds*. Boston: Houghton Mifflin Co., 1947.

Pough, Richard H. *Audubon Bird Guide*. New York: Doubleday & Co., 1949.

————. *Audubon Water Bird Guide*. New York: Doubleday & Co., 1956.

Robbins, Chandler S., Bruun, Bertel, and Zim, Herbert S. *Birds of North America*. New York: Golden Press, 1966.

How to Identify Birds

Barton, Roger. *How to Watch Birds*. New York: Bonanza Books, 1959.

Fisher, James. *Watching Birds*. New York: Penguin Books, 1951.

Hickey, Joseph J. *A Guide to Bird Watching*. Garden City, N.Y.: Garden City Books, 1953.

How to Watch Birds

Davidson, V. E. *Attracting Birds: From the Prairies to the Atlantic*. New York: Thomas Y. Crowell Co., 1967.

Lemmon, Robert S. *How to Attract Birds*. New York: American Garden Guild and Doubleday & Co., 1948.

McElroy, Thomas P., Jr. *The New Handbook of Attracting Birds*. 2nd ed. New York: Alfred A. Knopf, 1960.

How to Attract Birds

Petit, Ted S. *Birds in Your Back Yard*. New York: Harper & Brothers, 1949

Terres, John K. *Songbirds in Your Garden*. New York: Thomas Y. Crowell Co., 1968.

Bird Songs   Mathews, F. Schuyler. *Field Book of Wild Birds and Their Music*. New York: G. P. Putnam's Sons, 1921.

Saunders, Aretas A. *A Guide to Bird Songs*. New York: Doubleday & Co., Inc., 1951.

Bird Nests   Headstrom, Richard. *Birds' Nests: A Field Guide*. New York: Ives Washburn, 1949.

Berger, Andrew J. *Bird Study*. New York: John Wiley & Sons, 1961.

Dorst, Jean. *The Migration of Birds*. Boston: Houghton Mifflin Co., 1963.

Bird Study   Fisher, James, and Peterson, Roger Tory. *The World of Birds*. New York: Doubleday & Co., 1964.

Peterson, Roger Tory. *The Birds*. New York: Time-Life Books, 1970.

Pettingill, Olin Sewall, Jr. *Ornithology in Laboratory and Field*. 4th ed. Minneapolis: Burgess Publishing Co., 1970.

Stefferud, Alfred, and Nelson, Arnold L. *Birds in Our Lives*. Washington, D.C.: U.S. Government Printing Office, 1966.

Van Tyne, Josselyn, and Berger, Andrew J. *Fundamentals of Ornithology*. New York: John Wiley & Sons, 1959.

Welty, Joel Carl. *The Life of Birds*. New York: Alfred A. Knopf, 1963.

Wing, Leonard W. *Natural History of Birds*. New York: Ronald Press Co., 1956.

Life Histories   Bent, Arthur Cleveland. *Life Histories of North American Birds*. 26 vols. New York: Dover Publications, 1919–68.

Amos, W. H. *The Life of the Pond*. New York: McGraw-Hill Book Co., 1967.

Habitat Ecology   Berril, N. J. *The Living Tide*. New York: Fawcett Publications, 1956.

Buchsbaum, Ralph and Mildred. *Basic Ecology*. Pittsburgh: Boxwood Press, 1957.

Carson, Rachel. *The Edge of the Sea*. Boston: Houghton Mifflin Co., 1955.

Dice, Lee R. *Natural Communities*. Ann Arbor: University of Michigan Press, 1952.

Farb, Peter. *Face of North America: The Natural History of a Continent*. New York: Harper and Row, 1963.

Hylander, C. J. *Wildlife Communities: From the Tundra to the Tropics in North America*. Boston: Houghton Mifflin Co., 1966.

Macan, Thomas. *Freshwater Ecology*. New York: J. Wiley & Sons, 1963.

McCormick, Jack. *The Life of the Forest.* New York: McGraw-Hill Book Co., 1966.

————. *The Living Forest.* New York: Harper and Brothers, 1959.

Miner, Roy Waldo. *Field Book of Seashore Life.* New York: G. P. Putnam's Sons, 1950.

Neal, Ernest. *Woodland Ecology.* Cambridge, Mass.: Harvard University Press, 1958.

Niering, William A. *The Life of the Marsh.* New York: McGraw-Hill Book Co., 1966.

Reid, George K. *Ecology of Inland Waters and Estuaries.* New York: Reinhold Publishing Corporation, 1961.

Shelford, V. E. *The Ecology of North America.* Urbana: University of Illinois Press, 1963.

Usinger, R. L. *The Life of Rivers and Streams.* New York: McGraw-Hill Book Co., 1967.

CORNELL LABORATORY OF ORNITHOLOGY, The Sounds of Nature Series. Published by Houghton Mifflin Co., Boston.[*]

Some Helpful Recordings of Bird Songs

A Field Guide to Bird Songs. An album of two records. $10.95.

These two records contain the calls of more than 300 species and are designed to accompany, page by page, Roger Tory Peterson's *A Field Guide to the Birds.*

American Bird Songs. Volume I. $7.75.

Presents the songs of 60 of North America's most familiar birds. Divided into bands as follows: Birds of the North Woods, Birds of Northern Gardens and Shade Trees, Birds of Fields and Prairies, and American Game Birds.

American Bird Songs. Volume II. $7.75.

Presents the songs of 51 species, all different from those in Volume I. Divided into bands as follows: Some Familiar Birds of Gardens and Shade Trees, Some Familiar Birds of the Roadside, Some Birds of the Lakes and Marshes, More Birds of the Marshes, and Some North American Warblers.

Bird Songs in Your Garden. Record and spiral-bound album with full-color photographs. $6.95.

The record presents the songs of 25 of America's best-loved garden birds. The informative text is illustrated with 53 photographs, of which 31 are in full color.

Dawn in a Duckblind. Record and spiral-bound album with full-color photographs. $6.95.

A recording of the calls of North American waterfowl as they would be heard from a typical duckblind at daybreak on a marshy lake or bay in eastern United States.

*All records listed within this section are 33⅓ rpm.

Songbirds of America. Record and spiral-bound album with full-color photographs. $6.95.

This album contains the recordings of songs and the full-color photographs of 24 common birds. The commentary on the record takes the listener on an imaginary field trip.

FEDERATION OF ONTARIO NATURALISTS, The Sounds of Nature Series. Published by Houghton Mifflin Co., Boston.

Finches. $5.95

Approximately 400 songs from 43 species of the finch and sparrow families of eastern and central North America.

Songs of Spring. $5.95.

Presents the songs of 25 of the most common songbirds of the northeastern United States and Canada.

Thrushes, Wrens, and Mockingbirds. $5.95.

The songs of three bird families of eastern North America renowned for their singing prowess.

Warblers. $5.95.

Presenting more than 400 songs from 150 birds of the 38 species of warblers of eastern North America.

FICKER RECORDS, Old Greenwich, Conn.

Bird Songs of Dooryard, Field, and Forest. Volume I. $7.95.

Contains 135 songs and calls of 49 species of birds from the Great Plains to the Atlantic.

Bird Songs of Dooryard, Field, and Forest. Volume II. $7.95.

Contains 140 songs and calls of 58 species of birds from the Great Plains to the Atlantic.

Bird Songs of Dooryard, Field and Forest. Volume III. $7.95.

Contains 220 songs and calls of 68 species of birds from the Great Plains to the Pacific.

National Network of American Bird Songs. $19.95.

Volumes I, II, and III as described above.

Principal Ornithological Organizations and Their Journals

AMERICAN ORNITHOLOGISTS' UNION, Museum of Natural History, Smithsonian Institution, Washington, D.C. 20560. Aims to advance ornithological science through its publications, annual meetings, committees, and membership. Publication: *The Auk* (quarterly).

COOPER ORNITHOLOGICAL SOCIETY, Avian Biology Laboratory, San Jose State College, San Jose, Calif. 95114. Observation and cooperative study of birds; the spread of interest in bird study; the conservation of birds and wildlife in general; the publication of ornithological knowledge. Publication: *The Condor* (quarterly).

LABORATORY OF ORNITHOLOGY AT CORNELL UNIVERSITY, 159 Sapsucker Woods Road, Ithaca, N.Y. 14850. A world center for the study and cultural appreciation of birds. Publications: *The Living Bird* (annual), *Newsletter* (quarterly). Also books, phonograph records, record albums, and cassettes.

NATIONAL AUDUBON SOCIETY, 950 Third Avenue, New York, N.Y. 10022. For the conservation and appreciation of wildlife and wilderness, natural resources and natural beauty. Publications: *Audubon* (bimonthly), sent to all members; *American Birds* (bimonthly), summarizing the status, movements, and distribution of North American birds; and *Audubon Nature Bulletins*, for teachers and youth leaders.

NORTHEASTERN BIRD-BANDING ASSOCIATION, James Baird, President, Massachusetts Audubon Society, Lincoln, Mass. 01773. The advancement of ornithology through the banding of birds. Publications: *EBBA News* (issued 6 times a year), *Bird-banding* (quarterly).

WILSON ORNITHOLOGICAL SOCIETY, Division of Birds, Museum of Zoology, University of Michigan, Ann Arbor, Mich. 48104. The advancement of ornithological knowledge through publications, meetings, and activities. Publication: *The Wilson Bulletin* (quarterly).

References on Binoculars and Scopes

Binoculars and How to Choose Them, Bausch & Lomb, Inc., Rochester, N.Y. 14602. (12 pp.) Free.

Binoculars and Scopes, by Robert J. and Elsa Reichert. Published by Chilton Co. Available through Mirakel Optical Co., Inc., Mt. Vernon, N.Y. 10550. (128 pp.) $2.00.

How to Select, Enjoy, and Care for the Right Binocular, Swift Instruments, Inc., Boston, Mass. 02125. (12 pp.) Free.

How to Select the Right Binocular, Carl Zeiss, Inc., New York, N.Y. 10018. (10 pp.) Free.

How to Use Your New Spacemaster Telephoto Unit, D. P. Bushnell & Co., Inc., Pasadena, Calif. 91107. (6 pp.) Free.

Know Your Binoculars, by Robert J. and Elsa Reichert, *Audubon Magazine,* Vol. 53, No. 1 (Jan.–Feb., 1951). Reprints available from Mirakel Optical Co., Inc., Mt. Vernon, N.Y. 10550. Ten cents each, 20 for $1.00.

Bird Index

Ducks *(continued)*
    Ring-necked, 109, 115, 133
    Ruddy, 109
    Scaup, Greater, 133, 157
    Scaup, Lesser, 133, 157
    Scaups, 138, 158
    Scoter, Common, 157
    Scoters, 158, 189
    Scoter, Surf, 157
    Scoter, White-winged, 157
    Shoveler, 109, 115, 117, 133
    Teal, Blue-winged, 109, 115, 118–19, 133
    Teal, Green-winged, 109, 115, 118, 133
    Widgeon, American, 109, 119
    Widgeon, European, 133
    Wood, 40, 108–9, 113, 115, 119, 133, 171, 182
Dunlin, 133, 157

Eagles, 16, 91, 103, 115, 119, 166, 250
    Bald, 91, 97–8, 103, 115, 118–19
Egrets, 3, 17–18, 118, 128, 151, 157, 159, 164, 166–8, 170, 172, 182, 244–5
    Cattle, 119, 160–1
    Common, 115, 123, 126, 128, 160–1, 209
    Reddish, 161
    Snowy, 115, 123, 126, 128, 160–1

Falcons, 8, 67, 75, 91, 118, 133, 135, 212
Finches, 15, 25, 49, 51, 64, 67, 79, 91, 177, 179, 180, 190, 193, 195, 243
    House, 195
    Purple, 4, 49, 57, 175, 177, 180, 193, 195
Flicker, Yellow-shafted, 40, 42, 66, 79, 91, 177
Flycatchers, 15, 25–6, 33–4, 49, 64, 79, 91, 103, 150, 161, 171, 177, 179, 180, 184
    Acadian, 25, 34, 171
    Great Crested, 25, 33, 41–2, 79, 92–3
    Least, 21, 34
    Olive-sided, 49, 58
    Scissor-tailed, 161
    Trail's, 61
    Yellow-bellied, 49, 59
Frigatebird, Magnificent, 159, 161, 168

Gallinules, 17, 115, 119, 161, 166, 171, 202, 212
    Common, 115, 117, 119, 171
    Purple, 161, 171
Gannet, 144–6, 157
Geese, 3, 8, 17, 64, 103, 115, 118, 133, 212, 250
    Canada, 102–3, 115, 117, 133, 136
    Snow, 115, 133, 136
Gnatcatcher, Blue-gray, 25, 51, 80

A Note about the Author

Thomas P. McElroy, Jr., has spent fifteen years of his life in the fields of wildlife management and conservation education. For the past ten years he has been a free lance writer on outdoor subjects with special emphasis on birds, ecology, and environmentally related sports. He is author of the classic and still popular THE NEW HANDBOOK OF ATTRACTING BIRDS. Born in Chester County, Pennsylvania, in 1914, he now resides in West Palm Beach, Florida.

A Note on the Type

This book was set on the Linotype in Aster, a typeface designed by Francesco Simoncini (born in 1912 in Bologna, Italy) for Ludwig and Mayer, the German type foundry. Starting out with the basic old-face letterforms that can be traced back to Francesco Griffo in 1495, Simoncini emphasized the diagonal stress by the simple device of extending diagonals to the full height of the letterforms and squaring off. By modifying the weights of the individual letters to combat this stress, he has produced a type of rare balance and vigor. Introduced in 1958, Aster has steadily grown in popularity wherever type is used.

Composed by Cherry Hill Composition, Pennsauken, New Jersey, and Boro Typographers, Inc., New York, New York
Printed by Murray Printing, Forge Village, Massachusetts
Bound by The Book Press, Brattleboro, Vermont
Typography and binding design by Betty Anderson